McDougal Littell

Grammar for Writing

McDougal Littell
A HOUGHTON MIFFLIN COMPANY

McDougal Littell

Grammar for Writing

- GRAMMAR
- USAGE
- MECHANICS

McDougal Littell
A HOUGHTON MIFFLIN COMPANY

ISBN 13: 978-0-618-56617-4 ISBN 10: 0-618-56617-1

Printed in the United States of America.

Acknowledgments begin on page 373.

1 2 3 4 5 6 7 8 9—DCI—12 11 10 09 08 07

Contents Overview

Grammar, Usage, and Mechanics

Student Resources

Grammar, Usage, and Mechanics

3 Pronouns

9 Subject-Verb Agreement 206

10 Capitalization 228

HOT!
FASTER!
LISTEN!
DANCE!
NEW!
IMPROVED!
READ!

Quick-Fix Editing Machine

Special Features

Grammar Across the Curriculum

Grammar in Literature

Quick-Fix Editing Machine

Student Resources

Grammar, Usage, and Mechanics

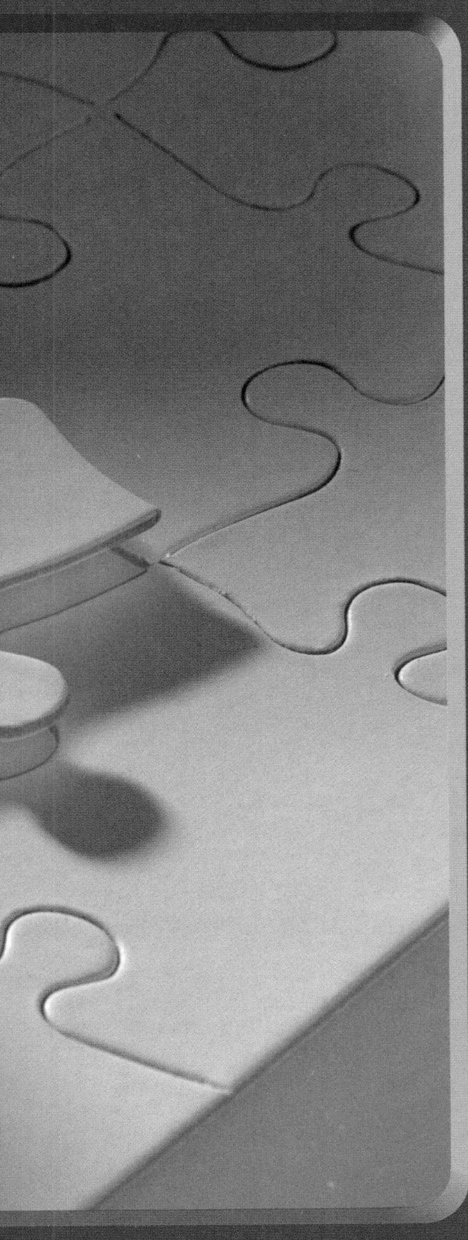

Putting the Pieces Together

When the pieces of a puzzle come together correctly, they form a clear picture. When words come together correctly, they form a clear message. By following the rules of grammar, you can be sure you've put it all together the right way.

Chapter 1

The Sentence and Its Parts

Theme: There's No Place Like Home

If You Build It . . .

A pile of bricks is not a home. To be a home, the bricks must be assembled and combined with doors and windows to make a building that will house a family.

In the same way, the pair of words *"Home is"* is not a sentence. To be a sentence, the words must be combined with other words to make a complete thought.

Write Away: Home Is . . . ?

Where do you feel most at home? Why? Write a paragraph answering these questions and place it in your **Working Portfolio.**

Diagnostic Test: What Do You Know?

Choose the letter that correctly identifies each underlined item.

What is a home? (1) That depends on the home. Skyscrapers, space stations, burrows, and nests (2) are all homes to living things. People and animals build (3) homes (4) from many different materials. However, for human beings a home (5) is more than a building. For some people home may be (6) the place where they were born. For others home is the place (7) where they feel most comfortable. We use the word (8) in many ways. Expressions like *home team, home plate, home page.* (9) You will (10) learn a lot about people by discussing their idea of home.

1. A. declarative sentence
   B. interrogative sentence
   C. exclamatory sentence
   D. imperative sentence

2. A. compound subject
   B. main verb
   C. helping verb
   D. indirect object

3. A. compound subject
   B. main verb
   C. helping verb
   D. object

4. A. simple subject
   B. direct object
   C. compound verb
   D. compound subject

5. A. simple subject
   B. simple predicate
   C. compound verb
   D. compound subject

6. A. indirect object
   B. subject
   C. direct object
   D. verb phrase

7. A. compound subject
   B. compound verb
   C. predicate noun
   D. verb phrase

8. A. subject
   B. predicate
   C. direct object
   D. indirect object

9. A. run-on sentence
   B. interrogative sentence
   C. sentence fragment
   D. exclamatory sentence

10. A. main verb
    B. helping verb
    C. complement
    D. subject

Complete Subjects and Predicates

1 Here's the Idea

In order to share ideas and information successfully, you need to use complete sentences.

A sentence is a group of words that expresses a complete thought.

Here is a group of words.

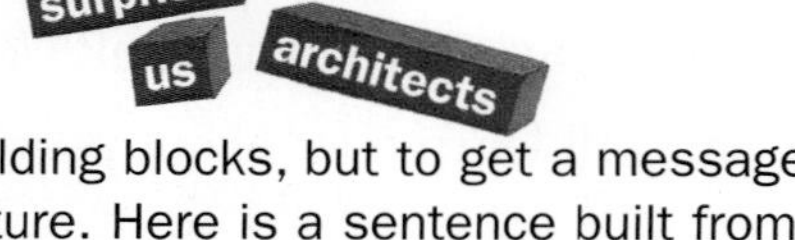

These words are good building blocks, but to get a message across, they need a structure. Here is a sentence built from the words. Notice that the sentence communicates a complete idea.

Architects can surprise us

Every complete sentence has two basic parts: a subject and a predicate.

1. The **complete subject** includes all the words that tell whom or what the sentence is about.

   COMPLETE SUBJECT

   Some architects bring nature indoors.

2. The **complete predicate** includes the verb and all the words that complete the verb's meaning.

   COMPLETE PREDICATE

   Some architects **bring nature indoors.**

Here's How Finding Complete Subjects and Predicates

Some architects bring nature indoors.

1. **To find the complete subject, ask who or what does something (or is something).**
   Who brings nature indoors? **Some architects**
2. **To find the complete predicate, ask what the subject does (or is).**
   What do some architects do? **bring nature indoors**

❷ Why It Matters in Writing

Jotting down ideas is a good way to prepare to write. For example, you might write down *Frank Lloyd Wright, didn't copy,* and *unique buildings* as you take notes or brainstorm. To share these ideas with others, though, you need both subjects and predicates. Notice what the writer has added in the paragraph below.

PROFESSIONAL MODEL

> **Frank Lloyd Wright** was different from other architects. **This dreamer from the prairie states** didn't copy other people's designs. **He** created his own unique buildings instead.
>
> —M. Carton

❸ Practice and Apply

CONCEPT CHECK: Complete Subjects and Predicates

In separate columns on a sheet of paper, write the complete subjects and complete predicates of these sentences.

Amazing Designs

Fallingwater

1. Frank Lloyd Wright designed an unusual home in the Pennsylvania woods.
2. The owners called the house Fallingwater.
3. Sections of the house jut over a waterfall.
4. Its stone walls blend in with the natural surroundings.
5. More than 130,000 people visit the site each year.
6. Tourists can see a very different house near Spring Green, Wisconsin.

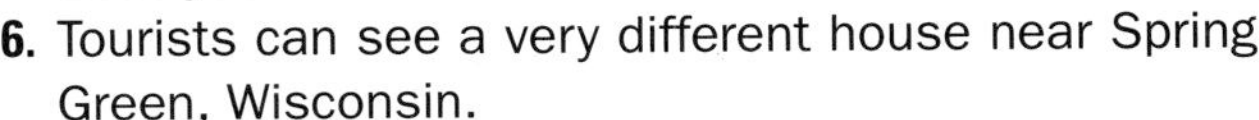

7. The architect Alex Jordan built House on the Rock on a column of sandstone.
8. Its many rooms contain unique furnishings.
9. An automated band plays music all day for the tourists.
10. This odd house attracts half a million visitors a year.

➜ **For a SELF-CHECK and more practice, see the EXERCISE BANK, p. 308.**

Simple Subjects

1 Here's the Idea

You have learned that one basic part of a sentence is the complete subject. Now you will learn about the key part of the complete subject.

The simple subject is the main word or words in the complete subject. Descriptive words are not part of the simple subject.

COMPLETE SUBJECT

An expectant seal builds a shelter in a snowdrift.

SIMPLE SUBJECT

The cozy shelter hides her newborn pup.

SIMPLE SUBJECT

When a proper name is used as a subject, all parts of the name make up the simple subject.

Robert Peary explored the North Pole.

SIMPLE SUBJECT

CHAPTER 1

2 Why It Matters in Writing

The simple subject tells the reader whom or what the sentence is about. Be sure to choose as accurate a word as possible for this key part.

STUDENT MODEL

Polar bears' ^noses stand out against the white snow. When bears lie in wait for a seal, their white ~~fur~~ paws serve~~s~~ as a mask. Then their ~~enemy~~ prey cannot see them.

3 Practice and Apply

A. CONCEPT CHECK: Simple Subjects

Write the simple subject of each sentence. Remember, descriptive words are not part of the simple subject.

Example: The river beavers built a new lodge.
Simple subject: beavers

Winter Lodges

1. Many animals need shelter from cold and predators.
2. Lodges on islands often give beavers the best protection.
3. These homes are built up from the bottom of the pond.
4. Strong saplings are anchored into the mud.
5. The sturdy rodents then pile debris into a mound.
6. Branches buried in the mud are food for the winter.
7. The whole family lives together in the snug burrow.
8. Their warm bodies keep the temperature comfortable.
9. Predators can claw at the frozen lodge.
10. The crafty beavers stay safe and warm inside.

→ **For a SELF-CHECK and more practice, see the EXERCISE BANK, p. 308.**

SENTENCE PARTS

B. WRITING: Synthesizing Information in Science

A classmate did research on how long young animals stay with their parents. Write one sentence about each animal described below. Underline the simple subject.

Example: An arctic seal <u>pup</u> spends two weeks in a shelter with its mother.

Leaving Home

Animal	Name of Young	Length of Time Spent with Parents
Arctic seal	pup	2 weeks in shelter with mother
Penguin	chick	23 days with parents
Kangaroo	joey	7 to10 months in mother's pouch
Beaver	kitten	more than a year with parents
Human	child	usually 18 years at home

Simple Predicates, or Verbs

1 Here's the Idea

You have learned about the simple subject of a sentence. You also need to know about the simple predicate.

The simple predicate, or verb, is the main word or words in the complete predicate.

COMPLETE PREDICATE

Prairie pioneers lived in sod houses.

SIMPLE PREDICATE

Few trees grow in the prairie grasslands.

SIMPLE PREDICATE

A verb is a word used to express an action, a condition, or a state of being. A **linking verb** tells what the subject *is*. An **action verb** tells what the subject *does,* even when the action cannot be seen.

Pioneers made sod bricks. (action you can see)

They wanted a sturdy home. (action you cannot see)

Sod houses stayed cool in hot weather. (linking)

2 Why It Matters in Writing

You can make your writing more interesting by substituting strong verbs for weaker ones. Strong verbs can add important information about the subject.

STUDENT MODEL

A prairie fire ~~burned~~ *destroyed* almost everything in its path. The fire ~~was~~ *grew* enormous. It ~~went~~ *stretched* from one end of the horizon to the other.

❸ Practice and Apply

A. CONCEPT CHECK: Simple Predicates, or Verbs

Write the simple predicate, or verb, in each sentence.

On the Lone Prairie

1. My great-grandparents lived in a sod house, or "soddy," on the Kansas prairie.
2. They traveled west from their home in Tennessee.
3. The men used nearly an acre of sod for the house.
4. The home had only two windows and one door.
5. My family built their soddy in the side of a hill.
6. Sometimes the cows ate the grass on the roof.
7. Once, a cow fell through the roof into the house!
8. Heavy rains at times soaked through the sod.
9. The dirt floor turned into a giant mud puddle.
10. Still, sod houses protected my family from harsh winters.

➜ **For a SELF-CHECK and more practice, see the EXERCISE BANK, p. 309.**

SENTENCE PARTS

B. WRITING: Preparing a Science Report

A science student drew this diagram and took notes about the soil in her neighborhood. Use a different verb with each note to create three sentences that describe the soil.

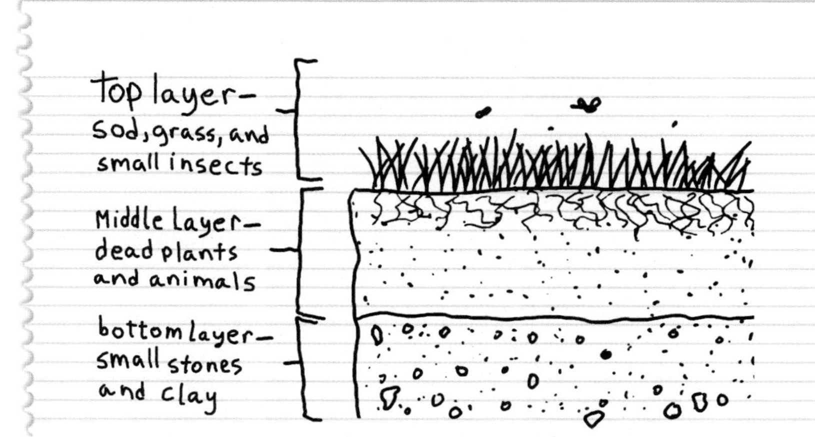

LESSON 4

Verb Phrases

1 Here's the Idea

The simple predicate, or verb, may consist of two or more words. These words are called a verb phrase.

▶ **A verb phrase is made up of a main verb and one or more helping verbs.**

VERB PHRASE

A "smart house" may cook your food for you.

HELPING VERB (may) MAIN VERB (cook)

Main Verbs and Helping Verbs

A **main verb** can stand by itself as the simple predicate of a sentence.

Computer networks run smart houses. (action)

MAIN VERB (run)

The network is the brain of the house. (linking)

MAIN VERB (is)

One or more **helping verbs** help main verbs express action or show time.

VERB PHRASE

Computer networks will run smart houses.

HELPING VERB (will) MAIN VERB (run)

The network has been turning the lights on and off.

It will have been programmed for all seasons.

Sometimes the main verb changes form when used with a helping verb. For more on these changes, see pages 108–110.

Common Helping Verbs	
Forms of *be*	is, am, are, was, were, be, been
Forms of *do*	do, does, did
Forms of *have*	has, have, had
Others	may, might, can, should, could, would, shall, will

CHAPTER 1

2 Why It Matters in Writing

Writers often use verb phrases to help show time. Notice how the verb phrases in the paragraph below show past, present, and future time.

PROFESSIONAL MODEL

Long before scientists or architects had considered the possibility, the author Ray Bradbury wrote about a smart house. In a 1950 story, he described a kind of super-automated house that technologists now are hoping they will make a reality.

—J. Timothy Bagwell

PAST

PRESENT

FUTURE

SENTENCE PARTS

3 Practice and Apply

CONCEPT CHECK: Verb Phrases

Write the verb phrase in each sentence below. Be sure to include all the helping verbs.

Smart Houses

1. The first "smart house" was developed in the early 1980s.
2. Its appliances could communicate with each other.
3. Suppose you were running the vacuum cleaner.
4. The noise might keep you from hearing the phone.
5. In that situation the house would stop the vacuum cleaner automatically.
6. Those with disabilities may benefit the most from a smart house.
7. The house will perform some of the tasks beyond their capability.
8. For example, meals could be brought to a person's bed.
9. The food will have been prepared by a smart kitchen.
10. Surely you can imagine other uses for a smart house.

➜ **For a SELF-CHECK and more practice, see the EXERCISE BANK, p. 309**

Compound Sentence Parts

1 Here's the Idea

Sentences can have **compound subjects** and **compound verbs**.

A compound subject is made up of two or more subjects that share the same verb. The subjects are joined by a conjunction, or connecting word, such as *and, or,* or *but.*

COMPOUND SUBJECT

***Salyut 1* and *Skylab* were the first space stations.**

SUBJECT SUBJECT

American astronauts or Russian cosmonauts lived aboard the stations.

A compound verb is made up of two or more verbs that have the same subject. The verbs are joined by a conjunction such as *and, or,* or *but.*

COMPOUND VERB

The *Skylab* crew worked and slept in close quarters.

VERB VERB

They worked hard but slept little.

CHAPTER 1

2 Why It Matters in Writing

You can use compound subjects and verbs to combine sentences and avoid repetition in your writing.

STUDENT MODEL

Weightlessness is fun ~~Weightlessness can have serious side effects~~ [but is dangerous]. In zero gravity, your muscles [and bones] do less work. ~~Your bones do less work, too~~. Without exercise, they lose strength quickly.

③ Practice and Apply

A. CONCEPT CHECK: Compound Sentence Parts

Write the compound subject or the compound verb in each sentence.

Home Away from Home

1. Space stations and orbiting platforms are our first step away from Earth.
2. In the future, we may design and build outer-space cities.
3. Several nations or international groups could pool their resources.
4. They could create and manage a colony on the moon.
5. Minerals and other raw materials would be shipped to colonies in space.
6. We already design and plan model cities.
7. In one design, two huge cylinders and their solar panels form the main body of the space city.
8. The cylinders rotate and create an artificial gravity.
9. Special greenhouses shelter and sustain the city's food.
10. These cities or other space colonies could bring us closer to the stars!

➜ **For a SELF-CHECK and more practice, see the EXERCISE BANK, p. 310.**

SENTENCE PARTS

B. REVISING: Using Compound Subjects and Verbs

Combine each pair of sentences, following the instructions in parentheses.

1. A group of nations is building an international space station. They are supplying it too. (Use a compound verb.)
2. Astronauts will be carried up on the space shuttle. Their supplies also will be carried on the shuttle. (Use a compound subject.)
3. Scientists will grow plants in zero gravity. They will study plants in zero gravity as well. (Use a compound verb.)

Skylab

Kinds of Sentences

1 Here's the Idea

A sentence can be used to make a statement, to ask a question, to make a request or give a command, or to show strong feelings.

Four Kinds of Sentences

	What It Does	Examples
Declarative .	Makes a statement; always ends with a period.	I see something weird in that tree. It looks like a gray basketball.
Interrogative ?	Asks a question; always ends with a question mark.	What do you think it is? Is it a hornet's nest?
Imperative . or !	Tells or asks someone to do something; usually ends with a period but may end with an exclamation point.	Please don't get too close to it. Be careful!
Exclamatory !	Shows strong feeling; always ends with an exclamation point.	I see hornets flying out! I'm getting out of here!

2 Why It Matters in Writing

You can use different kinds of sentences to imitate the way people really talk. Notice how three kinds of sentences are used in this conversation between Ebenezer Scrooge and his nephew, Fred.

LITERARY MODEL

Scrooge . . . . Come, come, what is it you want? Don't waste all day, Nephew.

Fred. I only want to wish you a Merry Christmas, Uncle. Don't be cross.

—Charles Dickens, *A Christmas Carol*, dramatized by Frederick Gaines

INTERROGATIVE
IMPERATIVE
DECLARATIVE

CHAPTER 1

3 Practice and Apply

A. CONCEPT CHECK: Kinds of Sentences

Identify each of the following sentences as declarative (D), interrogative (INT), exclamatory (E), or imperative (IMP).

Dangerous Nests

1. Did you know that some wasps build round, gray nests that can be as big as beach balls?
2. The nests are made from cellulose and are very strong.
3. Stay away from wasps.
4. Their sting is very painful!
5. Yellow jackets are really yellow and black.
6. Do they eat many insect pests?
7. They live in colonies and build papery nests in spaces underground or in walls and attics.
8. Did you know that their nests may have from 300 to more than 100,000 cells?
9. Yellow jackets are dangerous only if you get too close to their nest.
10. Don't ever try to move a nest yourself.

➜ **For a SELF-CHECK and more practice, see the EXERCISE BANK, p. 310.**

B. WRITING: Creating Dialogue

Read the following *Fox Trot* comic strip. Notice the kinds of sentences used in the first two frames. Then, on a sheet of paper, write dialogue for the last two frames. Use complete sentences and as many sentence types as you can.

Fox Trot by Bill Amend

Subjects in Unusual Order

1 Here's the Idea

In most declarative sentences, subjects come before verbs. In some kinds of sentences, however, subjects can come between verb parts, follow verbs, or not appear at all.

Questions

▶ **In a question, the subject usually comes after the verb or between parts of the verb phrase.**

Is she ready?

VERB PHRASE

Does the weather look good for the game?

SUBJECT

To find the subject, turn the question into a statement. Then ask who or what is or does something.

Are you staying home?

You are staying home. (Who is staying? *you*)

Commands

▶ **The subject of a command, or imperative sentence, is usually *you*.** Often, *you* doesn't appear in the sentence because it is implied.

(You) Meet us at the concession stand.

IMPLIED SUBJECT

(You) Bring money for snacks!

Inverted Sentences

In an inverted sentence, the subject comes after the verb. Writers use inverted sentences to emphasize particular words or ideas.

CHAPTER 1

Inverted Subject and Verb	
Normal	The first **batter walked** up to the plate.
Inverted	Up to the plate **walked** the first **batter.**
Normal	The **fans cheered** loud and long.
Inverted	Loud and long **cheered** the **fans.**

Sentences Beginning with *Here* or *There*

▶ **In some sentences beginning with *here* or *there,* subjects follow verbs. To find the subject in such a sentence, look for the verb and ask the question *who* or *what.*** Find the subject by looking at the words that follow the verb.

WHO COMES?

Here comes your all-state championship team.

VERB — SUBJECT

WHO GOES?

There goes our best rebounder.

VERB — SUBJECT

2 Why It Matters in Writing

You can add variety and interest to your sentences by changing the order of subjects and verbs. Notice how the inverted sentences in the revision below create a more suspenseful tone.

STUDENT MODEL

DRAFT

It was the bottom of the ninth inning, the score was tied, and two men were on base. Then the Yankees' best hitter stepped up to the plate. A deafening roar rolled from the upper decks.

REVISION

It was the bottom of the ninth inning, the score was tied, and two men were on base. **Then up to the plate stepped the Yankees' best hitter. From the upper decks rolled a deafening roar.**

3 Practice and Apply

A. CONCEPT CHECK: Subjects in Unusual Order

In separate columns on a sheet of paper, write the subjects and the verbs (or verb phrases) in these sentences.

Home Field Advantage

1. There are some benefits to games at the home stadium.
2. In the bleachers sit all your fans.
3. There are fewer hostile fans from the other team.
4. Is travel time shorter to and from the game?
5. On the field can be seen special landscaping.
6. Will the umpires give the home team a break?
7. Does the team usually play better on its own field?
8. Look at the team's record for the season.
9. There are more wins at home.
10. Plan more home games for next year.

→ **For a SELF-CHECK and more practice, see the EXERCISE BANK, p. 310.**

CHAPTER 1

B. REVISING: Adding Variety

Rewrite the following sentences according to the instructions given in parentheses.

1. You watched the Women's World Cup soccer games. (Change the sentence to a question.)
2. Women's soccer is becoming more popular for two reasons. (Begin the sentence with *There are.*)
3. Women with different backgrounds come from all over the United States. (Invert subject and verb, and begin with *From all over the United States.*)
4. Their schools have strong soccer programs for all grades. (Change the sentence to a question.)
5. The undefeated U.S. team ran onto the field. (Invert subject and verb, and begin with *Onto the field.*)

In your **Working Portfolio,** find the paragraph that you wrote for the **Write Away** on page 4. Add variety to the sentences by changing the position of the subjects in some of them.

Complements: Subject Complements

1 Here's the Idea

A complement is a word or a group of words that completes the meaning of a verb. Two kinds of complements are **subject complements** and **objects of verbs.**

▶ **A subject complement is a word or group of words that follows a linking verb and renames or describes the subject.** A linking verb links the subject with a noun or an adjective that tells more about it.

LINKING VERB
Butterflies are fragile.
SUBJECT COMPLEMENT

Common Linking Verbs	
Forms of *be*	am, is, are, was, were, be, been
Other linking verbs	appear, become, feel, look, sound, seem, taste

SENTENCE PARTS

Predicate Nouns and Predicate Adjectives

Both nouns and adjectives can serve as subject complements.

▶ **A predicate noun follows a linking verb and defines or renames the subject.**

DEFINES
Monarch butterflies are insects.
SUBJECT PREDICATE NOUN

RENAMES
Cocoons become butterfly nurseries.

▶ **A predicate adjective follows a linking verb and describes a quality of the subject.**

DESCRIBES
Monarchs look beautiful.
SUBJECT PREDICATE ADJECTIVE

❷ Why It Matters in Writing

Subject complements can provide important information and vivid details about your subjects.

PROFESSIONAL MODEL

Arctic terns **are** marathoners of the bird world. They **appear** too small and insignificant to be great athletes, but every year they fly from the Arctic to the Antarctic and back again.

—S. Baugh

PREDICATE NOUN

PREDICATE ADJECTIVES

❸ Practice and Apply

CHAPTER 1

A. CONCEPT CHECK: Subject Complements

Write the underlined word in each sentence, and identify it as a predicate noun (PN) or a predicate adjective (PA).

MIgration Matters

1. Migration routes are highways in the sky for birds.
2. The migration of songbirds is difficult to track.
3. The birds are too little to carry radio transmitters.
4. Identification bands can be useful in tracking migration.
5. The bands often become loose, however.
6. Fortunately, the isotope deuterium has been helpful.
7. Deuterium is a form of hydrogen found in rainwater.
8. Deuterium becomes part of plants, insects, and birds.
9. Deuterium levels become higher as you go farther south.
10. Now scientists feel hopeful about tracking migrations.

➜ **For a SELF-CHECK and more practice, see the EXERCISE BANK, p. 311.**

B. REVISING: Adding Subject Complements

Choose the word *time, residents,* or *remarkable* to fill in each missing subject complement below.

Monarch butterflies are **(1)** (predicate adjective). In the summer, the adults in the northern United States lay their eggs. Then, it is **(2)** (predicate noun) for them to die. By late summer, the great-grandchildren of the original butterflies migrate. They become **(3)** (predicate noun) of Mexico.

Complements: Objects of Verbs

1 Here's the Idea

In addition to subject complements, there are objects of verbs. Action verbs often need complements called direct objects and indirect objects to complete their meaning.

Direct Objects

▶ **A direct object is a word or group of words that names the receiver of the action of an action verb.** A direct object answers the question *what* or *whom.*

BORROW WHAT?

Movie producers often borrow real homes.

DIRECT OBJECT

The right house can charm viewers. (can charm whom? *viewers*)

Indirect Objects

▶ **An indirect object is a word or group of words that tells to whom or what (or for whom or what) an action is performed.** An indirect object usually comes between a verb and a direct object.

TO WHOM?

We lent the producer our house.

INDIRECT OBJECT — DIRECT OBJECT

She offered us free movie passes.

Verbs that are often followed by indirect objects include *bring, give, hand, lend, make, offer, send, show, teach, tell, write,* and *ask.*

Here's How **Finding Direct and Indirect Objects**

The producer paid us rent money.

1. Find the action verb in the sentence. ***paid***
2. To find the direct object, ask, Paid what? ***money***
3. To find the indirect object, ask, Paid to or for whom? ***us***

SENTENCE PARTS

2 Why It Matters in Writing

By using both direct and indirect objects, a writer can describe complicated events clearly and simply.

LITERARY MODEL

She **heated** some lima **beans** and **ham** she had in the icebox, **made** the **cocoa,** and **set** the **table.** The woman **did** not **ask** the **boy** **anything** about where he lived, or his folks, or anything else that **would embarrass** **him.**

—Langston Hughes, "Thank You, M'am"

DIRECT OBJECTS

INDIRECT OBJECT

3 Practice and Apply

CHAPTER 1

CONCEPT CHECK: Objects of Verbs

Write the objects in these sentences, identifying each as a direct object (DO) or an indirect object (IO).

One Person's Dream House

1. Bill Gates owns a very technologically advanced house.
2. The house gives its inhabitants a high level of comfort and convenience.
3. Each visitor to the house carries an electronic identifier.
4. The device gives the house information.
5. The house can then grant the visitor's wishes.
6. Such a house can teach researchers many things about homes for people with disabilities.
7. For example, the house can bring you music in every room.
8. A similar house could provide aids for the visually challenged.
9. Voice instructions could give a visually challenged person information about running appliances.
10. Gates's house also has a 32-screen video wall.

→ **For a SELF-CHECK and more practice, see the EXERCISE BANK, p. 311.**

LESSON 10 Fragments and Run-Ons

1 Here's the Idea

Sentence fragments and run-on sentences are writing errors that can make your writing difficult to understand.

Sentence Fragments

▶ **A sentence fragment is a part of a sentence that is written as if it were a complete sentence.** A sentence fragment is missing a subject, a predicate, or both.

FRAGMENTS

The Rungus people in Malaysia. (missing a predicate)

Build traditional homes called longhouses. (missing a subject)

On top of stilts away from floodwaters. (missing both)

To make a complete sentence, add a subject, a predicate, or both.

REVISION

The Rungus people live in Malaysia.

They build traditional homes called longhouses.

These homes often are constructed on top of stilts, away from floodwaters.

SENTENCE PARTS

Run-On Sentences

A run-on sentence is two or more sentences written as though they were a single sentence.

RUN-ON

The longhouse roof is made of palm leaves, the walls are made of tree bark.

REVISION

The longhouse roof is made of palm leaves. The walls are made of tree bark.

REVISION

The longhouse roof is made of palm leaves, and the walls are made of tree bark.

When combining two sentences with a conjunction, use a comma before the conjunction.

CHAPTER 1

2 Why It Matters in Writing

Fragments and run-on sentences can make your writing confusing and difficult to read. If you fix these problems, your writing will read more clearly.

STUDENT MODEL

DRAFT

Each Rungus family has its own apartment the family shares a common living area with other families. Many may live in a longhouse. Twenty to 40 families. In each apartment, a raised sleeping and dining area.

REVISION

Each Rungus family has its own apartment, **but** the family shares a common living area with other families. Twenty to 40 families **may live in a longhouse.** In each apartment **there is** a raised sleeping and dining area.

❸ Practice and Apply

A. CONCEPT CHECK: Sentence Fragments and Run-Ons

Identify each of the following sentences as a fragment (F), a run-on (RO), or a complete sentence (CS).

Mayan Homes

1. The Maya live in Mexico.
2. Their traditional homes.
3. Have been much the same for centuries.
4. Some were made of stucco or stone.
5. Today Mayan houses have electricity and telephones other things haven't changed.
6. Modern building materials.
7. The Maya now use such materials as cinder blocks and cement for walls.
8. They build roofs from corrugated metal they also use tarpaper.
9. The tombstones in some Mayan cemeteries.
10. Are shaped like little houses.

➜ **For a SELF-CHECK and more practice, see the EXERCISE BANK, p. 312.**

SENTENCE PARTS

B. REVISING: Clearing Up Confusion

You are out hiking on a beautiful sunny day when suddenly a thunderstorm rolls in. You pull out a friend's notes on building a temporary shelter. Yikes! The notes are hard to understand. Revise them so that the next person to use them won't be frustrated by fragments and run-ons.

BUILDING A TEMPORARY SHELTER

First, you need to find a small tree. Away from open areas. Won't be hit by lightning. Second, drive a three-foot stick into the ground nearby take out your rain poncho. Tie a string between the tree and the stick. Drape over the string. Sit underneath the poncho "tent" lie down if you hear thunder.

Grammar in Literature

Varying Your Sentences

Writers use sentences of different types to keep their writing interesting and to call attention to certain ideas. In the following passage, notice how Anna Quindlen varies her sentences effectively to describe and give readers a feel for her subject.

CHAPTER 1

from

Homeless

by Anna Quindlen

Her name was Ann, and we met in the Port Authority Bus terminal several Januarys ago. I was doing a story on homeless people. She said I was wasting my time talking to her; she was just passing through, although she'd been passing through for more than two weeks. To prove to me that this was true, she rummaged through a tote bag. . . and brought out her photographs.

They were not pictures of family, or friends. . . . They were pictures of a house. The house was yellow. I looked on the back for a date or name, but neither was there. There was no need for discussion. I knew what she was trying to tell me, for it was something I had often felt. She was not adrift, alone, anonymous, although her bags and her raincoat with the grime shadowing its creases had made me believe she was. She had a house, or at least once upon a time had had one. Inside were curtains, a couch, a stove, potholders. You are where you live. She was somebody.

SHORT DECLARATIVE SENTENCES help proclaim these simple statements of fact.

INVERTED SENTENCE draws the reader into the house.

SHORT SENTENCES neatly summarize the writer's feelings about Ann.

Practice and Apply

A. Using Sentence Variety

Follow the directions below to revise this passage by varying sentences.

(1) The temperature of 17 degrees below zero was dangerous. **(2)** People could die from exposure in only a few hours. **(3)** Volunteers tried to get homeless people into the city shelters. **(4)** The police tried to get them to go, too. **(5)** Homeless people could warm up. **(6)** They could eat hot meals, also. **(7)** A stubborn homeless man was on one street. **(8)** He refused to move, and at first no one knew why. **(9)** His wife was afraid to go to the shelter he wouldn't leave her, home was where she was, he said. **(10)** Volunteers finally got them into a warm shelter.

1. Revise sentences 1 and 2 to express a complete thought.
2. Revise sentences 3 and 4 by using a compound subject.
3. Use a compound predicate to combine sentences 5 and 6.
4. Revise sentence 7 by reversing the subject and the verb and beginning with *On one street*.
5. Revise run-on sentence 9 by creating three shorter sentences.

B. WRITING: Description

Use the ideas from this chapter or your own ideas to write a paragraph describing your ideal room or home. Save your paragraph in your **Working Portfolio.**

SENTENCE PARTS

Mixed Review

A. Subjects, Predicates, and Compound Sentence Parts Read the passage, then write the answers to the questions below it.

(1) The skies over many big cities echo with the cries of peregrine falcons. **(2)** These birds are raptors, or birds of prey. **(3)** Falcons and hawks were once nearly extinct in the eastern United States. **(4)** However, a restoration program has increased their numbers. **(5)** Falcons like the high ledges of skyscrapers and tall bridges. **(6)** There are perfect nesting sites in these places. **(7)** The birds' favorite foods are pigeons and starlings. **(8)** What happens when a soaring falcon spots its prey? **(9)** Down drops the hunter at nearly 200 miles an hour! **(10)** Falcons can live and hunt with ease in major cities.

1. What is the simple subject of sentence 1?
2. What kind of sentence is sentence 2?
3. What is the compound part in sentence 3?
4. What is the simple predicate of sentence 4?
5. What is the complete predicate of sentence 5?
6. What is the simple subject of sentence 6?
7. What is the complete subject of sentence 7?
8. What kind of sentence is sentence 8?
9. What is the simple subject of sentence 9?
10. What is the compound part in sentence 10?

B. Complements Identify each underlined word as a predicate noun (PN), a predicate adjective (PA), an indirect object (IO), or a direct object (DO).

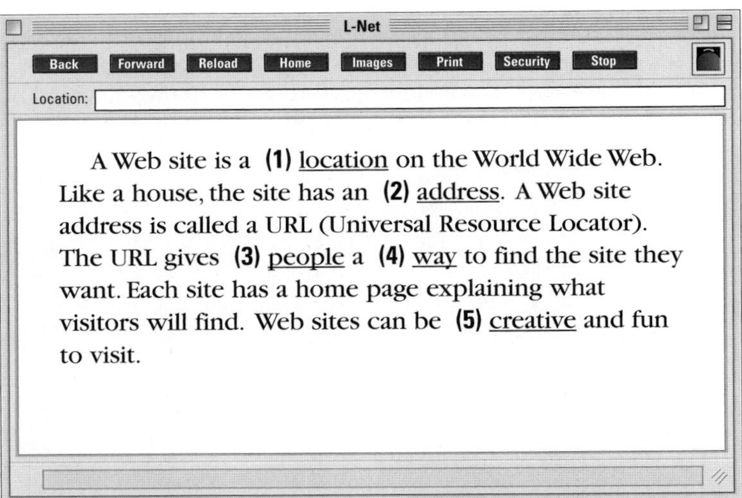

CHAPTER 1

Mastery Test: What Did You Learn?

Choose the letter of the term that correctly identifies each underlined part of this passage.

<u>Elevators made skyscrapers and high-rises possible.</u> (1) Why? There is a simple reason. Few people <u>would want</u> (2) to walk up 30 or 40 flights to their office or home each day. <u>Elevators offer other benefits too</u> (3). Their automated <u>cars</u> (4) are actually <u>safer</u> (5) than stairs. Every three days, elevators <u>collect and transport</u> (6) the equivalent of the world's population. The fastest elevator ever built is in Yokohama, Japan. It carries <u>people</u> (7) up 68 floors in 40 seconds. <u>Don't think this invention is always a convenience, though.</u> (8) Elevators can also cause <u>passengers</u> (9) real trouble. <u>A man in England was trapped in an elevator for 62 hours!</u> (10) He was finally rescued.

1. A. declarative sentence
   B. interrogative sentence
   C. exclamatory sentence
   D. imperative sentence

2. A. main verb
   B. helping verb
   C. complete predicate
   D. verb phrase

3. A. imperative sentence
   B. interrogative sentence
   C. exclamatory sentence
   D. declarative sentence

4. A. subject
   B. predicate
   C. complement
   D. indirect object

5. A. compound subject
   B. predicate noun
   C. simple subject
   D. predicate adjective

6. A. simple subject
   B. complement
   C. compound verb
   D. compound subject

7. A. simple subject
   B. verb phrase
   C. direct object
   D. indirect object

8. A. declarative sentence
   B. interrogative sentence
   C. exclamatory sentence
   D. imperative sentence

9. A. simple predicate
   B. direct object
   C. predicate noun
   D. indirect object

10. A. declarative sentence
    B. interrogative sentence
    C. exclamatory sentence
    D. imperative sentence

Student Help Desk

The Sentence at a Glance

A sentence has two basic parts, a complete subject and a complete predicate.

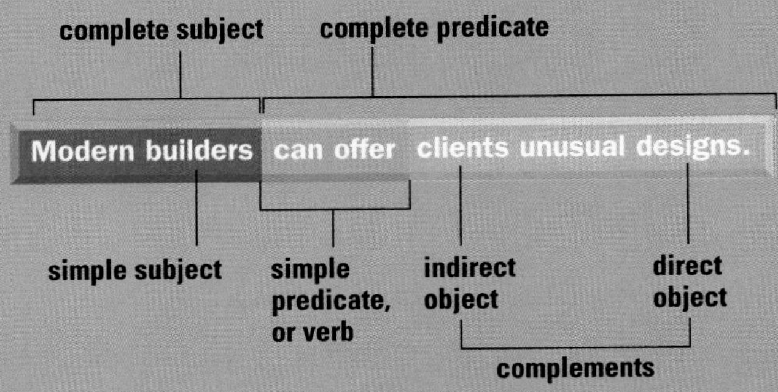

CHAPTER 1

Subjects and Predicates

Bricks and Mortar

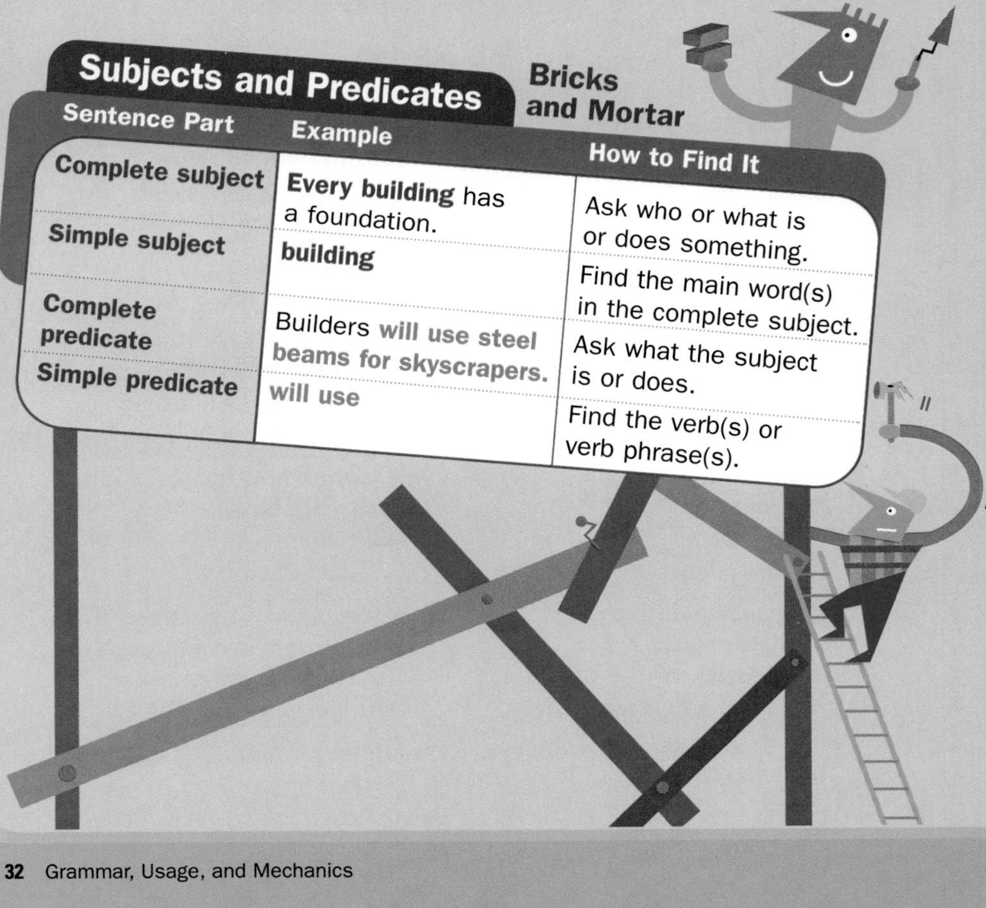

Sentence Part	Example	How to Find It
Complete subject	**Every building** has a foundation.	Ask who or what is or does something.
Simple subject	**building**	Find the main word(s) in the complete subject.
Complete predicate	Builders **will use steel beams for skyscrapers.**	Ask what the subject is or does.
Simple predicate	**will use**	Find the verb(s) or verb phrase(s).

Complements Finishing the Job

	Type of Complement	Example	What It Does
Linking verbs	Predicate noun	This building is my **home.**	Renames or defines the subject
	Predicate adjective	It is **gorgeous.**	Describes the subject
Action verbs	Direct object	We painted the **house.**	Completes the action of the verb
	Indirect object	A neighbor gave **us** some blue shutters.	Tells to whom/what or for whom/what the action is done

Kinds of Sentences Adding Interest

Declarative sentence	Someone is coming**.**
Interrogative sentence	Are you the repairman**?**
Imperative sentence	**(You)** Fix our furnace**.**
Exclamatory sentence	We are freezing**!**

SENTENCE PARTS

The Bottom Line

Checklist for Editing Sentences

Have I . . .

- ____ made sure that each sentence has a subject and a predicate?
- ____ corrected any fragments or run-on sentences?
- ____ combined sentences with similar ideas by using compound subjects or verbs?
- ____ used different kinds of sentences and different orders of sentence parts for variety?
- ____ used complements to make the meanings of sentences clear?

Nouns

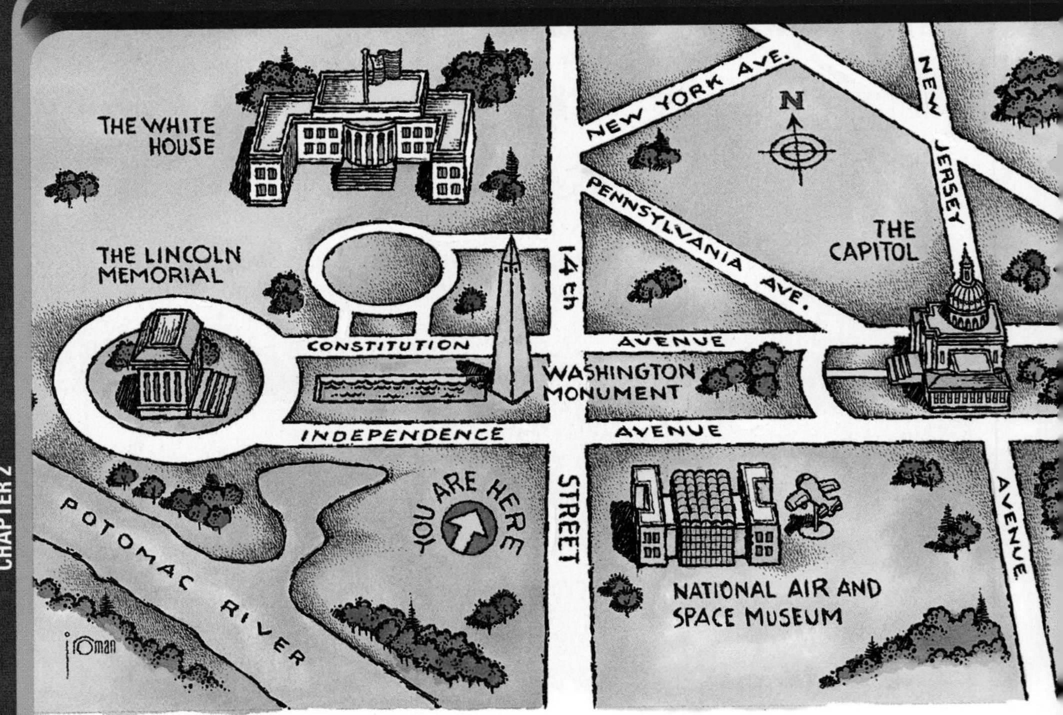

Topic: U.S. Landmarks and Attractions

You Are Here

If you were visiting Washington, D.C., a map like the one above could help you get to all the important sites. Using the map, explain how you would get from the White House to the National Air and Space Museum. What roads would you use? Which landmarks would you pass?

The labels for the roads and landmarks are nouns—important words that allow us to name persons, places, things, and ideas. Without nouns we'd all have trouble finding our way around.

Write Away: Roll Out the Plans

Write about a landmark you would design. What would it look like? Whom or what might it honor? Save your work in your **Working Portfolio.**

Diagnostic Test: What Do You Know?

For each underlined item, choose the letter of the term that correctly identifies it.

Each year, millions of people (1) visit the remarkable National Air and Space Museum (2) in Washington, D.C. Opened in 1976, this museum is part of the Smithsonian Institution. It features more than 20 galleries (3), a theater (4), and a planetarium. Among its displays of early aircraft are the Wright brothers' (5) original 1903 airplane (6), *Flyer,* and Charles Lindbergh's (7) *Spirit of St. Louis*. Other exhibits include spacecraft (8) from various missions, including *Columbia,* the command module of the *Apollo 11* spacecraft that carried astronauts Neil Armstrong (9), Buzz Aldrin, and Michael Collins to the moon and back. Those who want to learn more about the courage (10) of pilots and the history of flying should really stop in.

1. A. proper noun
   B. plural noun
   C. possessive noun
   D. compound noun

2. A. noun as subject
   B. noun as direct object
   C. noun as indirect object
   D. noun as predicate noun

3. A. collective noun
   B. plural noun
   C. possessive noun
   D. compound noun

4. A. common noun
   B. abstract noun
   C. proper noun
   D. compound noun

5. A. singular possessive noun
   B. plural possessive noun
   C. compound noun
   D. abstract noun

6. A. singular possessive noun
   B. plural possessive noun
   C. singular compound noun
   D. plural compound noun

7. A. singular common noun
   B. plural proper noun
   C. singular possessive noun
   D. plural possessive noun

8. A. proper noun
   B. abstract noun
   C. possessive noun
   D. compound noun

9. A. common noun
   B. abstract noun
   C. proper noun
   D. possessive noun

10. A. concrete noun
    B. abstract noun
    C. possessive noun
    D. compound noun

Kinds of Nouns

1 Here's the Idea

▶ **A noun is a word that names a person, place, thing, or idea.**

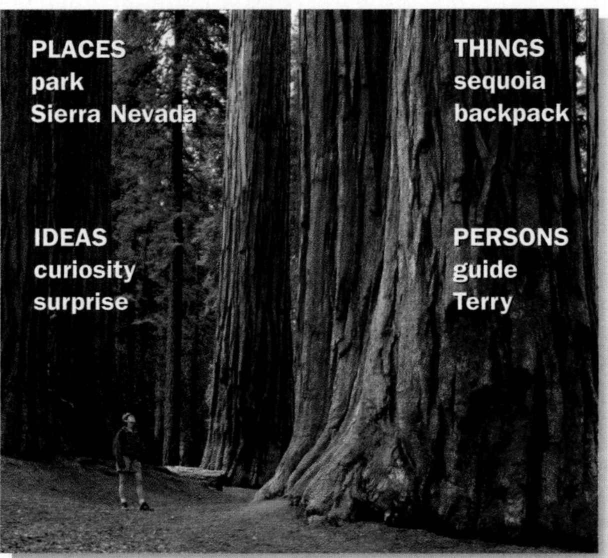

Common and Proper Nouns

A **common noun** is a general name for a person, place, thing, or idea. Common nouns are usually not capitalized. A **proper noun** is the name of a particular person, place, thing, or idea. Proper nouns are always capitalized.

Common	leader	forest	mountain
Proper	Sequoya	Giant Forest	Mount Whitney

Concrete and Abstract Nouns

A **concrete noun** names a thing that can be seen, heard, smelled, touched, or tasted. Examples include *rainbow, thunder, sapling, feather,* and *blueberry.*

On the path we spotted a large, slithery snake.

An **abstract noun** names an idea, feeling, quality, or characteristic. Examples include *happiness, beauty, freedom, humor,* and *greed.*

We felt tremendous relief after the snake passed us.

Every noun is either common or proper and either concrete or abstract. For example, *desert* is common and concrete; *Mohave Desert* is proper and concrete. *Nature* is common and abstract.

Collective Nouns

A **collective noun** is a word that names a group of people or things. Examples include *class, crowd, family, staff, trio,* and *team*.

Our family gathered around the campfire for breakfast.

Some collective nouns name specific groups of animals. Examples include *school, herd, pack,* and *colony*.

At night, a pack of wolves howled at the moon.

NOUNS

2 Why It Matters in Writing

Although common nouns can be very specific, the proper nouns in the passage below leave no doubt about exactly what trail or tree the writer means.

PROFESSIONAL MODEL

I began my park explorations on the **Congress Trail**—just up the road from my cabin in **Giant Forest**—for nowhere can you get a quicker grasp of the life cycle of the big trees. I set out early, when the air was bracing and few people stirred. For companions I had fussy Steller's jays and a trio of mule deer. The two-mile paved walkway starts right at the base of the **Sherman Tree.**

—Paul Martin, "California's Wilderness Sisters"

❸ Practice and Apply

A. CONCEPT CHECK: Kinds of Nouns

Write the nouns in these sentences, identifying each as common or proper. Then identify the two collective nouns.

California's Living Monuments

1. Among the largest living things on our planet are sequoias.
2. They are named for Sequoya, a Cherokee scholar and leader.
3. The most impressive example is the General Sherman Tree.
4. It bears the name of a Northern commander of the Civil War.
5. This sequoia weighs 12 million pounds and soars 275 feet, a symbol of strength and endurance.
6. The size of its trunk, as wide as a highway with three lanes, comes as a great surprise to many people.
7. A team of researchers estimated its age as between 2,200 and 2,500 years.
8. In past centuries sequoias grew across the Northern Hemisphere.
9. Now they are found chiefly in national reserves in California.
10. The beauty of these trees amazes crowds every day.

CHALLENGE Find two abstract nouns in the sentences above.

→ **For a SELF-CHECK and more practice, see the EXERCISE BANK, p. 312.**

B. WRITING: Collective Nouns

Flock is a collective noun referring to a group of birds. Of all the collective nouns, those referring to groups of animals may be the most unusual. Write a funny piece of dialogue about or between two members of an animal group. Be sure to use the right collective noun.

"Some of the guys in the flock think you're showing off."

Singular and Plural Nouns

1 Here's the Idea

A singular noun names one person, place, thing, or idea. A plural noun names more than one person, place, thing, or idea.

One tourist noticed a statue. (singular nouns)

Many tourists looked at statues. (plural nouns)

One of the hardest things about plural nouns is spelling them correctly. Use these rules in the Quick-Fix Spelling Machine.

QUICK–FIX SPELLING MACHINE: PLURALS OF NOUNS

	SINGULAR	RULE	PLURAL
1	statue dream	Add *-s* to most nouns.	statues dreams
2	wish sandwich	Add *-es* to a noun that ends in *s, sh, ch, x,* or *z.*	wishes sandwiches
3	photo	Add *-s* to most nouns that end in *o.*	photos
	hero	Add *-es* to a few nouns that end in *o.*	heroes
4	city	For most nouns ending in *y,* change the *y* to an *i* and add *-es.*	cities
	valley	When a vowel comes before the *y,* just add *-s.*	valleys
5	wolf life	For most nouns ending in *f* or *fe,* change the *f* to *v* and add *-es* or *-s.*	wolves lives
	chief	Just add *-s* to a few nouns that end in *f* or *fe.*	chiefs
6	deer buffalo	For some nouns, keep the same spelling.	deer buffalo

NOUNS

The plurals of some nouns are formed in irregular ways.

Singular	man	child	foot	mouse
Plural	men	children	feet	mice

2 Why It Matters in Writing

Imagine writing without plural nouns! Writers use so many plurals that learning the spelling rules is important.

LITERARY MODEL

Passengers all about us were crowding against the rail. Jabbered conversation, sharp **cries, laughs** and **cheers**—a steadily rising din filled the air. **Mothers** and **fathers** lifted up **babies** so that they too could see, off to the left, the Statue of Liberty.

—Russell Freedman, *Immigrant Kids*

CHAPTER 2

3 Practice and Apply

A. CONCEPT CHECK: Singular and Plural Nouns

Write the plural forms of the nouns in parentheses.

A Makeover for Lady Liberty

1. When the Statue of Liberty was almost a century old, (engineer) began to worry about her.
2. The copper (covering) had worn down, and (piece) of the torch were falling.
3. Photos showed that the head was 24 (inch) out of line.
4. This caused one of the (ray) in the crown to rub against the copper cover of the right arm.
5. Money for repairs came from (corporation), (individual), and (schoolchild).
6. A major job was repairing the arm and the torch, which had endured many (stress) over the (year).
7. Thin (leaf) of gold were applied to the torch's "flame" so that it would reflect the sun.

8. In addition to the anniversary celebration in New York, many (community) around the country held their own (celebration).
9. On July 3, 1986, (speech), (concert), and (party) were held.
10. Lady Liberty began her second century on July 4, 1986, with many (festivity) and fireworks (display).

➜ **For a SELF-CHECK and more practice, see the EXERCISE BANK, p. 313.**

B. PROOFREADING: Spelling Plural Nouns

Ten plural nouns in the following passage are misspelled. Find them and write the correct spellings.

Show Me Your Golden Gate

San Francisco is one of California's largest citys. It has bunchs of attractions, including cable cars, ferrys, and wharfes. Its most popular sight, however, is the Golden Gate Bridge. Completed in 1937, the bridge connects San Francisco to northern communitys. Its main span stretches more than 4,200 feet across the Golden Gate waterway. The bridge has withstood bad weather, strong winds, and earthquakies. Its steel structure remains solid, protected by coates of orange rustproof paint. The lifes of residents and touristes alike seem affected by the bridge's beauty. Few can resist snapping photoes of it.

C. WRITING: Interpreting Data

Using the table below, write a few sentences comparing two famous suspension bridges—New York City's Brooklyn Bridge and San Francisco's Golden Gate Bridge. Use a variety of plural nouns in your sentences.

Comparing Two Bridges

	Brooklyn Bridge	Golden Gate Bridge
Length of main span	1,595 feet	4,200 feet
Years to complete	14	4
Total cost	$15,000,000	$35,500,000
Construction deaths	21	0

NOUNS

LESSON 3

Possessive Nouns

1 Here's the Idea

▶ **The possessive form of a noun shows ownership or relationship.**

I held Corey's camera as she tied her shoe.
OWNERSHIP

Rick's parents met us at the train station.
RELATIONSHIP

You may use possessive nouns in place of longer phrases.

George Washington Carver's home.
We visited ~~the home of George Washington Carver~~.

QUICK–FIX SPELLING MACHINE: POSSESSIVES

	NOUN	RULE	POSSESSIVE
Singular	sun Charles	Add an apostrophe and *-s.*	The sun's heat Charles's souvenirs
Plural ending in *-s*	states farmers	Add an apostrophe.	states' border farmers' crops
Plural not ending in *-s*	children geese	Add an apostrophe and *-s.*	children's toys geese's migrations

2 Why It Matters in Writing

Possessive nouns can help writers show even the most unusual relationships, as in the model below.

PROFESSIONAL MODEL

In Ashburn, Georgia, stands an unusual monument. Here you will find the **world's** largest sculpture of a peanut, the local **growers'** pride. The **peanut's** length is an amazing ten feet, seven feet greater than that of its rival, **Oklahoma's** "big peanut."

❸ Practice and Apply

A. CONCEPT CHECK: Possessive Nouns

Write the possessive form of each noun in parentheses. Then label each possessive form as singular or plural.

George Washington Carver Slept Here

1. In (Missouri) southwestern corner stands a modest frame home.
2. The (farmhouse) appearance is like that of many others.
3. Visitors may not recognize one of our (country) monuments.
4. Yet, within its walls lived one of (history) finest agricultural scientists, George Washington Carver.
5. As a young boy he survived most (children) worst nightmare, the loss of both parents.
6. (Neighbors) actions helped him to overcome his greatest difficulties.
7. At the monument, children can walk through the (area) many woods and fields.
8. Here (Carver) own interest in plants and agriculture began.
9. In time his work benefited many (farmers) lives.
10. The (home) simplicity reminds visitors of this great (person) humble background.

➜ **For a SELF-CHECK and more practice, see the EXERCISE BANK, p. 313.**

B. REVISING: Using Possessive Nouns

Use possessive nouns to make these phrases short enough to fit on signposts.

Example: The Mammoth Caves of Kentucky
Answer: Kentucky's Mammoth Caves

1. the Space Needle in Seattle
2. Preservation Hall in New Orleans
3. the beaches of California
4. the Hermitage of Andrew Jackson
5. the Gateway Arch in St. Louis

Mixed Review

A. Kinds of Nouns Write the 12 nouns that appear in the message on the postcard below. Identify each as common or proper. Then identify two collective nouns.

MESSAGE

Dear Esperanza,

My family and I are here in Grand Canyon National Park. In an hour, we'll be riding a team of mules down into the actual canyon. I can't wait to see Phantom Ranch! I wonder if it will be scary. Ha! The whole experience has been like a dream.

See you later,

Taneah

P.S. Tell the class I say "Hi."

B. Plural and Possessive Nouns Choose the correct word in parentheses, and identify it as plural or possessive.

1. An incomplete sculpture of Chief Crazy Horse stands in the (Black Hills, Black Hill's) several (miles, mile's) from Mount Rushmore.
2. The (Lakotas, Lakota's) chose to celebrate the great (warriors, warrior's) spirit with this sculpture.
3. Work began over 50 years ago, and many (hands, hand's) continue to help in the process.
4. In 1998 the (statues, statue's) massive face was unveiled.
5. The (monuments, monument's) final form will show the (chiefs, chief's) entire figure seated on a horse.

In your **Working Portfolio,** return to the writing you did for the **Write Away** on page 34. Revise it to make the nouns more specific.

Compound Nouns

1 Here's the Idea

A compound noun is made of two or more words used together as a single noun. The parts of a compound noun may be written as

- a single word: **toothbrush, watermelon**
- two or more separate words: **sleeping bag, dining room**
- a hyphenated word: **runner-up, great-aunt**

Plural Compound Nouns

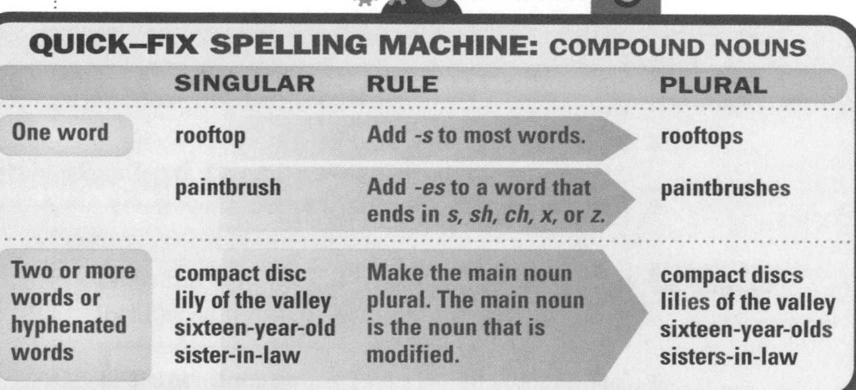

QUICK–FIX SPELLING MACHINE: COMPOUND NOUNS

	SINGULAR	RULE	PLURAL
One word	rooftop	Add *-s* to most words.	rooftops
	paintbrush	Add *-es* to a word that ends in *s, sh, ch, x,* or *z.*	paintbrushes
Two or more words or hyphenated words	compact disc lily of the valley sixteen-year-old sister-in-law	Make the main noun plural. The main noun is the noun that is modified.	compact discs lilies of the valley sixteen-year-olds sisters-in-law

2 Why It Matters in Writing

Compound nouns are very descriptive—they actually describe themselves. They also help writers paint clear pictures.

PROFESSIONAL MODEL

Dreamland Amusement Park is closed for the winter. . . . Taffy stands are shuttered, no **teenagers** screaming on the **roller coaster,** . . . and at the **merry-go-round,** the exquisite carousel which has been right here since 1915, the horses are frozen in their classical posture, waiting for another spring.

—Charles Kuralt, *On the Road with Charles Kuralt*

❸ Practice and Apply

A. CONCEPT CHECK: Compound Nouns

Write each compound noun in the sentences below, indicating whether it is singular or plural.

Not Corny to Farmers

1. The plains produce foodstuffs such as corn, wheat, and rye.
2. The cornstalks stand tall in South Dakota, a state that loves corn.
3. The Corn Palace is a famous building in Mitchell, a prairie town that welcomes cornhuskers.
4. Today it is called the agricultural show place of the world.
5. Each spring, the outside of the concrete building is covered with wall designs made of sweet corn, grains, and grasses.
6. Corn is so popular in Mitchell that the local radio station uses the call letters KORN.
7. Sportswriters cover the local high school's teams, which are named the Kernels.
8. Corn Palace Week celebrates harvest home, the end of the harvest, with themes such as "South Dakota birds."
9. The state produces other products: livestock are fattened in feedlots in eastern South Dakota.
10. Even though meatpacking is a major industry in Sioux Falls, corncribs throughout the state remind visitors that corn is king.

➜ **For a SELF-CHECK and more practice, see the EXERCISE BANK, p. 314.**

B. REVISING: Adding Compound Nouns

Read the following description. Then choose five compound nouns from the list to replace the words in parentheses.

During our summer vacation, my family usually visits the annual state fair. **(1)** Mom, Dad, and Cindy like to start off by riding the **(singular compound)**. **(2)** Cindy also enjoys petting animals, especially furry ones—sheep, rabbits, and **(plural compound)**. **(3)** My brother Tom and I, however, like to tear up the **(singular compound)** on our **(plural compound)**. **(4)** By evening, we all look forward to the rodeo and loud, sparkling **(plural compound)**.

skateboard
billy goats
thunderstorm
Ferris wheel
dirt bikes
fireworks
barnyard
rattlesnakes
racetrack

Nouns and Their Jobs

1 Here's the Idea

Because they name many things, nouns have different jobs in sentences.

Nouns as Subjects

A **subject** tells whom or what a sentence is about. Nouns are often subjects, as this description shows.

PROFESSIONAL MODEL

Independence Hall in Philadelphia is one of the nation's most popular landmarks. Here, the **Declaration of Independence** was approved by the 13 colonies on July 4, 1776.

NOUNS

Nouns as Complements

A **complement** is a word that completes the meaning of a verb. Three kinds of complements are predicate nouns, direct objects, and indirect objects.

Nouns as Complements

Predicate noun	Renames, identifies, or defines the subject after a linking verb.	Benjamin Franklin was a **Founding Father** of our country.
Direct object	Names the receiver of the action after an action verb.	Thomas Jefferson wrote the **Declaration of Independence.**
Indirect object	Tells to whom or what or for whom or what an action is done.	Mom gave my **brother** a miniature replica of the Liberty Bell.

Nouns as Objects of Prepositions

An **object of a preposition** is the noun or pronoun that follows a preposition.

Paul Revere left on his ride.

PREPOSITION (on) — OBJECT OF PREPOSITION (ride)

You'll learn more about prepositions on pp. 152–157.

2 Why It Matters in Writing

Specific complements can help you create a sharp picture. Notice how the complements in this description add specific details.

PROFESSIONAL MODEL

In the nation's capital, the Washington Monument seems a giant arrow, piercing the highest skies. This tremendous column climbs 555 feet into the air. The monument's sparkling beauty still astounds children and adults more than a century after its completion.

PREDICATE NOUN

DIRECT OBJECTS

CHAPTER 2

3 Practice and Apply

A. CONCEPT CHECK: Nouns and Their Jobs

Identify each underlined noun as a subject, a complement, or an object of a preposition.

Maya Lin and the Vietnam Veterans Memorial

1. The <u>Vietnam War</u> brought our <u>country</u> much <u>sorrow.</u>
2. More than 58,000 <u>Americans</u> died or remained missing in action.
3. <u>Veterans</u> of the <u>war</u> wished to honor those who died.
4. A <u>committee</u> set up a <u>contest</u> to choose someone to design a memorial.
5. <u>Maya Lin</u>, a young architect, visited <u>Washington, D.C.</u>, to view the memorial site.
6. The <u>landscape</u> gave <u>Lin</u> an <u>idea</u>.
7. The <u>architect</u> designed a <u>memorial</u> of two marble <u>walls</u>.
8. She created a meeting <u>place</u> between earth and sky.
9. The <u>names</u> of dead and missing <u>Americans</u> appear on the <u>walls</u>.
10. Visits to the <u>memorial</u> have been healing <u>experiences</u> for millions of <u>Americans</u>.

➜ **For a SELF-CHECK and more practice, see the EXERCISE BANK, p. 315.**

Label each complement as a predicate noun, a direct object, or an indirect object.

B. REVISING: Identifying Complements

Identify each underlined complement as a predicate noun, a direct object, or an indirect object.

The Cradle of Liberty

1. Boston, Massachusetts, is the <u>city</u> where American independence began.
2. Today, the Freedom Trail gives <u>tourists</u> a <u>walk</u> through history.
3. At Faneuil Hall colonists regularly protested the British <u>king</u> and his <u>taxation</u>.
4. In 1773, at Griffin's Wharf, patriots boarded three <u>ships</u>.
5. The patriots were active <u>participants</u> in the destruction of British property—tea.

C. WRITING: Using Nouns in Directions

A Tour of the White House

Imagine that you have been asked to prepare directions for tour guides at the White House. The tour begins in the Rose Garden and continues clockwise through the first floor. Using the floor plan shown below, write simple directions for the guides. Include nouns used as subjects, complements, and objects of prepositions. Then identify and label each.

NOUNS

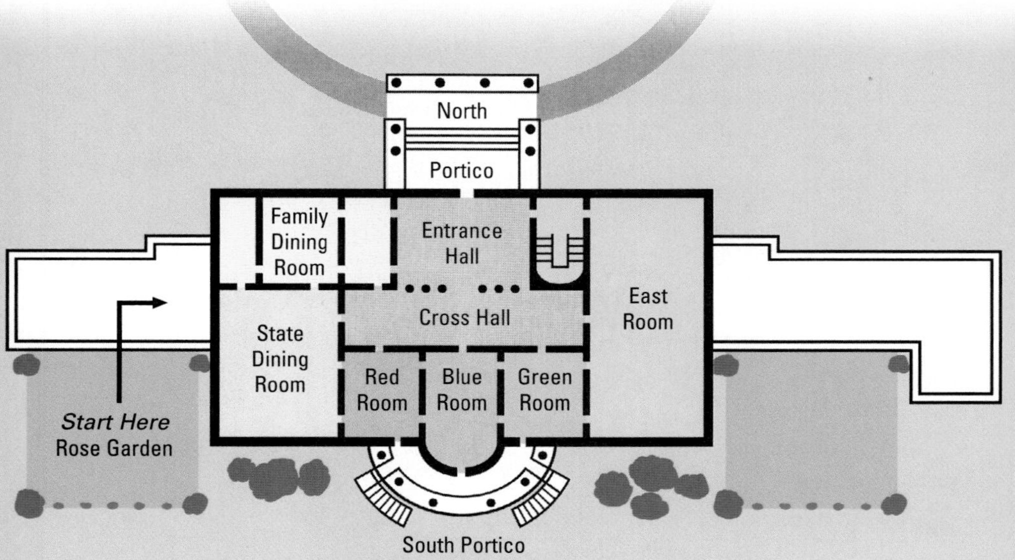

Grammar in Social Studies

Using Nouns Effectively

In social studies classes you learn about important people, places, and things,—and you use nouns to name them. Creating a map is a good way to show information rather than talking about it. Mapmaking allows you to present clearly where important places are and where important events took place. Notice how common and proper nouns are used on this map of the famous Route 66.

HISTORIC
ROUTE
66

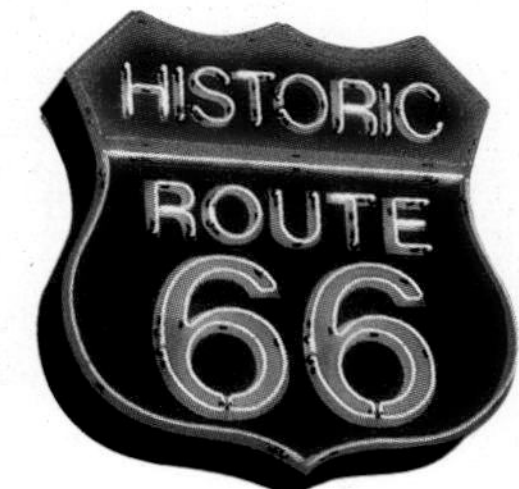

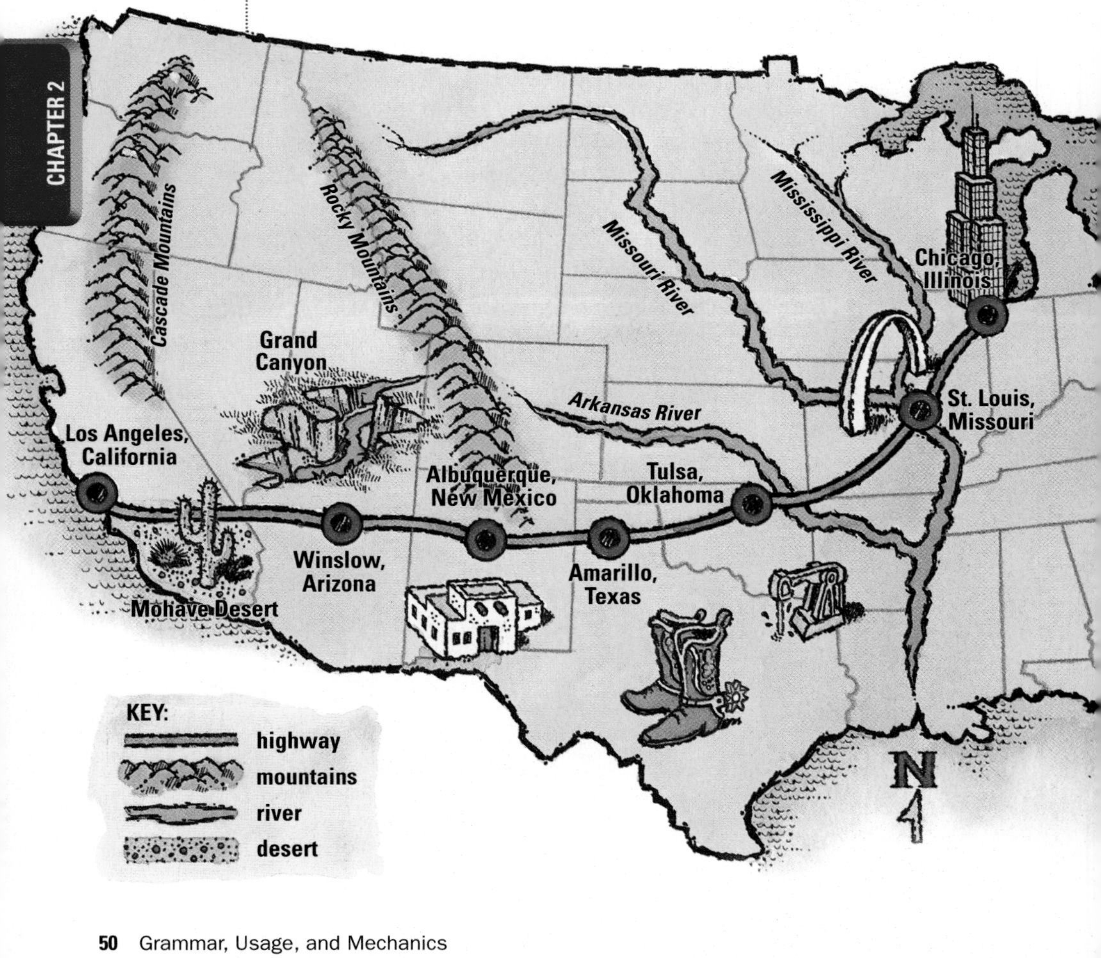
Cascade Mountains
Rocky Mountains
Missouri River
Mississippi River
Chicago, Illinois
Grand Canyon
Arkansas River
St. Louis, Missouri
Los Angeles, California
Albuquerque, New Mexico
Tulsa, Oklahoma
Winslow, Arizona
Amarillo, Texas
Mohave Desert
KEY:
highway
mountains
river
desert
N

Practice and Apply

A. REVISING: Using Proper Nouns

The message below is hard to understand because the writer uses many common nouns rather than specific proper ones. On a separate sheet of paper, write proper nouns to replace the underlined common nouns. Use the map to find the proper nouns.

Dear Anya,

Driving on <u>this road</u> is so cool. We started out at a lake and ended up at the ocean. We went through eight states and crossed <u>two of the country's major rivers</u>. <u>One city on a river</u> had a huge arch sticking up into the sky. Near the end of the trip, we passed by <u>one desert</u> and finally jumped into the surf at our final destination.

I wish you could have come with us.

See you soon,

Winona

Anya Taylor
501 S. Francisco Ave.
Chicago, IL 60601

B. WRITING: Make a map of your own.

Draw a map of your neighborhood, a nearby park, zoo, or any other area. Include the following landmarks:

- natural features such as rivers, lakes, and mountains
- streets
- buildings
- other interesting attractions

Be sure to label each landmark with an appropriate proper noun. Use different colors or symbols for features like streets, rivers, and bike paths. Use common nouns to create a key that explains the symbols.

A colorful strip along Route 66.

NOUNS

Mixed Review

A. Plurals, Possessives, and Compounds Read the following sign advertising a roadside attraction, and correct ten errors in spelling. Then identify each corrected noun as plural, possessive, or compound. For some of the nouns, you will use more than one label.

CHAPTER 2

B. Nouns and Their Jobs In the following sentences, nouns are used in various ways. Identify each underlined noun as a subject, a predicate noun, a direct object, an indirect object, or an object of a preposition.

1. A favorite site of many tourists is the <u>Everglades.</u>
2. The <u>Everglades</u> are wetlands in southern Florida.
3. The naturalist Marjory Stoneman Douglas saved the <u>Everglades</u> from <u>destruction</u> several decades ago.
4. Still, the <u>Everglades</u> continued to be drained, and much of the habitat of <u>alligators</u> and wading birds disappeared.
5. Now a congressional agreement gives the <u>Everglades</u> millions of dollars for preservation.
6. Every tourist should honor <u>John Muir</u> for his life and work.
7. <u>Muir</u> was a lifelong tourist himself.
8. His parents brought <u>Muir</u> and his sisters from Scotland to Wisconsin as children.
9. <u>Muir</u> later traveled the country and was responsible for saving Yosemite as a national park.
10. The conservationist who founded the Sierra Club was <u>John Muir.</u>

Mastery Test: What Did You Learn?

For each underlined item, choose the letter of the term that correctly identifies it.

In the East and the Midwest (1), travelers can visit many sites (2) associated with the Underground Railroad. This "railroad" consisted of people and places that helped Southern slaves escaping to the North and to Canada. Both blacks and whites were "conductors" (3) and guided the runaways (4). Some conductors were slaves who had already escaped and then traveled back south to lead others to safety. Over 2,000 slaves passed through Levi Coffin's (5) home in Newport, Indiana. A light (6) in the window (7) of John Rankin's home in Ohio showed slaves that no slave catchers were nearby. Today the homes of Levi Coffin (8), John Rankin, and others are open so that the public (9) can learn about the "railroad" of courage (10).

1. A. singular common noun
   B. plural common noun
   C. singular proper noun
   D. plural proper noun
2. A. noun as subject
   B. noun as predicate noun
   C. noun as direct object
   D. nouns as indirect object
3. A. noun as subject
   B. noun as predicate noun
   C. noun as direct object
   D. noun as indirect object
4. A. singular possessive noun
   B. plural possessive noun
   C. singular compound noun
   D. plural compound noun
5. A. singular collective noun
   B. plural collective noun
   C. singular possessive noun
   D. plural possessive noun
6. A. noun as subject
   B. noun as predicate noun
   C. noun as direct object
   D. noun as indirect object
7. A. concrete noun
   B. abstract noun
   C. possessive noun
   D. compound noun
8. A. noun as direct object
   B. noun as subject
   C. noun as predicate noun
   D. noun as object of a preposition
9. A. compound noun
   B. collective noun
   C. proper noun
   D. possessive noun
10. A. compound noun
    B. concrete noun
    C. abstract noun
    D. possessive noun

Student Help Desk

Nouns at a Glance

A noun names a person, place, thing, or idea. There are several ways to classify nouns.

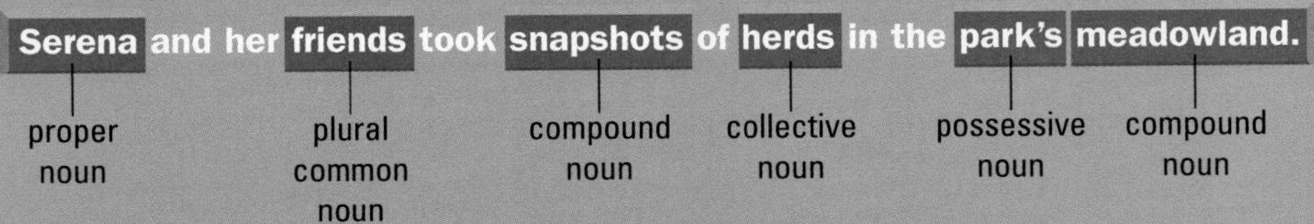

CHAPTER 2

QUICK–FIX SPELLING MACHINE: PLURALS OF NOUNS

	SINGULAR	RULE	PLURAL
1	tent	Add *-s* to most nouns.	tents
2	fox	Add *-es* to nouns that end in *s, sh, ch, x,* or *z.*	foxes
3	photo	Add *-s* to most nouns that end in *o.*	photos
	tomato	Add *-es* to a few nouns that end in *o.*	tomatoes
4	butterfly	For most nouns ending in *y,* change the *y* to *i* and add *-es.*	butterflies
	alley	When a vowel comes before the *y,* just add *-s.*	alleys
5	leaf	For most nouns ending in *f* or *fe,* change the *f* to *v* and add *-es.*	leaves
6	campfire	Add *-s* to most compound nouns.	campfires
7	pup tent	For a hyphenated compound or one written as separate words, make the main noun plural.	pup tents

Classifying Nouns

Sorting Your Stuff

Possessives of Nouns

Relationship	Ownership
Douglas's sister	Natalie's marshmallow

Collective Nouns

Collective Noun	Group of Animals
colony	colony of ants, badgers, or frogs
flock	flock of birds or sheep
school	school of fish
herd	herd of cattle, deer, or elephants

More Noun Types

Concrete	Abstract
tent	nature
lake	beauty

NOUNS

Nouns and Their Jobs

What's Happening at Camp?

Use of Noun	Example
Subject	**Mosquitoes** swarmed around Meg's head.
Predicate noun	The bullfrogs were our **entertainers** for the night.
Direct object	Tim tipped his **canoe** over in the icy river.
Indirect object	Kyra just handed **Jordan** a moldy plum.
Object of a preposition	We're hiking to **Old Faithful** this afternoon.

The Bottom Line

Checklist for Nouns

Have I . . .

___ chosen precise nouns?

___ spelled plural nouns correctly?

___ spelled possessive nouns correctly?

___ used possessive nouns to shorten my sentences?

___ spelled compound nouns correctly?

Pronouns

Theme: It's a Mystery

Who Did What?

Imagine this conversation without the words *it, I, your, what, that,* and *we.* These words, called **pronouns,** can streamline your writing by taking the place of nouns or other pronouns. Be careful though. If you don't use pronouns correctly, you may create a mystery for your readers.

Write Away: Real-Life Mysteries

You don't need to be a detective to solve mysteries. In a sense, you solve a mystery whenever you find the answer to a math problem or succeed in locating your new homeroom. Write a paragraph describing a mystery you've solved. Place the paragraph in your **Working Portfolio.**

Diagnostic Test: What Do You Know?

Choose the letter that correctly identifies each underlined word.

Ball lightning is one of nature's most baffling mysteries. Small glowing spheres appear during violent thunderstorms. No one knows what causes <u>them</u> (1). <u>Their</u> (2) behavior is truly weird. One eyewitness said <u>he</u> (3) saw a blue sphere go right through <u>his</u> (4) windowpane, burning a neat hole in the glass. If <u>you</u> (5) are in an airplane during a thunderstorm, you <u>yourself</u> (6) might see ball lightning rolling down the aisle! <u>This</u> (7) has actually happened on some flights. In one city, a multicolored sphere entered a factory, traveled along the metal girders, hit a window, and disappeared. The workers must have argued among <u>themselves</u> (8) about whether to tell <u>anyone</u> (9). <u>Who</u> (10) would believe such a strange story?

1. A. subject pronoun
   B. object pronoun
   C. possessive pronoun
   D. demonstrative pronoun

2. A. indefinite pronoun
   B. subject pronoun
   C. demonstrative pronoun
   D. possessive pronoun

3. A. first-person pronoun
   B. second-person pronoun
   C. third-person pronoun
   D. plural pronoun

4. A. plural possessive pronoun
   B. singular possessive pronoun
   C. plural object pronoun
   D. singular object pronoun

5. A. personal pronoun
   B. interrogative pronoun
   C. reflexive pronoun
   D. demonstrative pronoun

6. A. indefinite pronoun
   B. reflexive pronoun
   C. intensive pronoun
   D. interrogative pronoun

7. A. demonstrative pronoun
   B. intensive pronoun
   C. complement pronoun
   D. interrogative pronoun

8. A. personal pronoun
   B. indefinite pronoun
   C. reflexive pronoun
   D. possessive pronoun

9. A. demonstrative pronoun
   B. indefinite pronoun
   C. reflexive pronoun
   D. interrogative pronoun

10. A. demonstrative pronoun
    B. interrogative pronoun
    C. indefinite pronoun
    D. reflexive pronoun

What Is a Pronoun?

1 Here's the Idea

▶ **A pronoun is a word that is used in place of a noun or another pronoun.** A pronoun can refer to a person, place, thing, or idea. The word that a pronoun refers to is called its **antecedent.**

Ramon visited Death Valley, and he was impressed.

Death Valley is mysterious. It is silent.

Personal Pronouns

▶ **Pronouns such as *we, I, he, them,* and *it* are called personal pronouns.** Personal pronouns have a variety of forms to indicate different **persons, numbers,** and **cases.**

Person and Number There are first-person, second-person, and third-person personal pronouns, each having both singular and plural forms.

Singular	Plural
I went out.	**We left early.**
You left too.	**You are leaving.**
He came by bus.	**They came by car.**

Case Each personal pronoun has three cases: subject, object, and possessive. Which form to use depends on the pronoun's function in a sentence.

Subject: **He read about Death Valley.**

Object: **Julie asked him about the rocks.**

Possessive: **Ramon brought his book.**

The chart on the next page shows all the forms of the personal pronouns.

Personal Pronouns	Subject	Object	Possessive
Singular			
First person	I	me	my, mine
Second person	you	you	your, yours
Third person	he, she, it	him, her, it	his, her, hers, its
Plural			
First person	we	us	our, ours
Second person	you	you	your, yours
Third person	they	them	their, theirs

2 Why It Matters in Writing

Pronouns help you talk about people concisely when you're telling a story. Notice how pronouns are used in this passage.

PRONOUNS

LITERARY MODEL

I knew **I** had to be honest with Grandpa; **it** was **my** only chance. **He** saw **my** shadow and looked up.

He waited for **me** to speak. **I** cleared **my** throat nervously. . . .

—Marta Salinas, "The Scholarship Jacket"

3 Practice and Apply

A. CONCEPT CHECK: What Is a Pronoun?

Write the personal pronouns in these sentences.

Mystery in Death Valley

1. Death Valley is famous for its strange moving boulders.
2. They are found in a dry lake bed called Racetrack Playa.
3. The rocks slide on their own, leaving long tracks behind them.
4. Can you think of an explanation for this curious event?
5. Investigators offer two major theories for us to consider.

6. One geologist thinks that when floodwater freezes, an ice sheet can form under a rock and help it slide.
7. Other scientists disagree with his theory.
8. They believe that the wind alone can move the rocks.
9. Some scientists have hedged their bets, telling us that both theories could be true.
10. We still don't know for sure how the rocks move.

Name the antecedents of the personal pronouns in sentences 1, 3, 6, 7, and 8.

➜ **For a SELF-CHECK and more practice, see the EXERCISE BANK, p. 315.**

B. REVISING: Substituting Pronouns for Nouns

Rewrite this draft of a social studies report by changing each underlined noun to a pronoun.

STUDENT MODEL

Death Valley is a land of extremes. <u>Death Valley</u> contains the lowest point in the United States. Temperatures reflect the harsh, arid landscape. <u>Temperatures</u> range from 125°F in summer to near freezing in winter.

The valley was named in 1849 by pioneers after <u>the pioneers'</u> long, hard journey. In 1868 a California state geologist mentioned the valley in <u>the geologist's</u> published paper. The valley interested other geologists when <u>the geologists</u> heard about the valuable minerals discovered there.

C. WRITING: Dialogue

Use the information in exercise A to write a short dialogue between two people who are visiting Racetrack Playa. Use personal pronouns to make the dialogue sound natural.

Example:

SPEAKER 1. Did **you** see that boulder move?
SPEAKER 2. No, **I** didn't. Maybe **it** just wobbled a little.
SPEAKER 1. Don't tell **me** that. **You** can see the track!

Death Valley

CHAPTER 3

LESSON 2 Subject Pronouns

1 Here's the Idea

▶ **A subject pronoun is used as a subject in a sentence or as a predicate pronoun after a linking verb.**

Subject Pronouns	
Singular	**Plural**
I	we
you	you
he, she, it	they

PRONOUNS

Pronouns as Subjects

Use a subject pronoun when the pronoun is a subject or part of a compound subject.

The Hope diamond has a fascinating history.

It has been bad luck for many owners.
(*It,* referring to *The Hope diamond,* is the subject of the sentence.)

You and he think the diamond is cursed.

Predicate Pronouns

A predicate pronoun follows a linking verb and identifies the verb's subject. Use the subject case for predicate pronouns.

The owner was he.
SUBJECT PREDICATE PRONOUN

The buyers are you and she.

The royal jewelers are they.

Remember, the most common linking verbs are forms of the verb *be,* including *is, am, are, was, were, been, has been, have been, can be, will be, could be,* and *should be.*

② Why It Matters in Writing

A subject pronoun may not sound right to you. But as the writer of the passage below discovered, you can't always rely on sound to choose the correct case.

STUDENT MODEL

The huge French Blue diamond, later recut into the Hope diamond, was certainly bad luck for Marie Antoinette. The rulers of France in the years before the French Revolution were ~~her~~ *she* and Louis XVI. Marie Antoinette and ~~him~~ *he* were executed during the revolution.

CHAPTER 3

③ Practice and Apply

CONCEPT CHECK: Subject Pronouns

Write the correct pronoun form to complete each sentence.

Investigating the Hope Diamond Legend

1. The diamond detectives were Carla and (I, me).
2. According to legend the huge blue diamond has had many owners, and (they, them) all came to a bad end.
3. Jean Baptiste Tavernier brought the original blue diamond from India; the first owner to die was (him, he).
4. (He, him) is said to have been killed in India by wild dogs.
5. Marie Antoinette and Louis XVI inherited the diamond; (we, us) know that the next victims were (them, they).
6. Carla and (me, I) learned that a Dutch diamond cutter may have recut the stone to disguise it.
7. His son and (he, him) died tragically soon afterward.
8. In the 1830s Henry Hope bought the recut gem; the person for whom the diamond was named was (he, him).
9. (We, Us) discovered that the Hope diamond is now in the Smithsonian Institution in Washington, D.C.
10. "Hope diamond experts" are (us, we)!

➜ **For a SELF-CHECK and more practice, see the EXERCISE BANK, p. 316.**

Object Pronouns

Here's the Idea

▶ **An object pronoun is used as a direct object, an indirect object, or an object of a preposition.**

Object Pronouns	
Singular	**Plural**
me	us
you	you
him, her, it	them

Direct Object The pronoun receives the action of a verb and answers the question *whom or what.*

FASCINATES

The mysterious death of King Tut fascinates me.

DIRECT OBJECT

Did someone murder him? (murder whom? *him*)

Indirect Object The pronoun tells to whom or what or for whom or what an action is performed.

TO

Chu lent me a video on the topic.

INDIRECT OBJECT DIRECT OBJECT

I told her the whole story.

Object of a Preposition The pronoun follows a preposition (such as *to, from, for, against, by,* or *about*).

Will you save the video for them?

PREPOSITION

I can tell the story to you and him.

Always use object pronouns after the preposition *between.*

This secret is between you and me. (not *between you and I*)

PRONOUNS

❷ Why It Matters in Writing

In conversation, people sometimes misuse subject and object pronouns ("Him and me went to the store"). When you write for school, however, you should always use the correct forms.

STUDENT MODEL

The Egyptologist Bob Brier studied King Tut's mummy. Evidence uncovered by ~~he~~ *him* suggests that Tut was killed by a blow to the head. Others say he was poisoned. Brier and ~~them~~ *they* agree, however, that the king was murdered.

❸ Practice and Apply

MIXED REVIEW: Subject and Object Pronouns

Choose the correct pronoun in these sentences, and identify them as subject or object pronouns.

Who Killed King Tut?

1. King Tutankhamen was only about nine years old when the priests crowned (he, him) as the new pharaoh.
2. (He, Him) and his wife were not in power long before the young pharaoh died.
3. (I, Me) saw a video showing x-ray pictures of Tut's skull.
4. (They, Them) revealed that someone had struck Tut on the back of the head.
5. It occurred to (I, me) that only someone the king knew could get so close to (he, him).
6. There are several possible suspects, but two of (them, they) had the best opportunity—the queen and the royal minister, Ay.
7. (She, Her) and Ay married when Ay became pharaoh.
8. A ring discovered in 1931, however, shows that Ay married another queen after (she, her).
9. Just between you and (me, I), I believe that Ay is the most likely killer.
10. All the suspects may be long dead, but the evidence has outlived (they, them).

➜ **For a SELF-CHECK and more practice, see the EXERCISE BANK, p. 316.**

Possessive Pronouns

1 Here's the Idea

▶ **A possessive pronoun is a personal pronoun used to show ownership or relationship.**

Possessive Pronouns	
Singular	**Plural**
my, mine your, yours her, hers, his, its	our, ours your, yours their, theirs

The possessive pronouns *my, your, her, his, its, our,* and *their* come before nouns.

OWNERSHIP

The Chinese museum kept its amazing secret for years.

OWNERSHIP

No one saw the mummies in their colorful clothes.

RELATIONSHIP

Then Professor Mair and his tour group arrived.

The possessive pronouns *mine, yours, hers, his, ours* and *theirs* can stand alone in a sentence.

The secret was theirs. Now the secret is ours.

Is that book yours? No, mine has a blue cover.

His looks torn. Is hers in better shape?

Possessive Pronouns and Contractions

Some possessive pronouns sound like contractions (*its/it's, your/you're, their/they're*). Because these pairs sound alike, writers often confuse possessive pronouns with contractions.

Remember, a possessive pronoun *never* has an apostrophe. A contraction, however, *always* has an apostrophe. The apostrophe shows where a letter or letters have been left out after combining two words.

PRONOUNS

QUICK–FIX SPELLING MACHINE

Possessive pronouns		Contractions	
its	Its clothes look great.	it's	It's well preserved.
your	Your pictures are great.	you're	You're talented!
their	Their colors are vivid.	they're	They're beautiful.

2 Why It Matters in Writing

Proofread your work carefully to be sure you haven't confused possessive pronouns with contractions. The spell-checker on a computer will not catch these mistakes.

STUDENT MODEL

The desert, with ~~it's~~ its dry air, salt, and sand, is the best preserver of ancient textiles. Once these materials are uncovered, however, ~~their~~ they're easily damaged. Even the moisture from ~~you're~~ your hands and breath can harm the fibers. For this reason, archaeologists always wear masks when they work with ancient cloth.

Experts use tools in *their* work.

3 Practice and Apply

A. CONCEPT CHECK: Possessive Pronouns

Choose the pronoun or contraction to complete each sentence.

The Amazing Mummies of Ürümqi

1. Imagine (your, you're) visiting a museum in Ürümqi, in the desert of northwest China.
2. In one room, you find remarkable mummies in (their, they're) cases.
3. The leggings, shirts, and cloaks on the mummies look as colorful as (your, you're) clothes today.
4. This experience really happened to Professor Mair and his tour group on (their, they're) trip to China in 1987.
5. The mummies are about 3,000 years old, and (they're, their) European, not Chinese!
6. (It's, Its) a mystery why these Europeans went all the way to China.
7. Mair's astonishing report made (its, it's) way around the world.
8. Some 3,000 years ago, a group of European Celts may have started trading with (their, they're) Chinese neighbors.
9. When one of the Celts was buried, the dry, salty desert preserved the body and (it's, its) clothing perfectly.
10. You can satisfy (your, you're) curiosity about these mummies of Ürürmqi by reading articles about them.

➜ **For a SELF-CHECK and more practice, see the EXERCISE BANK, p. 317.**

B. PROOFREADING: Using Possessive Pronouns

Correct the errors in the use of pronouns and contractions in the paragraph below. If a sentence contains no error, write *Correct*.

(1) Its common for archaeologists to name the mummies they find. **(2)** Sometimes they're named for the way they look, other times for a person or place. **(3)** Your probably not aware that three mummies in the Smithsonian Institution are named Indiana Jones, Ancient Annie, and Minister Cox. **(4)** You can guess how the first two got they're names, but how did Minister Cox get him? **(5)** The mummy was named after a former diplomat, Mr. Cox, who donated the mummy to the museum for it's Egyptian collection.

PRONOUNS

Reflexive and Intensive Pronouns

Here's the Idea

A pronoun that ends in *self* or *selves* is either a reflexive or an intensive pronoun.

Reflexive and Intensive Pronouns		
myself ourselves	yourself yourselves	herself, himself, itself themselves

Reflexive Pronouns

A reflexive pronoun refers to the subject and directs the action of the verb back to the subject. Reflexive pronouns are necessary to the meaning of a sentence.

REFLECTS

Houdini called himself a master escape artist.

REFLECTS

Lynne dedicated herself to learning Houdini's secrets.

Notice that if you drop a reflexive pronoun, a sentence no longer makes sense ("Lynne dedicated to learning Houdini's secrets").

CHAPTER 3

Intensive Pronouns

An intensive pronoun emphasizes a noun or another pronoun in the same sentence. Intensive pronouns are not necessary to the meaning of a sentence.

You yourselves have seen magic shows on TV.

I myself like to perform magic tricks.

Notice that when you drop an intensive pronoun, a sentence still makes sense ("I like to perform magic tricks").

Hisself and *theirselves* may look like real words, but they are not. Use *himself* and *themselves* instead.

2 Why It Matters in Writing

You can use reflexive pronouns to describe a person's actions more clearly.

PROFESSIONAL MODEL

In the Water Torture Cell, Houdini doubled **himself** up and picked the lock that held his feet. Then, still holding his breath, he stood and unlocked the top of the tank. He hauled **himself** out.

—L. S. Baugh

3 Practice and Apply

CONCEPT CHECK: Reflexive and Intensive Pronouns

Write the reflexive or intensive pronoun in each sentence. Then label it *reflexive* or *intensive*.

Houdini's Great Escapes

1. During the 1920s, Harry Houdini labeled himself "the most daring escape artist in the world."
2. His name itself makes people think of magic.
3. In one famous trick, Houdini freed himself from a tank that was filled to the top with water and securely locked.
4. He also called himself "the handcuff king" and said no handcuffs in the world could hold him.
5. The police officers themselves were amazed at Houdini.
6. Some people convinced themselves that Houdini really had mysterious powers.
7. The magician himself said that wasn't true.
8. He said people could develop these skills themselves.
9. Still, we probably couldn't become Houdinis even if we taught ourselves his secrets.
10. Even today's professional magicians themselves don't try Houdini's dangerous escapes.

→ **For a SELF-CHECK and more practice, see the EXERCISE BANK, p. 317.**

Interrogatives and Demonstratives

1 Here's the Idea

Interrogative Pronouns

▶ **An interrogative pronoun is used to introduce a question.**

Who made up this riddle?

Which riddle are you talking about?

Using Interrogative Pronouns

Interrogative Pronoun	Use
who, whom	refers to people
what	refers to things
which	refers to people or things
whose	indicates ownership or relationship

CHAPTER 3

Using *Who* and *Whom*

▶ ***Who* is always used as a subject or a predicate pronoun.**

Subject: **Who knows the answer to the riddle?**

Predicate pronoun: **Your favorite comedian is who?**

▶ ***Whom* is always used as an object.**

Direct object: **Whom did you tell?**

Indirect object: **You gave whom the answer?**

Object of preposition: **To whom did you give my name?**

Don't confuse *whose* with *who's*. *Whose* is a pronoun. ("Whose book did you borrow?") *Who's* is a contraction that means *who is* or *who has.* ("Who's missing a book"? "Who's returned my book?")

Demonstrative Pronouns

▶ **A demonstrative pronoun points out a person, place, thing, or idea.**

The demonstrative pronouns—*this, that, these,* and *those*—are used alone in a sentence, as shown below.

Never use *here* or *there* with a demonstrative pronoun. The pronoun already tells which one or ones. *This* and *these* point out people or things that are near, or *here*. *That* and *those* point out people or things that are far away, or *there*.

This ~~here~~ is my playing piece.

That ~~there~~ is your playing piece.

❷ Why It Matters in Writing

Demonstrative pronouns call readers' attention to the people or things being discussed. In the riddles below, the demonstrative pronouns serve as the subjects of the riddles.

STUDENT MODEL

This has 18 legs and catches flies.

Answer: baseball team

These may fall far, but they never break.

Answer: leaves

Although **this** is small, it fills the house.

Answer: a lamp's light

These are bought by the yard and worn by the foot.

Answer: floor carpets

3 Practice and Apply

CHAPTER 3

A. CONCEPT CHECK: Interrogatives and Demonstratives

Write the correct word to complete each sentence.

Inventors' Guide to Creating Board Games

1. To create a great board game, you need to answer some basic questions. First, (what, who) is the goal of the game?

2. If several people make up rules, (who's, whose) will you follow?

3. (Who, What) will you use to represent each player?

4. (Who, Whom) will go first?

5. You have to think up penalties. (That, Those) are important to any game.

6. Also, to (who, whom) will you give extra points or turns?

7. You need to create some kind of trap along the way. (These, This) makes the game more challenging.

8. Be careful (which, what) people you tell about the game before you finish it.

9. (Who, Whom) knows—someone might try to copy it.

10. Once you finish the game, (who, whom) will you invite to play it?

→ **For a SELF-CHECK and more practice, see the EXERCISE BANK, p. 318.**

B. WRITING: What's Missing?

Geometry is important to quilters. Notice the many geometric pieces in the quilt. Can you find the sections that are missing from this quilt? Write a sentence about each missing section, describing its shape and telling how many sides it has. Then write another sentence to compare the missing sections to each other. Use four demonstrative pronouns in your sentences. Underline the demonstrative pronouns.

LESSON 7 Pronoun Agreement

1 Here's the Idea

▶ **The antecedent is the noun or pronoun that a pronoun replaces or refers to.** The antecedent and the pronoun can be in the same sentence or in difference sentences.

REFERS TO

Louis writes his own detective stories.
ANTECEDENT PRONOUN

REPLACES

Agatha Christie writes mysteries. Her stories are famous.

Pronouns must agree with their antecedents in number, person, and gender.

Agreement in Number

▶ **Use a singular pronoun to refer to a singular antecedent.**

REFERS TO

One story has its setting in Egypt.

▶ **Use a plural pronoun to refer to a plural antecedent.**

REFERS TO

The characters have their motives for murder.

Agreement in Person

▶ **The pronoun must agree in person with the antecedent.**

3RD PERSON

Louis likes his mysteries to have surprise endings.

2ND PERSON

You want a story to grab your attention.

PRONOUNS

Avoid switching from one person to another in the same sentence or paragraph.

INCORRECT:

Readers know you shouldn't read the ending first.
(*Readers* is third person; *you* is second person.)

CORRECT:

Readers know they shouldn't read the ending first.
(*Readers* and *they* are both third person.)

Agreement in Gender

▶ **The gender of a pronoun must be the same as the gender of its antecedent.**

Personal pronouns have three gender forms: masculine (*he, his, him*), feminine (*she, her, hers*), and neuter (*it, its*).

Agatha Christie sets many of her stories in England.

The hero has to use all his wits to solve the crime.

CHAPTER 3

Don't use only masculine or only feminine pronouns when you mean to refer to both genders.

DRAFT:

Each **character** has **his** alibi ready.
(character could be masculine or feminine.)

There are two ways to make this sentence gender free.

1. Use the phrase *his or her*.
   Each character has his or her alibi ready.

2. Rewrite the sentence, using a plural antecedent and a plural pronoun. Be careful! Other words may also need to be changed.
   The characters have their alibis ready.

2 Why It Matters in Writing

In your writing, you will sometimes refer to several people or groups of people. Correct pronoun-antecedent agreement will help your readers keep track of who is who in your writing.

STUDENT MODEL

Mystery lovers should read novels by Agatha Christie. ~~You~~ They will never guess who is the real **killer** in any of these stories. ~~They~~ He or she usually turn[s] out to be a surprise.

3 Practice and Apply

CONCEPT CHECK: Pronoun Agreement

Write the pronouns and their antecedents in these sentences.

Agatha Christie: Amateur Archaeologist

1. Agatha Christie loved real-life mysteries of the past. She helped to investigate them in the Middle East.
2. Max Mallowan was an English archaeologist. He was married to Christie for 45 years.
3. The couple went on many archaeological trips and found them exciting and a real source of inspiration.
4. Christie and Mallowan made important discoveries about Assyria. It was a wealthy country in the ancient world.
5. Pottery pieces revealed their secrets about the powerful Assyrian civilization.
6. Although Christie helped Mallowan at the site, she also kept writing mysteries.
7. A mystery writer may use exotic places as background for his or her stories.
8. Christie started *Murder in Mesopotamia* in the desert, but she finished it in England.
9. The story takes place at an archaeological dig. One of its main characters is Dr. Leidner.
10. When Mrs. Leidner is murdered, the detective Hercule Poirot must catch her killer.

Write the number and gender of each personal pronoun.

➜ **For a SELF-CHECK and more practice, see the EXERCISE BANK, p. 318.**

PRONOUNS

Indefinite-Pronoun Agreement

CHAPTER 3

1 Here's the Idea

▶ **An indefinite pronoun does not refer to a specific person, place, thing, or idea.**

Indefinite pronouns often do not have antecedents.

Something unusual is going on in Loch Ness.

Has anyone photographed the Loch Ness monster?

▶ **Some indefinite pronouns are always singular, some are always plural, and some can be either singular or plural.**

Indefinite Pronouns

Singular		Plural	Singular or Plural
another anybody anyone anything each either everybody everyone everything	neither nobody no one nothing one somebody someone something	both few many several	all any most none some

Any pronoun containing *one, thing,* or *body* is singular.

Singular Indefinite Pronouns

▶ **Use a singular personal pronoun to refer to a singular indefinite pronoun.**

REFERS TO

Everyone took his or her camera to the lake.

(*Everyone* could be masculine or feminine.)

REFERS TO

One dropped his camera in the water by mistake.

Plural Indefinite Pronouns

▶ **Use a plural personal pronoun to refer to a plural indefinite pronoun.**

REFERS TO

Several reported their sightings of the monster.

REFERS TO

Many could not believe their own eyes!

Singular or Plural Indefinite Pronouns

▶ **Some indefinite pronouns can be singular or plural.** The phrase that follows the indefinite pronoun will often tell you whether the pronoun is singular or plural.

Most of the monster story has its origin in fantasy.
↑SINGULAR INDEFINITE PRONOUN ↑SINGULAR PERSONAL PRONOUN

Most of the monster stories have their origins in fantasy.
↑PLURAL INDEFINITE PRONOUN ↑PLURAL PERSONAL PRONOUN

PRONOUNS

2 Why It Matters in Writing

Keep your facts and ideas clear. Make sure that all pronouns agree in number with their indefinite antecedents.

STUDENT MODEL

Not everyone has made up ~~their minds~~ *his or her mind* about the existence of the Loch Ness monster. A few have ~~his or her~~ *their* own ~~theory~~ *theories*.

Use singular pronoun to agree with *everyone*

Use plural pronoun to agree with *few*

❸ Practice and Apply

A. CONCEPT CHECK: Indefinite-Pronoun Agreement

Choose the pronoun that agrees with the indefinite pronoun antecedent.

The Quest for "Nessie"

1. All of the tourists want (his or her, their) own monster stories to tell.
2. None of the tourists have (his or her, their) questions answered.
3. Tourists wonder what the Loch Ness creature is. One said that in (their, her) opinion, it was an ancient reptile.
4. Several claim to have photos of (his or her, their) sightings.
5. Many display (his or her, their) very blurry photographs.
6. No one has proved that (their, his or her) pictures are genuine.
7. Everyone around Loch Ness has a nickname for the monster; (he or she, they) calls it "Nessie."
8. Scientists are curious about the mystery, and several have done (his or her, their) own underwater investigations.
9. Each has presented (his or her, their) theory about Nessie.
10. Most of the evidence has (their, its) problems, however.

➜ **For a SELF-CHECK and more practice, see the EXERCISE BANK, p. 319.**

B. PROOFREADING: Agreement Errors

Rewrite the paragraph, correcting errors in pronoun-antecedent agreement.

Famous Photo a Fake!

No one could believe their eyes when this famous photo was published. Most of the people had his or her opinions about the picture. Finally, the photographer, R. Kenneth Wilson, admitted it was a fake! Many were crushed that his or her favorite photo of Nessie was not real.

Return to your **Write Away** and correct any errors in pronoun-antecedent agreement.

CHAPTER 3

LESSON 9 Pronoun Problems

1 Here's the Idea

We and *Us* with Nouns

The pronoun *we* or *us* is sometimes followed by a noun that identifies the pronoun (*we students, us students*).

Use *we* when the pronoun is a subject or a predicate pronoun. Use *us* when the pronoun is an object.

We owners don't always understand our pets.
SUBJECT

Dogs and cats often surprise us owners.
OBJECT OF VERB

Here's How Choosing *We* or *Us*

Dogs think of (us, we) humans as their leaders.

1. Drop the identifying noun from the sentence.

Dogs think of (us, we) as their leaders.

2. Decide whether the sentence calls for a subject pronoun or an object pronoun. This sentence calls for the pronoun that is the object of the preposition *of.*

Dogs think of us as their leaders.

3. Use the correct pronoun with the noun.

Dogs think of us humans as their leaders.

Unclear Reference

Be sure that each personal pronoun refers clearly to only one person, place, or thing. If there is any chance your reader will be confused about whom or what you are talking about, use a noun instead of a pronoun.

Confusing: **Tony and Fred want to become veterinarians. He now works at an animal shelter.** (Who works? Tony or Fred?)

Clear: **Tony and Fred want to become veterinarians. Fred now works at an animal shelter.**

② Why It Matters in Writing

When you write a paper for school, or when you want to persuade someone in authority, your use of correct pronouns will help the reader take your ideas more seriously.

STUDENT MODEL

Dear Mayor Trimble:

~~Us~~ We students have some ideas about a special dog park for the city. Sarah Fein and Tanya Roberts have written a report on our ideas. ~~She~~ Tanya will send it to you soon.

Use *we—students* is a subject.

She could refer either to Sarah or to Tanya. Name the person to avoid confusion.

CHAPTER 3

③ Practice and Apply

A. CONCEPT CHECK: Pronoun Problems

Choose the correct word in parentheses.

Mysterious Cat Behavior

1. Cats baffle (us, we) owners by the things they do.
2. They often rub themselves against (we, us) humans.
3. My two cats, Pickles and Bert, do this. Surprisingly, (he, Bert) does this even with strangers.
4. However, (he, Pickles) hides when guests arrive.
5. This rubbing is simple. (We, Us) humans are being marked by the cat as part of its territory.

➜ **For a SELF-CHECK and more practice, see the EXERCISE BANK, p. 320.**

B. REVISING: Correcting Pronoun Errors

Correct the pronoun errors in the following paragraph.

A Cat's Point of View

Us cats have rights, too. A new puppy or pet bird in the house can upset us. It has very poor manners and will eat our food in one gulp. It will sit singing in its cage and drive us crazy. It will chase us through the house for fun. Owners need to consider the needs of we cats.

LESSON 10 More Pronoun Problems

1 Here's the Idea

Pronouns in Compounds

Pronouns sometimes cause difficulty when they are parts of compound subjects and compound objects.

Use the subject pronouns *I, she, he, we,* and *they* in a compound subject or with a predicate noun or pronoun.

Kathy and he decided to research a mystery.

The research team was Jim and I.

Use the object pronouns *me, her, him, us,* and *them* in a compound object.

Samantha asked Jim and me about the Bermuda Triangle.

Kathy loaned our report to Mac and her.

To choose the correct case of a pronoun in a compound part, read the sentence with only the pronoun in the compound part. Mentally screen out the noun. Then choose the correct case.

Intervening Phrases

Sometimes words and phrases come between a subject and a pronoun that refers to it. Don't be confused by those words in between. Mentally cross out the phrase to figure out agreement.

REFERS TO

Jim, like the others, brought his map. (*His* agrees with *Jim,* not with *others.*)

Five planes ~~from a Navy airfield~~ lost their way in the Bermuda Triangle. (*Their* agrees with *planes*, not with *airfield.*)

PRONOUNS

❷ Why It Matters in Writing

Some writers think that *between you and I* sounds more formal than *between you and me* and therefore is correct. Don't make that mistake in your writing—*between you and me* is correct.

STUDENT MODEL

To begin our project, my partner and ~~me~~ I did some research. However, between you and ~~I~~ me, I found many more sources than she did.

❸ Practice and Apply

CHAPTER 3

A. CONCEPT CHECK: More Pronoun Problems

Choose the correct word to complete each sentence.

The Bermuda Triangle: Mystery or Misinformation?

1. Terry, Kathy, Jim and (I, me) led a discussion about the Bermuda Triangle.
2. One student asked Jim and (I, me) where the Bermuda Triangle is.
3. Terry and (I, me) pointed out Bermuda, Puerto Rico, and the southeast coast of Florida.
4. The triangle, having three geographic boundaries, is named for (its, their) shape.
5. Another student asked Kathy and (we, us) about the strange disappearances that give the Bermuda Triangle its spooky reputation.
6. Jim and (I, me) explained that some ships and planes have mysteriously vanished in that area.
7. Angela, like several other classmates, had (her, their) doubts about the Bermuda Triangle stories.
8. Jim and (I, me) explained that many investigators agree with Angela.
9. Experts on the Bermuda Triangle said that in (its, their) opinion, many reports had been greatly exaggerated.
10. Between you and (I, me), I'm not sure how seriously to take this legend either.

➔ **For a SELF-CHECK and more practice, see the EXERCISE BANK, p. 320.**

B. PROOFREADING: Correct Use of Pronouns

Rewrite the passage below, correcting the pronoun errors.

Flight 19: The Mystery Is Solved!

Claire and me read about the mysterious disappearance of Flight 19 in the Bermuda Triangle. Us students discovered that Flight 19 consisted of five Avenger bombers led by Lt. Charles Taylor. Hours after they're take-off from Fort Lauderdale, Florida, they vanished in the Atlantic Ocean.

Whom is responsible for the bizarre disappearance of Flight 19? Interestingly, some think that UFOs may have been responsible. Which actually happened is less dramatic.

Lt. Taylor thought he was flying southwest when he really was flying east. Taylor, unlike two other crew members, did not recognize their mistake. It's clear Taylor led the team farther out into the Atlantic. His men and he finally crashed in the ocean.

The facts about Flight 19 taught Claire and I not to believe in the myth of the Bermuda Triangle.

C. WRITING: Interpreting a Map

This map illustrates what may have happened to Flight 19. Working with a partner, use the map and the information in exercise B to write a paragraph, explaining in your own words what probably happened to Flight 19.

Underline the pronouns you use. Proofread your work to be sure you have used the pronouns correctly.

Flight 19's Path

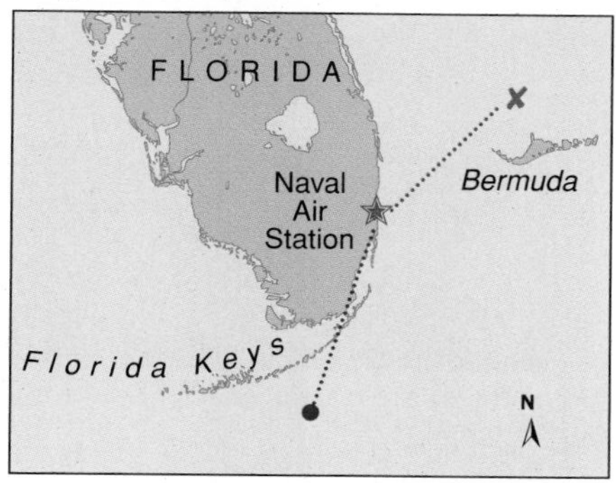

Example: The planes of Flight 19 left *their* base at the Naval Air Station in Fort Lauderdale, Florida.

Taylor's planned flight path, heading southwest

Taylor's actual flight path

Grammar in Literature

Using Pronouns in Dialogue

Look at the following sentences. Then, compare them with the dialogue in the following passage. How do pronouns change the effect of the words?

"The guard told Jimmy to go out in the morning, brace up, and make a man of himself. The guard told Jimmy he wasn't a bad fellow at heart."

from:

A Retrieved Reformation

by O. Henry

"Now, Valentine," said the warden, "**you**'ll go out in the morning. Brace up and make a man of **yourself**. **You**'re not a bad fellow at heart. Stop cracking safes, and live straight.

"**Me**?" said Jimmy, in surprise. "Why, **I** never cracked a safe in **my** life."

"Oh, no," laughed the warden. "Of course not, Let's see now. How was it **you** happened to get sent up on that Springfield job? Was it because you wouldn't prove an alibi for fear of compromising **somebody** in extremely high-toned society? Or was it simply a case of a mean old jury that had it in for **you**? It's always one or the other with **you** innocent victims."

"**Me**?" said Jimmy, still blankly virtuous. "Why, warden, **I** never was in Springfield in **my** life."

Portrait of Prince Eristoff (1925) Tamara de Lempicka. Private collection, New York. Copyright © 1996 Artists Rights Society (ARS), New York/SPADEM, Paris.

Practice and Apply

The following passage from "A Retrieved Reformation" does not include dialogue. Read the passage and follow the steps to create a dialogue for a skit about the passage.

> The Elmore Bank had just put in a new safe and vault. Mr. Adams was very proud of it, and insisted on an inspection by everyone. The vault was a small one, but it had a new patented door. It fastened with three solid steel bolts thrown simultaneously with a single handle, and had a time lock. . . . The two children, May and Agatha, were delighted by the shining metal and funny clock and knobs. . . .
>
> Suddenly there was a scream or two from the women, and a commotion. Unperceived by the elders, May, the nine-year-old girl, in a spirit of play, had shut Agatha in the vault. She had then shot the bolts and turned the knob of the combination as she had seen Mr. Adams do.
>
> The old banker sprang to the handle and tugged at it for a moment. "The door can't be opened," he groaned. "The clock hasn't been wound nor the combination set."

Writing About Literature

1. Identify the characters who will speak in your skit. You should include Mr. Adams, Agatha, and May. You might choose to add other visitors to the bank.
2. Write one or two lines of dialogue for each character you choose. Try reading your dialogue aloud to see if it sounds like a real conversation. Check to see if using pronouns instead of nouns will make your dialogue more natural.

Save your dialogue in your **Working Portfolio.**

Mixed Review

A. Pronouns Read this passage from "Waiting" by Budge Wilson. Then identify each underlined word as a subject pronoun, object pronoun, possessive pronoun, or contraction.

LITERARY MODEL

When the spring came, a gang of **(1)** us would always start going out to The Grove on weekends to start practicing for **(2)** our summer play. Year after year **(3)** we did this, and it had nothing to do with those school plays in which I made such a hit. **(4)** We'd all talk about what stories we liked, and then we'd pick one of **(5)** them and make a play out of **(6)** it. I would usually select the play because I was always the one who directed **(7)** it, so it was only fair that I'd get to do the choosing. If there was a king or a queen, I'd usually be the queen. If **(8)** you're the director, you can't be something like a page or a minor fairy, because then you don't seem important enough to be giving out instructions and bossing people around, and the kids maybe won't pay attention to all the orders. Besides, as **(9)** my mother pointed out, **(10)** I was smart and I could learn my lines fast. . . .

—Budge Wilson, "Waiting"

CHAPTER 3

B. Pronoun Use This passage about theater superstitions contains ten errors in pronoun usage. Rewrite the paragraph, correcting the errors.

When an actor goes on stage, their fellow actors don't say "Good luck." They say "Break a leg." Whom would wish someone a broken leg? What does this expression mean? To find out, my friend Kevin and me interviewed Ms. Kay Gilbert, an expert on theater traditions.

She told him and I, "Us theater people are more superstitious than people in most other fields. I think it's because plays are so unpredictable. If their a hit, everything is fine. If not, your out of work.

"We try to give ourself any advantage we can. All of the actors tell his or her fellow actors something insulting in order to confuse the forces of bad luck. Acting, like other jobs, has their own traditions to uphold."

So the next time you go on stage, don't worry if someone tells you to "break a leg"!

Mastery Test: What Did You Learn?

Choose the correct replacement for each underlined word, or indicate that the word is correct as is.

> Think of all the information that you have collected and saved over time. Who (1) was the first president of the United States? Name a favorite CD and picture their (2) cover. Recall for a moment what you're (3) elementary school looked like. You might say that we (4) humans are a little bit like computers; everyone stores countless memories in their (5) brain. If you wonder exactly how we store these memories in my (6) brains, you are not alone. These (7) is a question that scientists have asked theirselves (8) for years. Will themselves (9) find the explanation in the brain's physical structure, its complex chemistry, or both? It's (10) one more mystery that modern science has yet to solve.

1. A. Whom
   B. Whose
   C. Which
   D. Correct as is

2. A. his
   B. her
   C. its
   D. Correct as is

3. A. you
   B. your
   C. your are
   D. Correct as is

4. A. us
   B. they
   C. them
   D. Correct as is

5. A. his or her
   B. his
   C. her
   D. Correct as is

6. A. our
   B. their
   C. your
   D. Correct as is

7. A. What
   B. This
   C. Them
   D. Correct as is

8. A. theirs
   B. yourselves
   C. themselves
   D. Correct as is

9. A. them
   B. they
   C. he
   D. Correct as is

10. A. It
    B. Its
    C. Itself
    D. Correct as is

Student Help Desk

Pronouns at a Glance

Subject Case

I	it
you	we
he	you
she	they

Use this case when

- the pronoun is a **subject**
- the pronoun is a **predicate pronoun**

Object Case

me	it
you	us
him	you
her	them

Use this case when

- the pronoun is a **direct object**
- the pronoun is an **indirect object**
- the pronoun is the **object of a preposition**

Possessive Case

my/mine	its
your/yours	our/ours
his	your/yours
her/hers	their/theirs

Use this case for

- pronouns that show **ownership or relationship**

CHAPTER 3

Types of Pronouns

Who Did It?

Reflexive & Intensive	Interrogative	Demonstrative	Indefinite
myself	who	this	someone
herself	whom	that	anyone
himself	what	these	each
itself	which	those	several
yourself	whose		many
themselves			all
ourselves			most
yourselves			none

For a full list of indefinite pronouns, see page 76.

Pronoun-Antecedent Agreement

They Lost Their Marbles

A pronoun should agree with its antecedent in number, person, and gender.

A singular antecedent takes a singular pronoun.

Jewell is always writing **her** mystery stories. **(singular)**

A plural antecedent takes a plural pronoun.

The **plots** have **their** twists and turns. **(plural)**

Make sure you use the correct gender.

Each has **his or her** special skill.
They have **their** special skills.

Pronoun Problems

Solving the Case

We: Subject/predicate pronoun **Us:** Object	**We** students saw Nessie. No one believed **us** students.
Who: Subject/predicate pronoun **Whom:** Object	**Who** wants our story? To **whom** shall we write?

The Bottom Line

Checklist for Pronouns

Have I . . .

____ used the subject case for pronouns that are subjects and predicate pronouns?

____ used the object case for pronouns that are objects?

____ used the possessive case to show ownership or relationship?

____ made sure that pronouns agree with their antecedents in number, person, and gender?

____ used *who* and *whom* correctly?

PRONOUNS

Verbs

Theme: Lights, Camera, Action

A Giant Ape Did What?

Think about going with friends to see a really great movie. Talking about the movie afterward is almost as much fun as seeing it for the first time. You'll have to use plenty of verbs to recreate what you saw. In fact, whenever you speak or write, you use verbs to let people know exactly what is happening and how things look, feel, smell, sound, and taste.

Write Away: Tell Me a Movie

Write a paragraph describing an action scene from your favorite movie or one describing the scene from *King Kong* shown above. Put the paragraph in your **Working Portfolio.**

Diagnostic Test: What Do You Know?

Choose the best way to rewrite each underlined word or group of words.

Spending on entertainment will increase (1) sharply over the last several decades. In 1997 the average American household spends (2) almost as much on entertainment as it did on health care. Families now choose (3) from a wide selection of entertainment options. These included (4) books, TV, movies, games, CDs, and theme parks, to name a few. Think about how prices have rised (5) over the years. In 1939 a movie ticket to *Gone With The Wind* costed (6) 75 cents. When a major theme park first opened in 1955, visitors paid (7) only $1 to enter the park. Although people earned (8) more money today, many are spending (9) more of that money on entertainment. Can you predict how much prices raise (10) in the future?

1. A. increases
   B. has increased
   C. does increase
   D. Correct as is

2. A. spending
   B. spent
   C. will spend
   D. Correct as is

3. A. chose
   B. have choosen
   C. chosed
   D. Correct as is

4. A. will include
   B. include
   C. had included
   D. Correct as is

5. A. have rose
   B. raised
   C. have risen
   D. Correct as is

6. A. cost
   B. has cost
   C. will cost
   D. Correct as is

7. A. pay
   B. payed
   C. are paying
   D. Correct as is

8. A. will earn
   B. earn
   C. have earned
   D. Correct as is

9. A. spent
   B. have spent
   C. spended
   D. Correct as is

10. A. will rise
    B. will raise
    C. rise
    D. Correct as is

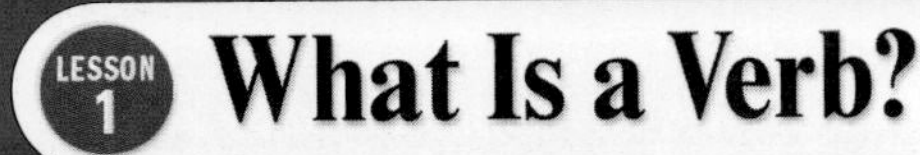

What Is a Verb?

Here's the Idea

A verb is a word used to express an action, a condition, or a state of being. The two main types of verbs are **action verbs** and **linking verbs.** Both kinds can be accompanied by helping verbs.

Action Verbs

An **action verb** tells what its subject does. The action it expresses can be either **physical** or **mental.**

King Kong stomps through the streets of New York. (physical action)

He climbs the Empire State Building. (physical action)

Everyone fears Kong. (mental action)

Kong loves a woman. (mental action)

CHAPTER 4

Linking Verbs

A **linking verb** links its subject to a word in the predicate. The most common linking verbs are forms of the verb *be.*

Linking Verbs	
Forms of *be*	is, am, are, was, were, been, being
Verbs that express condition	appear, become, feel, grow, look, remain, seem, smell, sound, taste

LINKS

King Kong is a huge gorilla.

LINKING VERB

He seems angry.

Some verbs can serve as either action or linking verbs.

LINKS

Kong looks at Ann Darrow. She looks frightened.

ACTION VERB — LINKING VERB

LINKS

He feels sad. She feels his hot breath.

LINKING VERB — ACTION VERB

Helping Verbs and Verb Phrases

Helping verbs help main verbs express precise shades of meaning. The combination of one or more helping verbs with a main verb is called a **verb phrase.**

VERB PHRASE

We have watched the movie *King Kong* four times.

HELPING — MAIN

I can rent it any time.

Some verbs can serve both as main verbs and as helping verbs. For example, *has* stands alone in the first sentence below but is a helping verb in the second sentence.

King Kong has no chance of survival.

MAIN VERB

He has angered too many people.

HELPING VERB

Common Helping Verbs	
Forms of *be*	be, am, is, are, was, were, been, being
Forms of *do*	do, does, did
Forms of *have*	have, has, had
Others	could, should, would, may, might, must, can, shall, will

Kong has terrorized New Yorkers.

VERBS

❷ Why It Matters in Writing

Strong verbs can make your writing powerful. Try to use verbs that are as specific as possible. Notice the difference that a change to a more precise verb makes in the sentence below.

The movie ~~had~~ *grabbed* my attention.

❸ Practice and Apply

A. CONCEPT CHECK: What Is a Verb?

Write the verb or verb phrase in each of the following sentences.

The King of the Monster Movies

1. *King Kong* may be the most famous monster movie ever.
2. At the start of the film, a producer is planning a movie.
3. He and a film crew sail to Skull Island.
4. There they find a giant ape, Kong.
5. Kong falls in love with Ann, the movie's star.
6. The producer takes Kong to New York in chains.
7. Kong escapes from his chains.
8. He climbs to the top of the Empire State Building.
9. There, he must struggle against fighter planes.
10. Kong's enemies win in the end.

Identify as action or linking each of the verbs you wrote.

➜ **For a SELF-CHECK and more practice, see the EXERCISE BANK, p. 321.**

B. WRITING: Using Specific Verbs

Special Effects

Write a more specific verb to replace each underlined verb in the paragraph below.

Willis O'Brien <u>did</u> the special effects for the *King Kong* movie of 1933. O'Brien <u>made</u> miniature models, including an 18-inch-tall Kong. To make Kong's muscles, he carefully <u>put</u> latex strips under the model's skin. Then he added air bladders in its chest. Now the model <u>was</u> real. O'Brien <u>took</u> many long hours at his task.

CHAPTER 4

Action Verbs and Objects

1 Here's the Idea

Action verbs are often accompanied by words that complete their meaning. These complements are **direct objects** and **indirect objects.**

Direct Objects

▶ **A direct object is a noun or pronoun that names the receiver of an action.** The direct object answers the question *what* or *whom.*

BEGINS WHAT?

The scriptwriter begins the process.

ACTION VERB — DIRECT OBJECT

The scriptwriter develops a story idea.

Indirect Objects

▶ **An indirect object tells *to what* or *whom* or *for what* or *whom* an action is done.** Verbs that often take indirect objects include *bring, give, hand, lend, make, send, show, teach, tell,* and *write.*

The scriptwriter sends a script. (sends to whom?)

TO WHOM?

The scriptwriter sends the director a script.

INDIRECT OBJECT — DIRECT OBJECT

The director gives the scriptwriter some advice.

If the preposition *to* or *for* appears in a sentence, the word that follows it is *not* an indirect object. It is the object of the preposition.

Tell the movie ending to us.

OBJECT OF PREPOSITION

Tell us the movie ending.

INDIRECT OBJECT

VERBS

Transitive and Intransitive Verbs

An action verb that has a direct object is called a **transitive verb.** A verb that does not have a direct object is called an **intransitive verb.**

Scriptwriters set the pace of their movies.
TRANSITIVE VERB (set) — DIRECT OBJECT (pace)

The action moves quickly or slowly.
INTRANSITIVE VERB (NO OBJECT) (moves)

Sometimes an intransitive verb is followed by a word that looks like a direct object but is really an adverb. An adverb tells where, when, how, or to what extent; a direct object answers the question whom or what.

CHOOSE WHAT?

Directors choose camera angles.
TRANSITIVE VERB (choose) — DIRECT OBJECT (angles)

CHOOSE HOW?

The good ones choose wisely.
INTRANSITIVE VERB (choose) — ADVERB (wisely)

CHAPTER 4

2 Why It Matters in Writing

The correct use of direct objects can help you give clear directions or specific advice. Notice how in the model below, Bradbury uses direct objects to show what he wants you to read and see.

LITERARY MODEL

> Read all the great **books.** Read all the great **poetry.** See all the great **films.** Fill your **life** with metaphors.
>
> —Ray Bradbury, "An Interview with Ray Bradbury"

❸ Practice and Apply

A. CONCEPT CHECK: Action Verbs and Objects

Write the 15 complements in these sentences, identifying each as a direct object or an indirect object.

A Crew of Dozens

1. A movie crew includes many people.
2. The director usually tells crew members their assignments.
3. The director of photography gives the director the film footage.
4. The sound crew includes a boom operator.
5. The director tells the composer the mood of the movie.
6. Members of the art department have an important function.
7. They show the director of photography the special effects.
8. The crew also includes wardrobe assistants.
9. Makeup artists give the actors the right look.
10. A movie set provides many creative jobs.

➜ **For a SELF-CHECK and more practice, see the EXERCISE BANK, p. 321.**

VERBS

B. REVISING: Adding Direct Objects

Read the movie proposal below. From the list at the top, select a direct object to fill in each blank.

world, powers, legs, evil, weights

Proposal for New Film

The movie begins as a sequel to *The Little Mermaid*. Ariel has changed, however. No longer a fragile little mermaid, she has two strong ___1___. She lifts ___2___ as a hobby. Now she has amazing ___3___. She can switch back and forth from a mermaid to a human. She travels the ___4___. She fights ___5___ everywhere.

Linking Verbs and Predicate Words

1 Here's the Idea

The word that a linking verb connects its subject to is called a **subject complement.** The subject complement identifies or describes the subject. Some common linking verbs are *is, feel, seem,* and *look.*

IDENTIFIES

A movie is a complicated project.
SUBJECT VERB SUBJECT COMPLEMENT

DESCRIBES

A movie must seem real.
SUBJECT VERB SUBJECT COMPLEMENT

CHAPTER 4

Predicate Nouns and Predicate Adjectives

A subject complement can be a **predicate noun** or a **predicate adjective.**

▶ **A predicate noun is a noun that follows a linking verb and identifies, renames, or defines the subject.**

IDENTIFIES

***Star Wars* is a science fiction film.**
SUBJECT VERB PREDICATE NOUN

I am a science fiction fan.

▶ **A predicate adjective is an adjective that follows a linking verb and modifies the subject.**

MODIFIES

Science fiction films are popular.
SUBJECT VERB PREDICATE ADJECTIVE

They look so futuristic.

2 Why It Matters in Writing

Predicate adjectives let you describe subjects with just a word or two. They can help you create vivid descriptions. Notice how predicate adjectives are used in the model below to contrast the characters and briefly convey the situation.

STUDENT MODEL

Look at the characters in *Star Wars.* Princess Leia is **brave.** Luke Skywalker is **tough.** And Han Solo is basically **honest.** Throughout the movie their situation seems **hopeless.** But their cause is **just.** In the end, they triumph.

Predicate adjectives describe the subjects.

3 Practice and Apply

CONCEPT CHECK: Linking Verbs and Predicate Words

Identify each linking verb, predicate noun, and predicate adjective in the sentences below.

Creature Features

1. Not all creatures in science fiction movies are scary.
2. Some seem downright friendly.
3. For example, *E.T. the Extra-Terrestrial* was a hit.
4. The movie's alien creature appeared lovable.
5. E.T. seemed afraid of the children at first.
6. In *Close Encounters of the Third Kind* the aliens were a mystery for most of the movie.
7. In the end the inhabitants of the giant UFO were friendly to humans.
8. In *The Empire Strikes Back* one alien was very wise.
9. Yoda was a 900-year-old Jedi sage.
10. With Yoda's help Luke Skywalker became a Jedi too.

➜ **For a SELF-CHECK and more practice, see the EXERCISE BANK, p. 322.**

Principal Parts of Verbs

1 Here's the Idea

Every verb has four basic forms, called its principal parts: the present, the present participle, the past, and the past participle. These principal parts are used to make all of the forms and tenses of the verb. Here are some examples.

Stunt people take risks on screen.
PRESENT

Stunt people are doing dangerous things all the time.
PRESENT PARTICIPLE

Polly Berson performed stunts for 27 years.
PAST

Most stunt people have trained for many years.
PAST PARTICIPLE

The Four Principal Parts of a Verb

Present	Present Participle	Past	Past Participle
jump	(is) jumping	jumped	(has) jumped
crash	(is) crashing	crashed	(has) crashed

Notice that helping verbs are used with the present participle and the past participles.

Regular Verbs

There are two kinds of verbs: regular and irregular.

A regular verb is a verb whose past and past participle are formed by adding *-ed* or *-d* to the present. The present participle is formed by adding *-ing* to the present.

Present	Present Participle	Past	Past Participle
look	(is) look + -ing	look + -ed	(has) look + -ed

You will learn about irregular verbs in the next lesson.

CHAPTER 4

② Why It Matters in Writing

The principal parts of verbs let you express changes in time in your writing. In the model below, notice how the writer uses the past and the present to show a shift in time.

PROFESSIONAL MODEL

An accident paralyzed stuntwoman Heidi von Beltz during a car stunt for the movie *The Cannonball Run.* Still, she exercises daily with a special trainer.

—S. Atlas

PAST

PRESENT

VERBS

③ Practice and Apply

CONCEPT CHECK: Principal Parts of Verbs

Identify each underlined principal part as the present, the present participle, the past, or the past participle.

Stunt Stand-ins

Stunt people **(1)** perform the dangerous scenes in movies and TV shows. Many are athletes who have **(2)** decided to pursue careers in show business. When the hero of a movie is **(3)** leaping from a galloping horse or the villain is **(4)** jumping out of a burning helicopter, the person you see is probably a stunt person. Most stunts **(5)** belong to five categories: falls, fights, fires, car stunts, and horse stunts. A safety crew **(6)** stays on hand in case of problems. Some stunt people have fatally **(7)** injured themselves. For example, Vic Rivers once **(8)** jumped a truck into a lake and **(9)** drowned. Despite the dangers, most stunters **(10)** love their exciting jobs.

→ **For a SELF-CHECK and more practice, see the EXERCISE BANK, p. 322.**

Irregular Verbs

LESSON 5

1 Here's the Idea

▶ **Irregular verbs are verbs whose past and past participle forms are not made by adding *-ed* or *-d* to the present.** The following chart shows you how to form the past and past-participle forms of many irregular verbs.

Common Irregular Verbs

	Present	Past	Past Participle
Group 1 The forms of the present, the past, and the past participle are all the same.	**burst** cost cut hit hurt let put set shut	**burst** cost cut hit hurt let put set shut	(has) **burst** (has) cost (has) cut (has) hit (has) hurt (has) let (has) put (has) set (has) shut
Group 2 The forms of the past and the past participle are the same.	**bring** build buy catch feel have keep lay leave lose make pay say sell shine sit sleep teach think win wind	**brought** built bought caught felt had kept laid left lost made paid said sold shone sat slept taught thought won wound	(has) **brought** (has) built (has) bought (has) caught (has) felt (has) had (has) kept (has) laid (has) left (has) lost (has) made (has) paid (has) said (has) sold (has) shone (has) sat (has) slept (has) taught (has) thought (has) won (has) wound

Common Irregular Verbs *(continued)*			
	Present	**Past**	**Past Participle**
Group 3 The past participle is formed by adding *-n* or *-en* to the past.	**bite** break choose freeze lie speak steal tear wear	**bit** broke chose froze lay spoke stole tore wore	(has) **bitten** (has) broken (has) chosen (has) frozen (has) lain (has) spoken (has) stolen (has) torn (has) worn
Group 4 The past participle is formed from the present, usually by adding *-n* or *-en.*	**blow** do draw drive eat fall give go grow know rise run see take throw write	**blew** did drew drove ate fell gave went grew knew rose ran saw took threw wrote	(has) **blown** (has) done (has) drawn (has) driven (has) eaten (has) fallen (has) given (has) gone (has) grown (has) known (has) risen (has) run (has) seen (has) taken (has) thrown (has) written
Group 5 A vowel in the verb changes from *i* in the present to *a* in the past and to *u* in the past participle.	**begin** drink ring shrink sing sink spring swim	**began** drank rang shrank sang sank sprang swam	(has) **begun** (has) drunk (has) rung (has) shrunk (has) sung (has) sunk (has) sprung (has) swum

The Irregular Verb *Be*			
	Present	**Past**	**Past Participle**
The past and past participle do not follow any pattern.	**am, are, is**	**was, were**	(has) **been**

VERBS

❷ Why It Matters in Writing

To be a skilled writer, you need to use irregular verb forms correctly. They can be tricky, though. The best way to avoid mistakes is to memorize the principal parts of the most common irregular verbs.

STUDENT MODEL

Special effects ~~maked~~ *made* a skyscraper fall in an instant. Then a gigantic tornado ~~blowed~~ *blew* away the rubble.

❸ Practice and Apply

CONCEPT CHECK: Irregular Verbs

In the sentences below, choose the correct forms of the verbs in parentheses.

Movie Magic

1. Movies can convince us that we have (saw, seen) real events on screen.
2. Special effects have (let, letted) filmmakers fool us.
3. They have (bringed, brought) to the screen cloud cities, giant apes, and telephones with teeth.
4. Even in the early days of movies, directors (made, maked) impossible scenes look real.
5. A famous story shows that the Lumière brothers (knowed, knew) how to create a special effect in 1896.
6. A pile of rubble quickly (built, builded) itself into a wall.
7. The brothers had filmed as workers (teared, tore) down a wall.
8. Then they (runned, ran) the film backward.
9. Often filmmakers have (shrank, shrunk) huge monsters to miniature size for filming.
10. In the 1990s filmmakers (beginned, began) using computer-generated effects.

→ **For a SELF-CHECK and more practice, see the EXERCISE BANK, p. 323.**

LESSON 6 Simple Tenses

❶ Here's the Idea

▶ **A tense is a verb form that shows the time of an action or condition.** Verbs have three **simple tenses:** the present, the past, and the future.

Understanding Simple Tenses

Simple Tenses

The water rushes swiftly by the raft.	The **present tense** shows that an action or condition occurs now.
The raft passed the point of no return earlier.	The **past tense** shows that an action or condition was completed in the past.
Soon someone will fall into the water.	The **future tense** shows that an action or condition will occur in the future.

A **progressive** form of a tense expresses an action or condition in progress. The progressive forms of the three simple tenses are used to show that actions or conditions are, were, or will be in progress.

Progressive Forms

People on shore are calling for help.	Present Progressive
They were fishing before.	Past Progressive
They will be watching for the rescue boat.	Future Progressive

Forming Simple Tenses

The present tense of a verb is the present principal part. The past tense is the past principal part. To form the future tense, add *will* to the present principal part.

Forming Simple Tenses

	Singular	Plural
Present (present principal part)	I direct you direct he, she, it directs	we direct you direct they direct
Past (past principal part)	I directed you directed he, she, it directed	we directed you directed they directed
Future (*will* + present principal part)	I will direct you will direct he, she, it will direct	we will direct you will direct they will direct

CHAPTER 4

To make the progressive form of one of these tenses, add the present, past, or future form of *be* to the present participle.

Present progressive: **I am directing.**

Past progressive: **I was directing.**

Future progressive: **I will be directing.**

2 Why It Matters in Writing

Changing tenses allows you to be clear about the order in which things happen. Notice how the writer uses the past, the present, and the future tense in the sentence below.

PROFESSIONAL MODEL

Until recently, people considered digital films inferior. Now better cameras produce good, clear images. Soon many filmmakers will produce their movies digitally.

PAST
PRESENT
FUTURE

—Eliza Blackburn

❸ Practice and Apply

A. CONCEPT CHECK: Simple Tenses

Identify each underlined verb as present, past, future, present progressive, past progressive, or future progressive.

The Digital Revolution Arrives

1. DVDs were developed in the mid-1990s.
2. These shiny platters transformed movie distribution.
3. A DVD holds up to 25 times as much information as a CD.
4. It provides high-quality video images, interactive multimedia features, and surround sound.
5. The movie *Ghostbusters* came out in 1984.
6. It did well at the box office.
7. Now it is available in DVD format.
8. Besides the movie, the DVD contains commentary by the director, production notes, and a photo gallery.
9. It also includes a complete script and ten scenes that were cut from the movie.
10. In the next few years, companies will be releasing nearly 100,000 movies on DVD.

➜ **For a SELF-CHECK and more practice, see the EXERCISE BANK, p. 323.**

Working Portfolio: Find the paragraph you wrote for the **Write Away** on page 90 or a sample of your most recent work. Identify any errors in the use of simple tenses and correct them.

B. REVISING: Correcting Simple Tenses

Rewrite the following paragraph, correcting the tenses of the underlined verbs.

Advantages of DVDs

In the early 1990s, VHS videotapes **(1)** will be the standard format for movie distributors. In the late 1990s, DVD format slowly **(2)** takes over, and in 2003 it **(3)** surpasses videotapes in popularity. Today, DVDs **(4)** included many subtitle tracks in different languages. Because DVDs **(5)** will have so much more storage capacity, they can include interviews, deleted scenes, trailers, and more. Eventually, a new technological format **(6)** has even greater storage capacity and **(7)** replaced the DVD.

LESSON 7 Perfect Tenses

1 Here's the Idea

Understanding Perfect Tenses

The **present perfect tense** places an action or condition in a stretch of time leading up to the present.

The scientist has created a monster.

The scientist created the monster at some unspecified time before the present.

The **past perfect tense** places a past action or condition before another past action or condition.

When the scientist had tinkered with him, the monster awakened.

The tinkering occurred before the awakening.

The **future perfect tense** places a future action or condition before another future action or condition.

The monster will have escaped before the scientist notices.

The escaping will occur before the scientist's noticing.

CHAPTER 4

Forming Perfect Tenses

To form the present perfect, past perfect, or future perfect tense of a verb, add the present, past, or future form of *have* to the past participle.

Forming Perfect Tenses	Singular	Plural
Present perfect (*has* or *have* + past participle)	I have screamed you have screamed he, she, it has screamed	we have screamed you have screamed they have screamed
Past perfect (*had* + past participle)	I had screamed you had screamed he, she, it had screamed	we had screamed you had screamed they had screamed
Future perfect (*will* + *have* + past participle)	I will have screamed you will have screamed he, she, it will have screamed	we will have screamed you will have screamed they will have screamed

VERBS

In perfect forms of verbs, the tense of the helping verb *have* shows the verb's tense.

❷ Why It Matters in Writing

By using perfect tenses, you can help your readers understand when events occur in relation to other events. Notice the effective use of the past perfect and present perfect tenses in the model.

PROFESSIONAL MODEL

Within a year the brute **had returned** in *Godzilla's Counterattack* and over the years he **has battled** The Thing.

—Jeremy Pascall, *The King Kong Story*

This action occurred before other events in the past.

This action occurred sometime between the previous action and the present.

3 Practice and Apply

A. CONCEPT CHECK: Perfect Tenses

Identify the verb in each sentence, and indicate whether its tense is present perfect, past perfect, or future perfect.

Horrors!

1. For years we had looked for a funny werewolf movie.
2. Now we have found *An American Werewolf in London.*
3. By tomorrow morning we will have watched it four times.
4. *Young Frankenstein* has amused us too.
5. Many serious Frankenstein movies had appeared before that comedy.
6. Filmmakers had created the first such horror films not long after the invention of movies.
7. Even before the 1931 *Frankenstein* there had been a silent version of the Frankenstein story.
8. All Frankenstein movies have drawn on Mary Shelley's 1818 novel.
9. Filmmakers have produced at least eight versions of *Dr. Jekyll and Mr. Hyde*.
10. What new versions of horror classics will have come out by next year?

→ **For a SELF-CHECK and more practice, see the EXERCISE BANK, p. 324.**

CHAPTER 4

B. WRITING: Using Perfect Tenses

The scene described below could happen in a horror movie. Rewrite each underlined verb in the tense named in parentheses.

Horror Scene: Take One

Three girls cut (present perfect) through a cemetery. They thought (past perfect) it would be a good shortcut, but they were (present perfect) sorry ever since. Suddenly they see a strange light that appeared (present perfect) ahead of them. By the time they round the next tombstone, they discovered (future perfect) the light's source—a mummy!

Using Verb Tenses

1 Here's the Idea

A good writer uses different verb tenses to indicate that events occur at different times. If you do not need to indicate a change of time, do not switch from one tense to another.

Writing About the Present

You can write about the present using the present tense, the present perfect tense, and the present progressive form.

Motion pictures work because of our vision.

The brain sees a series of still pictures as moving.

The **present tense** places the actions in the present.

Filmmakers have created fantastic special effects.

They have brought dinosaurs and alien beings to life.

The **present perfect tense** places the actions in the period of time leading up to the present.

Directors are learning the use of computer effects.

They are becoming extremely skilled artists.

The **present progressive forms** show the actions are in progress now.

Many futuristic movies are becoming classics.

VERBS

Writing About the Past

The past tense conveys actions and conditions that came to an end in the past. When you write about the past, you can use past verb forms to indicate the order in which events occurred. Using these forms correctly will make it easier for readers to follow the events.

Thomas Edison's company launched the motion-picture industry.

His employee William Dickson devised a way of moving film through a camera.

The **past tense** shows action that began and was completed in the past.

Other inventors had put sound with pictures before Edison did.

After the Lumière brothers had developed a projector, Edison began projecting his films.

The **past perfect tense** places the actions before other past actions.

Filmmakers were inventing new technologies for years before they began using computers.

They were trying to make unreal events look real.

The **past progressive forms** show that the actions in the past were in progress.

CHAPTER 4

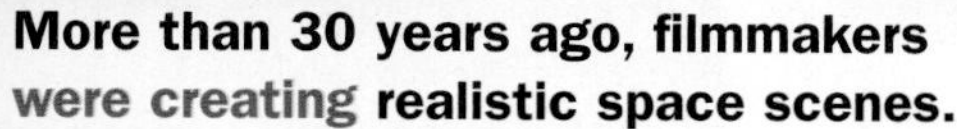
More than 30 years ago, filmmakers were creating realistic space scenes.

Writing About the Future

▶ **The future tenses convey actions and conditions that are yet to come.** By using the different future verb forms, you can show how future events are related in time.

Maybe everyone will make movies someday.

The line between home movies and professional ones will blur.

The **future tense** shows that the actions have not yet occurred.

Before they can read, children already will have learned to use a camera.

Studio films will be less important because the Internet will have increased people's access to one another's films.

The **future perfect tense** places the actions before other future actions.

People will be making movies ever more cheaply.

Everyone will be watching everyone else's movies.

The **future progressive forms** show that the actions in the future will be continuing.

VERBS

2 Why It Matters in Writing

When you use the right tenses, you help your readers keep sequences of events straight.

1850 No movies existed.

1900 Few people owned cameras and projectors.

Today Big studios make movies for profit.

2050 Anyone will be able to make movies.

3 Practice and Apply

A. CONCEPT CHECK: Using Verb Tenses

In each sentence, choose the correct verb form in parentheses.

Hollywood Goes High-Tech

1. In the 1930s, makers of monster movies (were using, will be using) laughably bad special effects.
2. They (lacked, have lacked) the technology to create realistic monsters.
3. Recently filmmakers (have improved, improved) special-effects technology considerably.
4. As early as the 1980s, filmmakers (will be using, were using) computer-generated, or CG, graphics.
5. They (added, will have added) effects on a background.
6. Now they (are refining, were refining) CG technology further.
7. They (will build, are building) characters on a computer.
8. They already (create, will create) everything from aliens to giant gorillas.
9. Soon they (had shown, will show) realistic animated human figures.
10. Yet the story (will remain, remained) the most important element.

Name the tense or form of each verb you chose in the sentences above.

→ **For a SELF-CHECK and more practice, see the EXERCISE BANK, p. 324.**

B. EDITING: Arranging Verb Tenses

Pretend you are a film director. List the numbers of the following directions in a logical order, so that the tenses of the verbs make sense. (Hint: Read all the sentences before you begin.)

1. Now that you know what the scene is about, we will begin.
2. This scene starts just after an alien has made video contact with the reporter Colleen McKay.
3. Colleen is surprised because she expected the alien to look like a bug.
4. First, Colleen sees the alien, who looks like a cat.
5. The alien will tell Colleen his name, Rxxd.

LESSON 9 Troublesome Verb Pairs

1 Here's the Idea

Some pairs of verbs seem similar but are actually different words with different meanings. Troublesome verb pairs include *lie* and *lay, sit* and *set, rise* and *raise,* and *may* and *can.*

Lie and *Lay*

Lie means "to rest in a flat position." It does not take an object. *Lay* means "to put or place." It does take an object.

The tigers lie at the trainer's feet.

The trainer lays the tiger treats on a tray.

Lie and *Lay*		
Present	**Past**	**Past Participle**
lie Fido **lies** down.	**lay** Fido **lay** down.	**lain** Fido has **lain** down.
lay Fido **lays** the toy down.	**laid** Fido **laid** the toy down.	**laid** Fido has **laid** the toy down.

Lie and *lay* are confusing because the present principal part of *lay* is spelled the same as the past principal part of *lie*.

Sit and *Set*

Sit means "to be seated." It does not take an object.

Set means "to put or place." It does take an object.

My cat, Luna, sits on the couch.

I set the flea powder down somewhere.

Sit and *Set*		
Present	**Past**	**Past Participle**
sit We **sit** on the floor.	**sat** We **sat** on the floor.	**sat** I had **sat** for hours.
set Tiff **sets** down the bug.	**set** Tiff **set** down the bug.	**set** Tiff had **set** down the bug.

VERBS

Rise and *Raise*

Rise means "to move upward" or "to get out of bed." It does not take an object. *Raise* means "to lift" or "to care for or bring up." It does take an object.

The sun rises every morning.

King Kong raises a car easily.

CHAPTER 4

Rise and *Raise*		
Present	**Past**	**Past Participle**
rise The water **rises.**	**rose** The water **rose.**	**risen** The water had **risen** earlier.
raise Kong **raises** the car.	**raised** Kong **raised** the car.	**raised** Kong had **raised** the car earlier.

May and *Can*

May means "to be allowed to" or "to be likely to." *Can* means "to be able to." *Might* and *could* serve as the past tense forms of *may* and *can.*

May I pet your dog?

Can he do any tricks?

Can and *may* do not have past participles. They are usually used as helping verbs.

❷ Practice and Apply

A. CONCEPT CHECK: Troublesome Verb Pairs

Choose the correct word in parentheses in each of the following sentences.

The Gentle Jungle

1. With love, patience, understanding, and respect, you (can, may) teach an animal almost anything.
2. The animal trainer Ralph Helfer teaches his animals what they (can, may) do with a system called affection training.
3. To show affection, Helfer (lies, lays) down with a lion.
4. Helfer (lies, lays) his hands on his animals carefully.
5. When Helfer's daughter Tana was little, she often (sat, set) on the trunk of Margie the elephant.
6. Margie the elephant (rose, raised) her trunk.
7. Tana would (rise, raise) in the air.
8. Then Margie would (sit, set) the child on her back.
9. Helfer (rose, raised) the orangutan who costarred with Clint Eastwood in two movies.
10. He even taught a sick chimp to (lie, lay) down and give itself a shot.

➜ **For a SELF-CHECK and more practice, see the EXERCISE BANK, p. 325.**

B. PROOFREADING: What Do They Mean?

List the five verbs that are used incorrectly in the following paragraph. Then change them to the correct verb forms.

Elvis and the Chimp

May you believe this story about Elvis Presley? Elvis used to set on Helfer's floor and play with baby tigers. One day when Elvis arrived, a chimp named Coffee jumped off the roof and knocked him down. Elvis laid on the ground while Coffee jumped up and down on him. After Helfer helped rise Elvis to his feet, Coffee apologized by brushing the dust off the singer. Coffee learned that he should not sit his feet on Elvis Presley!

VERBS

Grammar in Fine Arts

Using Verbs in Drama

When you present a dramatic scene, you perform actions. When you write a dramatic scene, you use verbs to indicate those actions. Stage directions are very important because they tell the actors exactly what to do. The verbs in stage directions must clearly describe the desired movements. Notice the verbs in these scenes from *A Christmas Carol.*

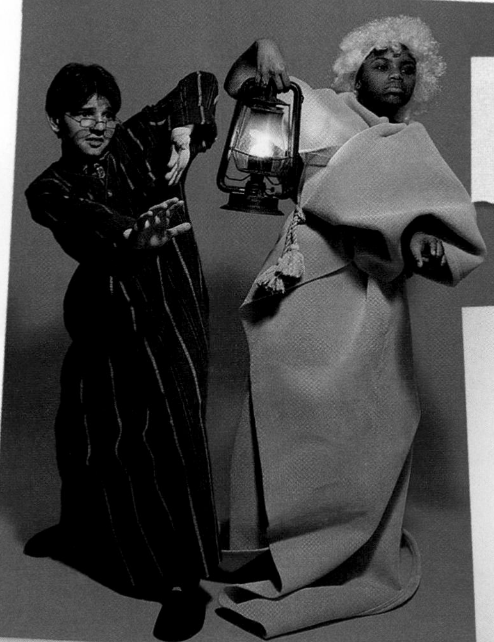

(The spirit motions for Scrooge to turn. Scrooge trembles and shakes his head.)

(Dancers whirl around the stage. Fezziwhig's wife applauds.)

Practice and Apply

A. WRITING: Describing a Scene

Use your own ideas and the actions shown on page 118 to write a one-minute scene. Include interesting, scary, or funny actions in your scene. Write clear stage directions for your actors. You may use some of the sentences beside the characters to get started.

B. Creating a Blocking Diagram

A director's plans for how actors should move on stage are called blocking. When you are working on a dramatic performance, you may need to write plans for blocking the action. The picture shows a blocking diagram for another scene in the play.

Make your own diagram showing the blocking for your scene. In your diagram, include each of the actors who will be on stage. Indicate who should move. Use arrows to indicate directions. Add verbs on labels that give additional information about how actors should move.

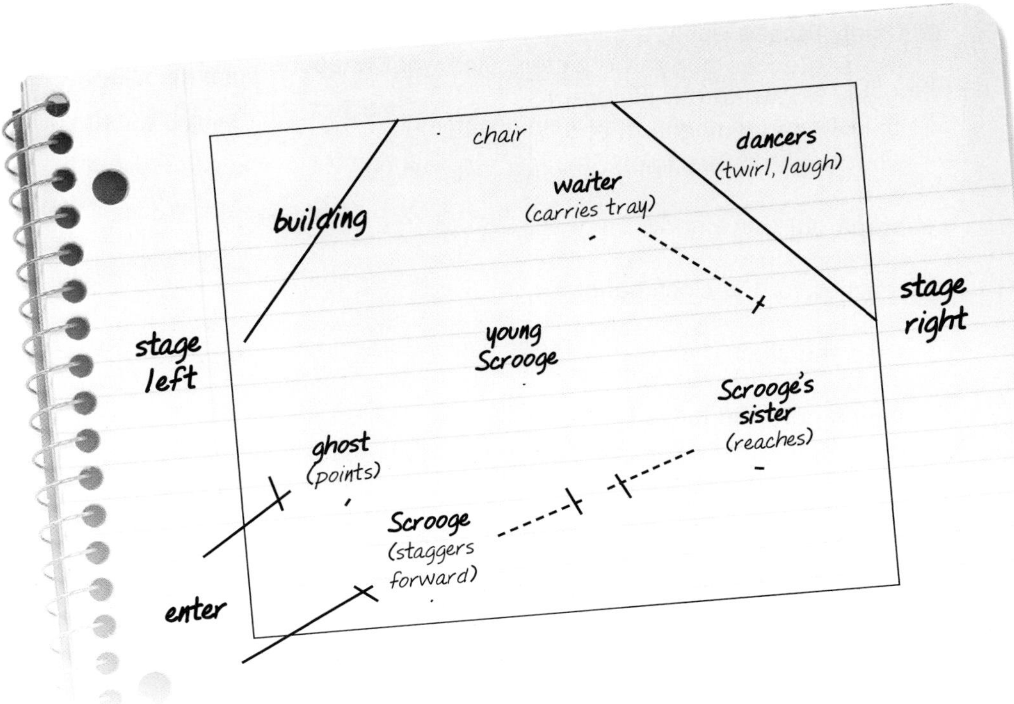

VERBS

chair
dancers (twirl, laugh)
waiter (carries tray)
building
stage right
young Scrooge
stage left
Scrooge's sister (reaches)
ghost (points)
Scrooge (staggers forward)
enter

Mixed Review

A. Revising Incorrect Verbs Find and correct the incorrect verb in each of the following sentences. Watch out for irregular verbs, troublesome verbs, and incorrect verb tenses.

Preserving Our Past in Movies

1. Today, some movie fans currently have worried about the rate at which movie prints are deteriorating.
2. They rose the alarm when they found that many early movies have disappeared forever.
3. Already, time will be destroying nine-tenths of all the movies from the 1920s.
4. The world has lost half of all the movies that were maked before 1950.
5. Thousands of movies are being losed in studios' vaults right now.
6. The biggest problem had been the decay of the film that moviemakers use.
7. Most directors in the future filmed digitally, without celluloid.
8. Yet electronic ways of recording movies were becoming out of date very fast.
9. Because equipment has changed, most TV stations today were unable to broadcast from the movie tape of 20 years ago.
10. Film restorers work hard now so that people have enjoyed today's movies in the future.

B. Using Tenses Using the ideas in the phrases listed below, write five sentences about the picture. Tell what happened before the scene shown in the picture, what is happening in it, and what might happen next.

steps out the window

reaches for the clock hands

fixes the clock

jumps onto the ledge

climbs up a rope to the flagpole

Mastery Test: What Did You Learn?

Choose the best way to rewrite each underlined word or group of words.

Money <u>has been</u> (1) an issue in movies since the beginning. In fact, before movies became popular, Thomas Edison <u>vows</u> (2) never to invent anything he couldn't sell. He <u>seen</u> (3) the movie camera as a product that would make money. As technology improved, some costs decreased. Other costs <u>rised</u> (4). For example, in 1959 it <u>costed</u> (5) about $70,000 to film a minute of the epic movie *Ben-Hur.* In 1998 the filming of *Titanic* cost $1 million per minute. However, soon the cost of special effects <u>will come</u> (6) down as computer-generated graphics are used more widely. In the next 25 years the cost of effects <u>had dropped</u> (7) by half. Today, all the studios together <u>spent</u> (8) $400 million each year on prints of their movies. Soon filmmakers <u>sent</u> (9) their movies worldwide by satellite, and the cost <u>sinks</u> (10).

1. A. had been
   B. will be
   C. was
   D. Correct as is

2. A. will vow
   B. has vowed
   C. had vowed
   D. Correct as is

3. A. saw
   B. has seen
   C. had saw
   D. Correct as is

4. A. rise
   B. rose
   C. raised
   D. Correct as is

5. A. cost
   B. will cost
   C. is costing
   D. Correct as is

6. A. came
   B. are coming
   C. have come
   D. Correct as is

7. A. drop
   B. have dropped
   C. will drop
   D. Correct as is

8. A. spend
   B. spended
   C. will spend
   D. Correct as is

9. A. send
   B. have sent
   C. will send
   D. Correct as is

10. A. sank
    B. have sunk
    C. will sink
    D. Correct as is

Student Help Desk

Verbs at a Glance

A verb expresses action, condition, or state of being.

People **eat** popcorn at the movies.
ACTION VERB

Popcorn **is** a noisy treat.
LINKING VERB

They **have eaten** too much popcorn.
HELPING VERB ↑ ↑ MAIN VERB

CHAPTER 4

Principal Parts of Regular Verbs

Present	Present Participle	Past	Past Participle
present	**present + *-ing***	**present + *-ed* or *-d***	**present + *-ed* or *-d***
act	**(is) acting**	**acted**	**(has) acted**
bellow	(is) bellowing	bellowed	(has) bellowed
cry	(is) crying	cried	(has) cried
drag	(is) dragging	dragged	(has) dragged
emote	(is) emoting	emoted	(has) emoted
film	(is) filming	filmed	(has) filmed
gesture	(is) gesturing	gestured	(has) gestured
help	(is) helping	helped	(has) helped
imitate	(is) imitating	imitated	(has) imitated
join	(is) joining	joined	(has) joined

...It's about Time!

Keeping Tenses Straight

Tense	What It Conveys	Example
Present	Action or condition occurring in the present	I **watch** movies.
Past	Action or condition occurring in the past	I **watched** a movie.
Future	Action or condition occurring in the future	I **will watch** a movie.
Present perfect	Action or condition occurring in the period leading up to the present	I **have watched** movies.
Past perfect	Past action or condition preceding another past action or condition	I **had watched** the movie before I went to bed.
Future perfect	Future action or condition preceding another future action or condition	I **will have watched** five movies by next Tuesday.

VERBS

The Bottom Line

Checklist for Verbs

Have I . . .

____ used action verbs to express actions?

____ used linking verbs with predicate nouns and predicate adjectives?

____ used direct objects and indirect objects to answer the questions *whom, what,* and *to whom* or *to what?*

____ used the correct principal parts of irregular verbs?

____ used tenses correctly to express the times of actions and conditions?

____ used *sit* and *set, lie* and *lay, rise* and *raise,* and *may* and *can* correctly?

Chapter 5

Adjectives and Adverbs

Theme: Accidents and Inventions

Back to the Drawing Board

How did inventors bring us from a primitive glider that barely carried one person to the incredibly sophisticated Boeing 777 that easily carries 300 passengers? It took a long time—and many modifications, or changes. Otto Lilienthal, who invented the first piloted glider (on the left above) in 1891, died after crashing one of his gliders. But other eager inventors continued to fine-tune their vehicles until they created the huge, fast, sleek jets of today.

Writers, like inventors, are fine-tuners. They use adjectives and adverbs to modify, or make more specific, their words. What words would you use to describe the three aircraft above?

Write Away: Moving into the Future

Imagine a transportation invention of the future. Freewrite a paragraph that describes what it does and how it looks. Save the paragraph in your **Working Portfolio.**

Diagnostic Test: What Do You Know?

For each underlined item, choose the letter of the term that correctly identifies it.

In the late 1700s two French (1) brothers, Jacques and Joseph Montgolfier, began experiments that led to the invention of the modern (2) hot-air balloon. The (3) brothers started really (4) simply, using small paper bags and wood fires. In these (5) tests the Montgolfiers saw that a bag would rise when completely (6) filled with hot air. The brothers conducted a more important (7) experiment when they filled a large cloth balloon with hot air and launched it. The flight was successful (8)! Today's balloonists couldn't hardly fly (9) without the methods perfected by the Montgolfiers. Today, by using modern technologies, modern balloonists fly even farther (10) than the Montgolfiers flew.

1. A. adverb
   B. comparative adjective
   C. proper adjective
   D. predicate adjective
2. A. adjective
   B. comparative adjective
   C. proper adjective
   D. predicate adjective
3. A. proper adjective
   B. definite article
   C. predicate adjective
   D. indefinite article
4. A. adverb describing *simply*
   B. adverb describing *started*
   C. adverb describing *brothers*
   D. adverb describing *bags*
5. A. pronoun used as adjective
   B. noun used as adjective
   C. pronoun used as adverb
   D. noun used as adverb
6. A. adverb telling how
   B. adverb telling when
   C. adverb telling where
   D. adverb telling to what extent
7. A. comparative adjective
   B. superlative adjective
   C. comparative adverb
   D. superlative adverb
8. A. adverb
   B. comparative adjective
   C. proper adjective
   D. predicate adjective
9. A. adjective
   B. double negative
   C. statement
   D. question
10. A. comparative adverb
    B. superlative adverb
    C. comparative adjective
    D. superlative adjective

What Is an Adjective?

1 Here's the Idea

▶ **An adjective is a word that modifies, or describes, a noun or a pronoun.**

MODIFIES

The noisy crowd cheered for Daria.

ADJECTIVE ↑ ↑ NOUN

Adjectives help you see, feel, taste, hear, and smell all the things you read about. Notice how adjectives make the second sentence in the following pair more descriptive.

She sped along the track on her bicycle.

She sped along the narrow track on her sleek bicycle.

Adjectives answer the questions *what kind, which one, how many,* and *how much.*

Adjectives			
What kind?	**fast** riders	**crowded** stadium	**steamy** afternoon
Which one or ones?	**first** lap	**inner** lanes	**final** race
How many or how much?	**five** teams	**many** fans	**more** applause

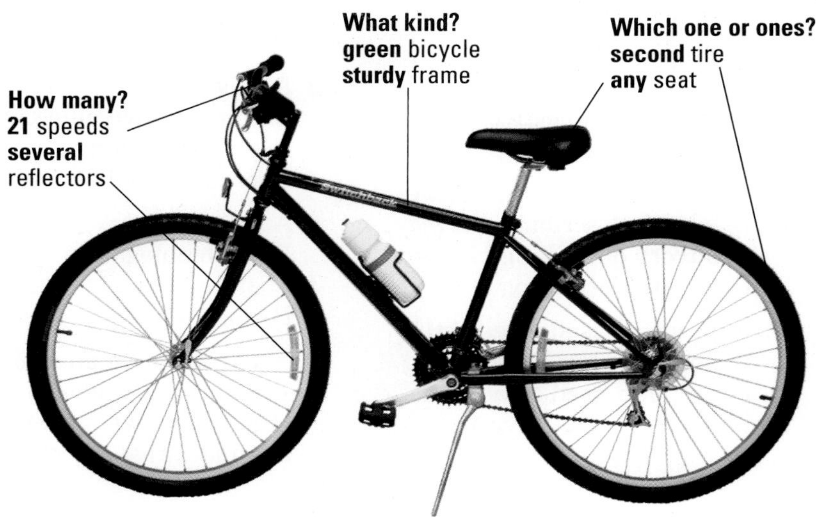

CHAPTER 5

Articles

The most commonly used adjectives are the **articles** *a, an,* and *the. A* and *an* are forms of the **indefinite article.** The indefinite article is used before a noun that names a nonspecific person, place, thing, or idea.

A sudden turn can cause an accident.
↑ INDEFINITE ARTICLE ↑ INDEFINITE ARTICLE

Use *a* before a word beginning with a consonant sound ("a ball"); use *an* before a word beginning with a vowel sound ("an egg").

The is the **definite article.** It points to a particular person, place, thing, or idea.

The competition continued through the afternoon.
↑ DEFINITE ARTICLE ↑ DEFINITE ARTICLE

ADJ. & ADV.

Forming Adjectives

Many adjectives are formed from common nouns.

Nouns and Adjectives

Noun	Adjective
storm	stormy
child	childish
music	musical
beauty	beautiful

A **proper adjective** is formed from a proper noun. Proper adjectives are always capitalized.

Proper Nouns and Proper Adjectives

Proper Noun	Proper Adjective
Shakespeare	Shakespearean
Asia	Asian
Spain	Spanish
Islam	Islamic

2 Why It Matters in Writing

Adjectives can provide important details. Imagine this description without adjectives.

PROFESSIONAL MODEL

The **first** bicycle was made of wood. This model was **hard** on shoes. Riders moved the bike in an **awkward** way. They pushed their feet backward against the ground. Later, a **Scottish** blacksmith made a **better** model, one with **two** pedals. This **new** bicycle was **easier** to ride and **easier** on shoes.

—L.C. Chaveriat

CHAPTER 5

3 Practice and Apply

CONCEPT CHECK: What Is an Adjective?

Write each adjective in these sentences, along with the noun or pronoun it modifies. Do not include articles.

Cold Ears, Warm Invention

1. Some successful inventors are mature scientists.
2. Chester Greenwood, however, was a creative teenager when he made the first pair of earmuffs.
3. Chester's cold, red ears bothered him during the harsh Northeastern winters.
4. He didn't like itchy woolen mufflers.
5. One day, Chester had a brilliant idea.
6. He took a piece of flexible wire.
7. His grandmother sewed soft fur to the wire.
8. Chester then put on the strange contraption.
9. Earmuffs made Chester a rich man.
10. Chester received an American patent for the earmuffs at the age of 18.

➜ **For a SELF-CHECK and more practice, see the EXERCISE BANK, p. 326.**

Identify the proper adjectives in the sentences above. For each, write the proper noun from which it is formed.

LESSON 2 Predicate Adjectives

1 Here's the Idea

▶ **A predicate adjective is an adjective that follows a linking verb and describes the verb's subject.** The linking verb connects the predicate adjective with the subject.

DESCRIBES

The airplanes were strange.
SUBJECT LINKING VERB

DESCRIBE

They were large, heavy, and often dangerous.

Predicate adjectives can follow linking verbs other than forms of *be.* Forms of *taste, smell, feel, look, become,* and *seem* are often used as linking verbs.

DESCRIBES

Sam felt anxious about the airplane flight.
LINKING VERB PREDICATE ADJECTIVE

DESCRIBES

The airplane's compartments felt warm.

For more about linking verbs, see page 98.

2 Why It Matters in Writing

Predicate adjectives help you paint pictures with words. Notice how the adjectives in this passage help you visualize the wings.

LITERARY MODEL

The wings themselves were **finer** than the finest rice paper, and yet they were **strong**. . . .

Right then I spread my wings and saw the glory of them! They had been **gold** at first, but now I saw how they shone iridescently—like the rainbow colors you see on a soap bubble. . . .

—Laurence Yep, *Dragonwings*

❸ Practice and Apply

A. CONCEPT CHECK: Predicate Adjectives

Write each predicate adjective in these sentences, along with the noun or pronoun it modifies. There may be more than one predicate adjective in a sentence.

Clear and Safe

1. Because of a trolley rider's fear, windshield wipers are common today.
2. To Mary Anderson electric trolleys seemed dangerous.
3. The drivers were alert.
4. The windshields, however, looked blurry and cloudy.
5. The windshields became clean when drivers rubbed them with damp tobacco and onions.
6. Anderson was creative, so she invented a windshield wiper.
7. Her first wiper was clumsy.
8. It was manual, and the driver had to crank a handle.
9. Today's wipers are automatic.
10. Because of Mary Anderson's invention, transportation became safer than it had been.

→ **For a SELF-CHECK and more practice, see the EXERCISE BANK, p. 326.**

Write the linking verb in each sentence above.

B. WRITING: Creating Riddles

Choose three of the common inventions in the list below. For each, write a riddle containing one or more predicate adjectives. Then exchange riddles with a partner. Solve your partner's riddles, and underline the predicate adjectives in them.

Example: What is shiny and twisted and keeps papers together? (a paper clip)

television set	toaster
portable radio	doorbell
pencil	bubble gum
computer	cereal
in-line skates	wristwatch

Other Words Used as Adjectives

1 Here's the Idea

In addition to their usual uses, many nouns and pronouns can be used as adjectives. They can modify nouns to make their meanings more specific.

Pronouns as Adjectives

Demonstrative Pronouns *This, that, these,* and *those* are demonstrative pronouns that can be used as adjectives.

This phone has a dial.

That phone has a keypad.

This phone has a cord.

That phone has a battery.

Possessive Pronouns *My, our, your, her, his, its,* and *their* are possessive pronouns that are used as adjectives.

Your phone is lighter. My phone has better reception.

Indefinite Pronouns Indefinite pronouns such as *all, each, both, few, most,* and *some* can be used as adjectives.

Originally, few people believed in the idea of the telephone.

Today, most households have at least two phones.

Nouns as Adjectives

Like pronouns, nouns can be used as adjectives. In the expression "computer keyboard," for example, the word *computer* (normally a noun) is used to modify *keyboard.* Notice the following examples of nouns used as adjectives.

MODIFIES

Renata's family just opened up an Internet account.

MODIFIES

This account should help her complete school projects.

2 Why It Matters in Writing

You can't gesture in writing the way you can in a face-to-face conversation. But you can use demonstrative pronouns as adjectives to "point to" people, and possessive pronouns in order to make relationships clear.

LITERARY MODEL

Transistors, chips, integrated circuits, Teflon, new medicines, new ways of treating diseases, new ways of performing operations, . . . are linked to the space effort. Most of these developments have been so incorporated into our day-to-day life that they are taken for granted, their origin not considered.

—Louis L'Amour, "The Eternal Frontier"

DEMONSTRATIVE PRONOUN

POSSESSIVE PRONOUNS

3 Practice and Apply

A. CONCEPT CHECK: Other Words Used as Adjectives

Write each noun or pronoun that is used as an adjective in these sentences.

Inventions from Nature

1. Most inventions are made by human beings.
2. But beavers may have inspired those huge dams that we build across rivers.

3. Our inventions often imitate the contrivances of nature.
4. To escape their enemies, insects mimic flowers and tree limbs.
5. A human army uses camouflage to hide its tanks.
6. Birds adjust their wings to the airflow as they fly.
7. Most airplanes have adjustable wing surfaces, too.
8. Bats use sound waves to locate their prey.
9. With sonar, we use sound waves to map the ocean floor.
10. I'm watching my cat for new ideas!

➜ **For a SELF-CHECK and more practice, see the EXERCISE BANK, p. 327.**

B. REVISING: Adding Pronouns Used as Adjectives

Write a demonstrative, possessive, or indefinite pronoun that can be used as an adjective to fill in each blank in this paragraph.

Young Inventors

Some late-night talk shows feature child inventors. __1__ children use __2__ imaginations to solve everyday problems. Many of __3__ inventions have to do with pets. For example, one girl who didn't like putting __4__ hand on cat food invented a device that feeds __5__ cat automatically. Another invented a doggie entertainment center for times when a dog's owners are away from __6__ home. A boy created a device for petting __7__ dog. __8__ children have used ordinary household items to create __9__ unusual inventions. For __10__ clever ideas, they have sometimes won prizes.

C. WRITING: Using Nouns as Adjectives

Many nouns used as adjectives name the materials used to make something. Write a different noun used as an adjective for each of the following phrases.

Example stone wall
brick wall

glass door	gravel road
paper bag	plastic tube
marble statue	leather jacket

ADJ. & ADV.

What Is an Adverb?

1 Here's the Idea

▶ **An adverb is a word that modifies a verb, an adjective, or another adverb.**

Historians strongly believe that the Chinese invented rockets.
(strongly — ADVERB; believe — VERB; MODIFIES)

Ancient Chinese warriors fired very powerful rockets.
(very — ADVERB; powerful — ADJECTIVE; MODIFIES)

Today, rockets almost always power missiles and spacecraft.
(almost — ADVERB; always — ADVERB; MODIFIES)

CHAPTER 5

Adverbs answer the questions *how, when, where,* and *to what extent*.

Adverbs	
How?	patiently, loudly, carefully
When?	sometimes, daily, always
Where?	inside, there, everywhere
To what extent?	extremely, nearly, almost

The position of adverbs can vary. An adverb that modifies an adjective or another adverb is generally placed just before the word it modifies. An adverb that modifies a verb can be placed after the verb, before the verb, or at the beginning of the sentence.

The rocket ascended suddenly. (after verb)

The rocket suddenly ascended. (before verb)

Suddenly, the rocket ascended. (at beginning of sentence)

Intensifiers are adverbs that modify adjectives or other adverbs. They are usually placed directly before the words they modify. Intensifiers usually answer the question *to what extent.*

MODIFIES

We covered our ears very quickly at the shuttle launch.

Intensifiers				
almost	extremely	quite	so	usually
especially	nearly	really	too	very

Forming Adverbs

Many adverbs are formed by adding the suffix *-ly* to adjectives. Sometimes a base word's spelling changes when *-ly* is added.

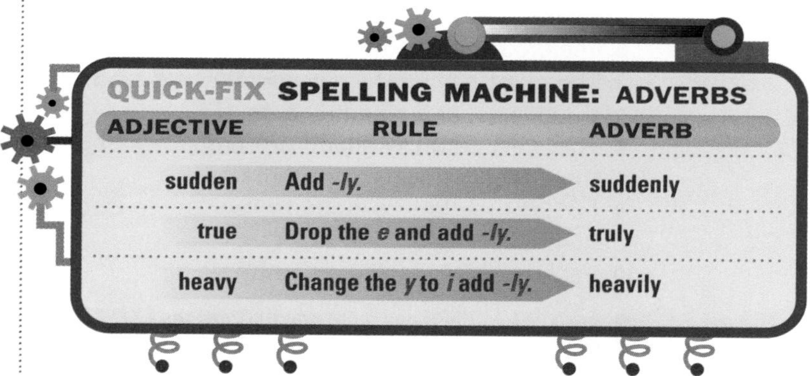

QUICK-FIX SPELLING MACHINE: ADVERBS

ADJECTIVE	RULE	ADVERB
sudden	Add *-ly.*	suddenly
true	Drop the *e* and add *-ly.*	truly
heavy	Change the *y* to *i* add *-ly.*	heavily

2 Why It Matters in Writing

You will find adverbs helpful when you're writing about historical events. The adverbs in this model help tell readers when and how blue jeans were invented.

PROFESSIONAL MODEL

During the California gold rush, a tailor named Levi Strauss saw miners daily. Their pants were often extremely worn. Strauss worked very carefully to fashion stiff canvas into overalls. These tough pants ultimately became today's blue jeans.

TELLS WHEN

TELLS TO WHAT EXTENT

TELLS HOW

ADJ. & ADV.

3 Practice and Apply

A. CONCEPT CHECK: What Is an Adverb?

Write each adverb and the word it modifies. Identify the modified word as a verb, an adjective, or an adverb. There may be more than one adverb in a sentence.

Like the Birds

1. People were flying gliders experimentally in the early 1900s.
2. No one had yet flown a powered aircraft successfully.
3. In Dayton, Ohio, Orville and Wilbur Wright expertly repaired bicycles.
4. They were quite popular members of the community.
5. They bicycled enthusiastically and also studied gliders there.
6. The brothers worked fanatically to invent a powered aircraft.
7. Their first plane, which was quite crude, was made from wood, wire, and cotton sheets.
8. They very carefully added two propellers and hitched them together with bicycle chains.
9. In 1903 the Wright brothers flew and landed their *Flyer* quite successfully.
10. Each brother flew the plane twice.

➜ **For a SELF-CHECK and more practice, see the EXERCISE BANK, p. 327.**

B. WRITING: Adding Adverbs

Read the paragraph below. Choose five adverbs from the following list to replace the words in parentheses.

thoughtfully	cruelly	there	almost	soon
energetically	tiredly	very	daily	

Shopping-Cart Convenience

(1) Sylvan Goldman lived in Oklahoma City and owned a grocery store (answers *where*). **(2)** He watched shoppers (answers *how*) carry items from aisle to aisle. **(3)** To help his customers, Goldman (answers *how*) set out wheeled carts for them to use. **(4)** He (answers *to what extent*) sadly noted that no one wanted the carts. Goldman outsmarted them, however. He hired phony shoppers to push around the carts. **(5)** The real shoppers (answers *when*) began to use the carts throughout the store.

LESSON 5 Making Comparisons

1 Here's the Idea

Adjectives and adverbs can be used to compare people or things. Special forms of these words are used to make comparisons.

Use the comparative form of an adjective or adverb when you compare a person or thing with one other person or thing.

The *Titanic* was larger than the *Olympic.*

It traveled faster than the other ship.

Use the superlative form of an adjective or adverb when you compare someone or something with more than one other thing.

In fact, the *Titanic* was the largest ship of all.

Of the fleet's ships, the *Titanic* raced the fastest.

ADJ. & ADV.

Regular Forms of Comparison

For most one-syllable modifiers, add *-er* to form the comparative and *-est* to form the superlative.

One-Syllable Modifiers

	Base Form	Comparative	Superlative
Adjectives	tall shiny	taller shinier	tallest shiniest
Adverbs	close soon	closer sooner	closest soonest

You can also add *-er* and *-est* to some two-syllable adjectives. With others, and with two-syllable adverbs, use the words *more* and *most.*

Two-Syllable Modifiers

	Base Form	Comparative	Superlative
Adjectives	easy cheerful	easier more cheerful	easiest most cheerful
Adverbs	brightly swiftly	more brightly more swiftly	most brightly most swiftly

With adjectives and adverbs having three or more syllables, use *more* and *most.*

Modifiers with More Than Two Syllables	Base Form	Comparative	Superlative
Adjectives	powerful energetic	**more** powerful **more** energetic	**most** powerful **most** energetic
Adverbs	peacefully comfortably	**more** peacefully **more** comfortably	**most** peacefully **most** comfortably

Use only one sign of comparison at a time. Don't use more and *-er* together or most and *-est* together.

INCORRECT: **The *Titanic* was the most greatest ship.**

CORRECT: **The Titanic was the greatest ship.**

CHAPTER 5

Irregular Forms of Comparison

The comparatives and superlatives of some adjectives and adverbs are formed in irregular ways.

Irregular Modifiers	Base Form	Comparative	Superlative
Adjectives	good bad	better worse	best worst
Adverbs	well much little	better more less	best most least

2 Why It Matters in Writing

Use comparative and superlative forms of modifiers when you need to compare or contrast things in history or science class.

STUDENT MODEL

Although the *Californian* was the ship **nearest** the *Titanic,* it was the *Carpathia* that rescued the survivors. Those in the lifeboats were **most likely** to survive.

❸ Practice and Apply

A. CONCEPT CHECK: Making Comparisons

Choose the correct comparative or superlative form to complete each sentence.

Stronger Than Steel

1. Stephanie Kwolek invented one of the (more original, most original) materials ever developed.
2. She believed that creativity was (more important, most important) for an inventor than technical knowledge.
3. Kwolek planned to study medicine, but she found chemistry (more interesting, most interesting).
4. She was intrigued by all the (most new, newest) chemical processes.
5. She studied the (best, most best) ways of making artificial materials.
6. When Kwolek was working with chemicals, petroleum was the (more, most) common source of plastic.
7. Kwolek invented a chemical fiber called Kevlar, which is five times (more strong, stronger) than steel.
8. Kevlar was one of the (more, most) influential inventions of the 20th century.
9. Kevlar vests are (most, more) famous as police vests.
10. Kwolek's work inventing Kevlar and other materials made her one of the (better-known, best-known) chemists in the United States.

➜ **For a SELF-CHECK and more practice, see the EXERCISE BANK, p. 328.**

ADJ. & ADV.

B. WRITING: Creating Comparisons

Examine the three photographs of different kinds of boats. Write five sentences comparing them in terms of appearance, speed, power, or capacity. Use comparative and superlative forms in your writing.

Adjective or Adverb?

1 Here's the Idea

Some pairs of adjectives and adverbs are often a source of confusion and mistakes in speaking and writing.

Good and *Well*

Good is always an adjective; it modifies a noun or pronoun. *Well* is usually an adverb, modifying a verb, an adverb, or an adjective. *Well* is an adjective when it refers to health.

The ice-cream sundae was a good invention. (MODIFIES: ADJECTIVE → NOUN)

Ice cream sold well. (MODIFIES: ADVERB → VERB) **He doesn't feel well.** (MODIFIES: ADJECTIVE → PRONOUN)

Real and *Really*

Real is always an adjective; it modifies a noun or pronoun. *Really* is always an adverb; it modifies a verb, an adverb, or an adjective.

Medical inventions can make a real difference. (MODIFIES: ADJECTIVE → NOUN)

A few inventions have really changed how we live. (MODIFIES: ADVERB → VERB)

Bad and *Badly*

Bad is always an adjective; it modifies a noun or pronoun. *Badly* is always an adverb; it modifies a verb, an adverb, or an adjective.

A bad illness can require medicine. (MODIFIES: ADJECTIVE → NOUN)

I did badly on the last science quiz. (MODIFIES: ADVERB → VERB)

❷ Why It Matters in Writing

Watch out for these tricky pairs of adjectives and adverbs. Mistakes are so common that you need to double-check your work every time you use a form of good, real, or bad.

STUDENT MODEL

I want to enter this year's science fair because I think my experiment on lasers will be ~~real~~ *really* interesting. I'm planning on talking about the different uses of lasers in grocery stores, hospitals, and banks. All of the lasers seem to work ~~good~~ *well*.

Sincerely,

Jamie D.

ADJ. & ADV.

❸ Practice and Apply

CONCEPT CHECK: Adjective or Adverb?

For each sentence, choose the correct modifier from those given in parentheses. Identify each word you choose as an adjective or an adverb.

Medicine's History—Good or Bad?

1. Today we take (real, really) good medical care for granted, but history is full of examples of ineffective medicine.
2. Many early treatments were (badly, bad).
3. Unsuccessful treatments were (bad, badly) for both patients and doctors.
4. But if they got well, patients thought their doctors were (good, well).
5. The ancient Greek physician Hippocrates helped rid medicine of magic, superstition, and other (real, really) bad elements.

→ **For a SELF-CHECK and more practice, see the EXERCISE BANK, p. 328.**

Avoiding Double Negatives

1 Here's the Idea

A **negative word** is a word that implies that something does not exist or happen. Some common negative words are listed below.

Common Negative Words

barely	hardly	never	none	nothing
can't	hasn't	no	no one	nowhere
don't	neither	nobody	not	scarcely

If two negative words are used where only one is needed, the result is a **double negative.** Avoid double negatives in your speaking and writing.

Nonstandard

I can't hardly believe someone created pajamas for dogs.

Standard

I can hardly believe someone created pajamas for dogs.

I can't believe someone created pajamas for dogs.

CHAPTER 5

2 Why It Matters in Writing

Don't let double negatives creep into your writing when you're trying to make an important point. Double negatives are almost always nonstandard.

STUDENT MODEL

During World War II, pilots flew planes higher than ever before. They didn't have ~~no~~ enough air to breathe at very high altitudes. Alice Chatham, a sculptor, designed a mask to supply pilots with oxygen so that they wouldn't ~~never~~ ever black out from lack of oxygen.

3 Practice and Apply

A. CONCEPT CHECK: Avoiding Double Negatives

Write the word in parentheses that correctly completes each sentence.

Sticky Stuff

1. You (can, can't) scarcely imagine a time before sticky notes, can you?
2. You (can't, can) barely put a note in a book without them.
3. Sticky notes (aren't, are) nothing like other bookmarks.
4. They (were, weren't) scarcely Art Fry's first invention.
5. In the 1970s Fry (hadn't, had) nothing but pieces of paper for bookmarks.
6. These scraps of paper (could, couldn't) hardly stay in a book.
7. Fry wanted something that (wouldn't, would) never fall out but wouldn't harm the page.
8. His colleague discovered a glue that (did, didn't) not stick as tightly as other glues.
9. Nobody had (never, ever) made a sticky bookmark that you could pull off a page.
10. Now there (aren't, are) hardly any homes or offices without sticky notes.

→ **For a SELF-CHECK and more practice, see the EXERCISE BANK, p. 329.**

B. PROOFREADING: Eliminating Double Negatives

Find and correct the double negatives in the paragraph below.

Cat Feeding for Fun

Suzanna Goodin never wanted to feed her cats. Was she a cat hater? No, she loved her cats. She just didn't want nothing to do with feeding them. One day Suzanna's teacher told the class to think of problems they hadn't never been able to solve. Then they should invent solutions. Suzanna invented a cat-feeding spoon that didn't leave nothing to clean up. The spoon was made from dough baked in the oven.

ADJ. & ADV.

Grammar in Literature

Inventing with Adjectives and Adverbs

One of the gifts an inventor needs is the ability to notice details. Writers use the same gift when they create literature. In your own writing, you can use adjectives and adverbs to help communicate details and convey the tone of your passage.

In the following excerpt, Gish Jen uses adjectives and adverbs to describe an umbrella. Her use of details lets readers sense the speaker's feelings of wonder.

CHAPTER 5

The White Umbrella

by Gish Jen

I stared at the umbrella. I wanted to open it, twirl it around by its **slender silver** handle. . . .

ADJECTIVE

ADVERB

I could not believe that I was **actually** holding the umbrella, opening it. It sprang up by itself as if it were alive, as if that were what it wanted to do—as if it belonged in my hands, above my head. I stared at the network of **silver** spokes, and then spun the umbrella **around** and **around** and **around.** It was so **clean** and **white** that it seemed to glow, to illuminate everything around it. "It's **beautiful,**" I said.

Practice and Apply

A. DRAFTING: Write a Description

As the speaker and her sister wait for a ride, it begins to rain. Follow the directions to invent two descriptions about rain.

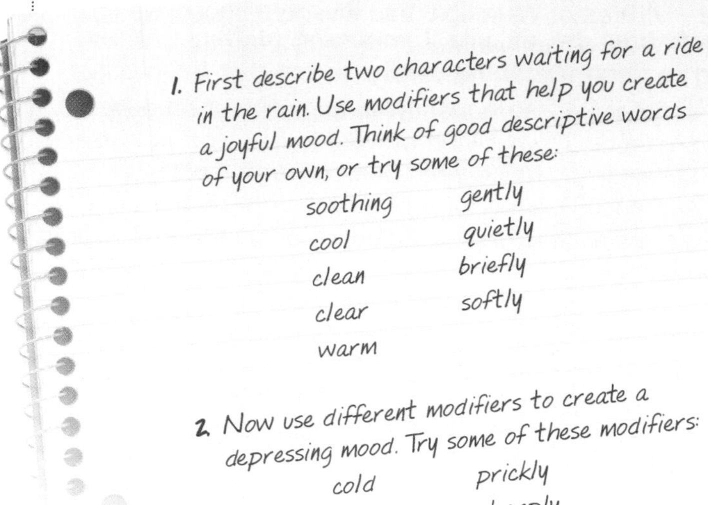

B. WRITING: Create a Scene

Put ideas from your two descriptions together to create a scene in which two people are together in the rain and waiting for a ride. One of the people is enjoying the rain. The other is miserable. Save your descriptions in your **Working Portfolio.**

Mixed Review

A. Using Modifiers Read this passage and answer the questions below it.

(1) Ruth Wakefield, owner of the Toll House Inn, frequently baked a kind of cookie that had melted chocolate in its batter. **(2)** One day she didn't have enough time to melt the chocolate. **(3)** So she cut the large slab of chocolate into smaller bits and added them to the batter. **(4)** She thought they would melt in the oven just as if she had melted the chocolate first. **(5)** But the chocolate bits didn't melt. **(6)** They poked up here and there in the cookies' surface. **(7)** Presto! Wakefield had invented chocolate chip cookies, an invention for which we are all hungrily grateful.

1. In sentence 1, is *frequently* an adjective or an adverb?
2. In sentence 1, what kind of word is *its*? How is it used?
3. In sentence 2, which word does *enough* modify?
4. In sentence 3, what form of adjective is *smaller*?
5. In sentence 4, is *first* an adjective or an adverb? How do you know?
6. In sentence 5, how is *chocolate* used?
7. In sentence 6, what kind of words are *here* and *there,* and what question do they answer?
8. In sentence 7, how is *chocolate chip* used?
9. In sentence 7, which word does *hungrily* modify? What part of speech is *hungrily?*
10. In sentence 7, is *grateful* an adjective or adverb? Which word does it modify?

B. Choosing the Right Modifier Choose the correct words from those given in parentheses.

1. George Crum, a chef, made a (real, really) good discovery in 1853.
2. One guest complained (loud, loudly) that his French fries were too (large, larger).
3. Crum sliced some (thinner, more thin) ones, but the guest (wouldn't say nothing, wouldn't say anything) good about the potatoes.
4. Finally Crum (angerly, angrily) sliced some potatoes (real, really) thin and fried them.
5. The guest loved the dish so (good, well) that potato chips became a specialty of the restaurant.

Mastery Test: What Did You Learn?

For each underlined item, choose the letter of the term that correctly identifies it.

We don't never (1) run out of discoveries about space. Space is really (2) infinite (3). Recently in the *New York Times Magazine,* James Gleick stated: "It wasn't until the year 4.5 billion or so . . . that an earthly life form managed to hurl some (4) stuff into orbit . . . high enough to look down (5) and see our tiny globe for what it is. Counted another way, it was Oct. 4, 1957 [when Russian (6) scientists launched the artificial satellite *Sputnik.*] . . . Plenty of scientists and rocket buffs were listening down below and hatching grander (7) plans. Already (8), Arthur C. Clarke, the science-fiction writer, had performed one of the millennium's most astounding (9) feats of invention. In 1945, he . . . published a complete plan for using satellites to relay radio (10) "signals."

1. A. adjective
   B. double negative
   C. statement
   D. question
2. A. adverb
   B. adjective
   C. demonstrative pronoun
   D. predicate adjective
3. A. adverb
   B. predicate adjective
   C. proper adjective
   D. demonstrative pronoun
4. A. pronoun used as adjective
   B. noun used as adjective
   C. pronoun used as adverb
   D. noun used as adverb
5. A. adverb telling when
   B. adverb telling how
   C. adverb telling how much
   D. adverb telling where
6. A. possessive pronoun
   B. adverb
   C. predicate adjective
   D. proper adjective
7. A. comparative adverb
   B. superlative adverb
   C. comparative adjective
   D. superlative adjective
8. A. adverb describing *Clarke*
   B. adverb describing *had performed*
   C. adjective describing *writer*
   D. adjective describing *Clarke*
9. A. comparative adverb
   B. superlative adverb
   C. comparative adjective
   D. superlative adjective
10. A. pronoun used as adjective
    B. noun used as adjective
    C. pronoun used as adverb
    D. noun used as adverb

Student Help Desk

Adjectives and Adverbs at a Glance

Adjectives modify nouns and pronouns.

The nifty invention was helpful. It was silver.

Adverbs modify verbs, adjectives, and other adverbs.

The unusually quiet hole puncher worked very efficiently.

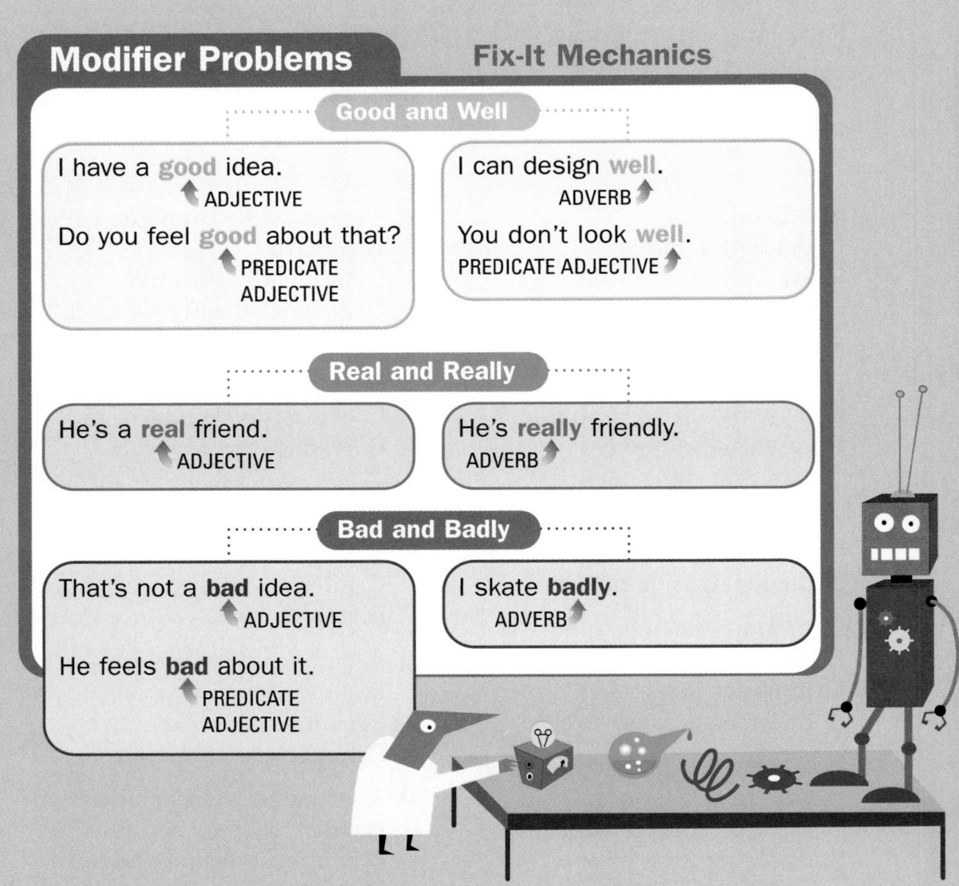

Modifiers in Comparisons

Size Adjustments

	Comparative	Superlative
far	farther	farthest
shiny	shinier	shiniest
useful	more useful	most useful
intelligent	more intelligent	most intelligent
happily	more happily	most happily
good	better	best
bad	worse	worst

Avoiding Double Forms

Double Trouble

Double Negative	Fix
we can't never	we can never we can't
we don't hardly	we hardly we don't
Double Comparison	**Fix**
more better	better
most luckiest	luckiest

The Bottom Line

Checklist for Adjectives and Adverbs

Have I remembered to . . .

____ use adjectives to fine-tune my nouns?

____ capitalize proper adjectives?

____ use adverbs to fine-tune descriptions of actions?

____ use correct forms of adverbs and adjectives in comparisons?

____ avoid double negatives?

ADJ. & ADV.

Chapter 6

Prepositions, Conjunctions, Interjections

Theme: Bugs!

Little Things Mean a Lot

What would you say if you came face to face with this bug? You might express yourself with a small but powerful interjection like the one in the balloon above. Like bugs, interjections, conjunctions, and prepositions are often small but powerful. They not only express emotion but also connect other words and show relationships between words.

Write Away: What Bugs You?

Recall a time when you were up close and personal with a bug. Was the bug disgusting? fascinating? weird? beautiful, perhaps? Write a short paragraph about your bug. Save the paragraph in your **Working Portfolio.**

Diagnostic Test: What Do You Know?

Choose the letter of the term that correctly identifies each underlined item.

Bugs! Ugh! (1) Do you shriek in horror (2) when you see bugs? Many people are terrified of bugs (3). Their alien shapes inspire fear, and (4) the way they swarm around their target (5) often causes panic. Bugs include both (6) 700,000 known species of insects and (6) more than 30,000 known species of spiders. Ecologists are glad that bugs live among (7) us. Their contributions to the environment (8) are important. For example, bees pollinate flowers. Bugs may seem strange, but (9) life as we know it would be impossible without (10) them.

1. A. preposition
   B. interjection
   C. conjunction
   D. adverb
2. A. preposition
   B. object of a preposition
   C. prepositional phrase
   D. interjection
3. A. preposition
   B. object of a preposition
   C. conjunction
   D. interjection
4. A. coordinating conjunction
   B. correlative conjunction
   C. adjective phrase
   D. preposition
5. A. conjunction
   B. interjection
   C. adjective phrase
   D. adverb phrase
6. A. preposition
   B. object of a preposition
   C. coordinating conjunction
   D. correlative conjunction
7. A. preposition
   B. interjection
   C. coordinating conjunction
   D. prepositional phrase
8. A. conjunction
   B. interjection
   C. adjective phrase
   D. adverb phrase
9. A. coordinating conjunction
   B. correlative conjunction
   C. preposition
   D. interjection
10. A. interjection
    B. preposition
    C. object of a preposition
    D. adjective

What Is a Preposition?

1 Here's the Idea

A preposition is a word that shows a relationship between a noun or pronoun and some other word in the sentence. A preposition is always followed by an object, either a noun or a pronoun.

The article about insects is interesting.
PREPOSITION

Here, the preposition *about* shows the relationship between the words *article* and *insects.* In the sentences below, notice how each preposition expresses a different relationship between the worm and the apple.

The worm is on the apple.

The worm is beside the apple.

The worm is under the apple.

The worm is in the apple.

CHAPTER 6

Common Prepositions

about	at	despite	like	to
above	before	down	near	toward
across	behind	during	of	under
after	below	except	off	until
against	beneath	for	on	up
along	beside	from	out	with
among	between	in	over	within
around	beyond	inside	past	without
as	by	into	through	

This jewelry is inspired by a beetle.

Prepositional Phrases

A prepositional phrase consists of a preposition, its object, and any modifiers of the object. The object of the preposition is the noun or pronoun following the preposition.

PREPOSITIONAL PHRASE
Some peoples have depicted insects in art.
PREPOSITION ↑ ↑ OBJECT

Beetle images decorate the jewelry of many cultures.
PREPOSITION ↑ ↑ MODIFIER ↑ OBJECT

Some believed that dreams come from a butterfly.

Use *between* when the object of the preposition refers to two people or things. Use *among* when speaking of three or more.

Ants share food *between* two nestmates.

Ants share food *among* all the colony members.

PREPOSITIONS

Preposition or Adverb?

Sometimes the same word can be used as a preposition or as an adverb. If the word has no object, then it is an adverb.

PREPOSITIONAL PHRASE
The ant scurried out the door.
PREPOSITION ↑ ↑ OBJECT

The ant scurried out.
↑ ADVERB

For more on adverbs, see pp. 134–136.

❷ Why It Matters in Writing

Use prepositional phrases in descriptive writing to add detailed information to sentences. For example, a prepositional phrase can tell an exact location. The prepositional phrases in this model tell where the ant found the grain and where she put it.

LITERARY MODEL

. . . she had taken it from the fields and stowed it away in a hole in the bank, under a hawthorn bush.

—Aesop, "Ant and Grasshopper," retold by James Reeves

PREPOSITIONAL PHRASES

CHAPTER 6

❸ Practice and Apply

CONCEPT CHECK: What Is a Preposition?

Write the preposition in each sentence, along with its object.

Smoky the Beetle

1. Some jewel beetles are attracted to forest fires.
2. They can sense a forest fire from 30 miles.
3. Often they fly straight into the flames.
4. Sometimes they swarm around firefighters!
5. With their own infrared detectors, they sense heat.
6. Some scientists now believe that the beetles smell fire through their antennae.
7. Information from the beetles may improve the accuracy of fire alarms.
8. Currently, many fire alarms detect carbon dioxide levels in the air.
9. But the alarms can be fooled by car fumes.
10. Scientists are testing a more accurate alarm that is outfitted with actual insect antennae.

→ **For a SELF-CHECK and more practice, see the EXERCISE BANK, p. 330.**

LESSON 2 Using Prepositional Phrases

1 Here's the Idea

A prepositional phrase is always related to another word in a sentence. It modifies the word in the same way an adjective or adverb would.

Adjective Phrases

▶ **An adjective prepositional phrase modifies a noun or a pronoun.** Like an adjective, a prepositional phrase can tell which one, how many, or what kind.

WHAT KIND?

This spider is a type of jumping spider.

NOUN — ADJECTIVE PHRASE

WHICH ONE?

The tiny bug on the windowsill is also a jumping spider.

PREPOSITIONS

Adverb Phrases

▶ **An adverb prepositional phrase modifies a verb, an adjective, or an adverb.** Like an adverb, a prepositional phrase can tell where, when, how, why, or to what extent.

WHERE?

Jumping spiders live in many places.

VERB — ADVERB PHRASE

WHY?

These spiders are famous for their eight eyes.

ADJECTIVE

HOW?

They jump far for their size.

ADVERB

Several prepositional phrases can work together. Each phrase after the first often modifies the object of the phrase before it.

A spider sat on the tip of a twig in a tree.

Placement of Prepositional Phrases

When you write, try to place each prepositional phrase as close as possible to the word it modifies. Otherwise, you may confuse—or unintentionally amuse—your readers.

Unclear

With eight hairy legs, the bird chased the spider.

(This must be the world's weirdest bird!)

Clear

The bird chased the spider with eight hairy legs.

(Now the reader can tell who has the hairy legs!)

2 Why It Matters in Writing

When you write about science, use prepositional phrases to answer such questions as *where, how, which one,* and *what kind.* Notice how much information the prepositional phrases supply in the caption of the photograph below.

A jumping spider, photographed while jumping **from one berry to another.**

❸ Practice and Apply

A. CONCEPT CHECK: Using Prepositional Phrases

Write the prepositional phrase in each sentence, along with the word it modifies. Then indicate whether the phrase is an adjective phrase or an adverb phrase. Warning: One sentence contains two prepositional phrases.

Eight-Legged Heroes

1. Nearly 36,000 known kinds of spiders inhabit the earth.
2. Very few spiders are dangerous to people.
3. Spiders eat millions of disease-bearing mosquitoes.
4. They also control huge populations of garden pests.
5. The spider, with its many useful qualities, is often helpful.
6. Spiders live in many habitats.
7. Some spiders survive in cold climates.
8. Spiders with brilliant colors are beautiful.
9. Dewdrops on spider webs sparkle in the morning light.
10. The dewdrops usually evaporate by afternoon.

➜ **For a SELF-CHECK and more practice, see the EXERCISE BANK, p. 330**

B. WRITING: Using Prepositional Phrases in Science

Suppose that on a field trip you discovered an interesting spider and took this photograph of it. Write a very detailed description of the spider and of the place where you found it. Use adverb phrases to answer questions like *how, when,* and *where.*

PREPOSITIONS

LESSON 3

Conjunctions

1 Here's the Idea

▶ **A conjunction is a word used to join words or groups of words.** Different kinds of conjunctions are used in different ways.

Coordinating Conjunctions

▶ **A coordinating conjunction connects words used in the same way.** The words joined by a conjunction can be subjects, objects, predicates, or any other kind of sentence parts.

SUBJECTS

Insects and crustaceans have eyes with many lenses.

COORDINATING CONJUNCTION

OBJECTS

Light enters the front or the side of their eyes.

COORDINATING CONJUNCTION

Common Coordinating Conjunctions						
and	but	or	nor	yet	so	for

Use *and* to connect similar ideas. Use *but* to contrast ideas.

Each lens can receive light and form a separate image.
(*And* connects two things each lens can do.)

Insects' eyes are smaller than ours, but their vision is more complex.
(*But* contrasts vision in insects and people.)

A greenbottle fly is small, but its eyes contain many lenses.

Correlative Conjunctions

▶ **Correlative conjunctions are pairs of words that connect words used in the same way.** Like coordinating conjunctions, correlative conjunctions can join subjects, objects, predicates, and other sentence parts.

SUBJECTS

Both flies and mosquitoes have compound eyes.

CORRELATIVE CONJUNCTION

PREDICATE ADJECTIVES

Their eye lenses are not only long but also cylindrical.

CORRELATIVE CONJUNCTION

Common Correlative Conjunctions		
both . . . and	either . . . or	not only . . . but also
neither . . . nor	whether . . . or	

CONJUNCTIONS

2 Why It Matters in Writing

A writer's use of the right conjunction helps readers know which words or ideas are joined together and how they relate to each other. Notice how conjunctions in the model connect similar ideas.

PROFESSIONAL MODEL

Insects **and** spiders have many different kinds of eyes. Some spiders have eight eyes, **so** they can see in several directions at once. Some insects have two compound eyes **and** three simple eyes called ocelli.

—S. Lieb

And connects two subjects in the sentence.

So connects two complete ideas.

And connects the two objects of *have.*

3 Practice and Apply

A. CONCEPT CHECK: Conjunctions

Write the conjunction in each sentence, along with the words or groups of words that it joins.

Seeing with Electrons

1. To magnify things, optical microscopes make use of lenses and light waves.
2. Light waves show the details of ordinary objects, but the waves are too long to reveal the smallest structures.
3. Electron microscopes open new worlds, for they show smaller details.
4. They use magnetic "lenses" and electron beams instead of light waves.
5. The beams of electrons have only 1/8,000 the wavelength of visible light, so they can show much more detail.
6. Electron microscopes can be scanning or transmission microscopes.
7. Scanning microscopes and transmission microscopes are much more powerful than optical microscopes.
8. Scanning microscopes not only magnify but also produce a TV picture.
9. They can magnify an object over 100,000 times, but transmission microscopes can magnify up to 1 million times.
10. Bugs can keep no secrets from either scanning or transmission microscopes!

➔ **For a SELF-CHECK and more practice, see the EXERCISE BANK, p. 330.**

B. REVISING: Changing Conjunctions

The right conjunctions help you say what you mean. Rewrite the conjunctions so that the meaning is clear.

Catch Me If You Can

Flies always see the swatter but flit away from it. Are flies smart and alert? Which characteristic do they have? They are probably alert but sharp-eyed. Their eyes have many parts, or they can see motion even at the edges of their vision. You can hide the swatter, and the fly might still see it.

LESSON 4 Interjections

1 Here's the Idea

An interjection is a word or phrase used to express emotion.

Hey, look at that bug.

It's a cockroach! Yuck!

2 Why It Matters in Writing

"Whoa! Time out! Something's wrong. We have only ten players on the field!"

Writers often use interjections to express strong emotions, such as concern, terror, anger, and disgust.

3 Practice and Apply

In the cartoon above, the interjection *whoa* shows surprise and confusion. (Where *is* that other player?) Try writing your own caption for the cartoon, using at least one interjection. Add your caption to your **Working Portfolio.**

Grammar in Science

1 Using Prepositions to Write about Science

When you write your observations and conclusions in a lab report, the proper use of prepositions can make a difference. Prepositions are especially important if you are describing the physical features of animals or their behavior. In the notebook below, a student has used arrows on her drawing to show the location of certain features. For her field notes, she has used prepositional phrases to express the information shown in her drawing.

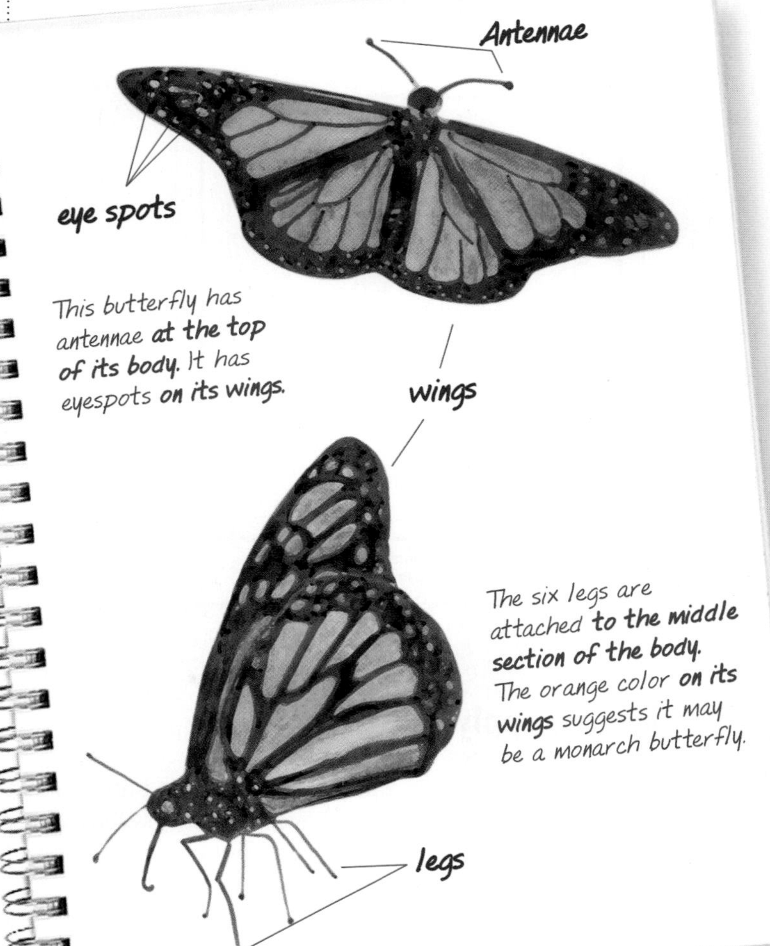

CHAPTER 6

2 Practice and Apply

USING PREPOSITIONS

For a project on insect metamorphosis, your class has observed videos of caterpillars developing into butterflies and moths. You have taken notes on your observations. Write a summary of your observations using your notes as a guide. Use prepositional phrases to explain details about the caterpillar's behavior, the cocoon or pupa stage, and the butterfly or moth. Useful prepositions might include the words *around, inside, before, after, from.* Underline the prepositional phrases in your summary. Save your work in your **Working Portfolio.**

- caterpillar stuck to the leaf
- film formed around caterpillar

- insect begins breaking from pupa or cocoon

- insect out of pupa or cocoon
- pumps fluids through its wings

PREP. & CONJ.

Mixed Review

A. Prepositions, Conjunctions, Interjections Choose the correct word in parentheses to complete each sentence. Then identify the word as a preposition, a conjunction, or an interjection.

1. New Orleans has many wooden buildings built (on, out) swampland.
2. (For, Off) termites these buildings are like a buffet.
3. The Algiers Public Library (near, up) New Orleans had 79 antitermite treatments.
4. Yet experts examined the ground afterward and found 70 million Formosan termites (beneath, above) the library.
5. (Ugh!, To!) It was the largest known termite colony on earth.
6. Each of the termites was small, (or, yet) together they were like a 500-pound animal eating the building 24 hours a day.
7. A typical Formosan colony is made up of 5 million termites (and, but) eats 1,000 pounds of wood a year.
8. The termites probably traveled (to, until) the United States in wooden crates after World War II.
9. People thought they were relatively harmless, (not, but) by 1965 they had infested a Houston warehouse.
10. (Except, Both) Galveston, Texas, (for, and) Charleston, South Carolina, are also victims of Formosan termites.

B. Prepositional Phrases Write the prepositional phrases in the paragraph below. Identify each as an adjective or an adverb phrase.

(1) Butterflies are the darlings of the insect world. **(2)** Like bugs in elaborate costumes, they grace our gardens. **(3)** Yet butterflies work hard despite their delicate appearance. **(4)** Some migrate for 2,000 miles. **(5)** They can soar 7,000 feet above the earth. **(6)** There are more than 20,000 species of butterflies. **(7)** But environmental changes in the modern world have reduced their numbers. **(8)** Industrial and residential development destroys the food and shelter needed by butterflies. **(9)** Pesticides are deadly to them. **(10)** However, "habitat gardening" helps provide butterflies with shelter and food plants.

Mastery Test: What Did You Learn?

Choose the letter of the term that correctly identifies each underlined item.

Jumping spiders are the cats <u>of the spider world</u> (1). Their quick gait <u>and</u> (2) short, sudden jumps help them catch their prey. When they get close <u>to</u> (3) an insect, they pounce. A jumping spider can leap 40 times its body length. In human terms, it is like a person 6 feet tall who can jump 240 feet. <u>Wow!</u> (4) The spider is also famous <u>for its excellent vision</u> (5). <u>With</u> (6) four <u>of</u> (7) its eight eyes very large, it has the best vision of any <u>spider</u> (8) its size. Jumping spiders do not build webs. They spin a dragline attached to a wall <u>or</u> (9) a tree. Jumping spiders live in almost every environment—you can find them <u>both</u> (10) on your own windowsill <u>and</u> (10) 22,000 feet up the slopes of Mount Everest.

1. A. adjective phrase
   B. adverb phrase
   C. coordinating conjunction
   D. correlative conjunction

2. A. preposition
   B. object of a preposition
   C. coordinating conjunction
   D. correlative conjunction

3. A. interjection
   B. preposition
   C. correlative conjunction
   D. object of a preposition

4. A. object of a preposition
   B. coordinating conjunction
   C. correlative conjunction
   D. interjection

5. A. conjunction
   B. interjection
   C. adverb phrase
   D. adjective phrase

6. A. preposition
   B. conjunction
   C. adverb
   D. interjection

7. A. object of a preposition
   B. preposition
   C. correlative conjunction
   D. coordinating conjunction

8. A. interjection
   B. conjunction
   C. prepositional phrase
   D. object of a preposition

9. A. preposition
   B. adverb
   C. conjunction
   D. interjection

10. A. coordinating conjunction
    B. correlative conjunction
    C. preposition
    D. object of a preposition

Student Help Desk

Prepositions, Conjunctions, Interjections at a Glance

Interjections show emotion.

Prepositions show relationships.

Conjunctions connect.

Prepositions, Conjunctions, Interjections

Preposition

Shows a relationship. Has an object.

RELATIONSHIP

flypaper on the ceiling

PREPOSITION (on) OBJECT (ceiling)

Conjunction

Joins words or groups of words.

mosquitoes or gnats

Mosquitoes bite, and so do gnats.

- Coordinating conjunction: fleas and ticks
- Correlative conjunction: both fleas and ticks

Interjection

Expresses emotion.

Ouch! A mosquito bit me!

Prepositional Phrases

What Do They Do?

Adjective Phrase

Modifies a noun or a pronoun

Tells which one	That little spider **on the wall**
Tells what kind	is a type **of jumping spider.**

Adverb Phrase

Modifies a verb, an adjective, or an adverb

Tells when	**During our recent picnic,**
Tells where	ants came **from everywhere**
Tells why	**for the free food**
Tells how	**in a big rush.**

Interjections!

Splat! Just a Few Ideas . . .

To express concern	oh-oh, oh no, oops
To express disgust	yuck, ick, gross
To express joy	awesome, hooray, yea
To express surprise	wow, what, whoops
To draw attention to	hey, yo, look, wait

The Bottom Line

Checklist for Prepositions, Conjunctions, Interjections

Have I . . .

____ used prepositions to show relationships between things?

____ placed prepositional phrases close to the words they modify?

____ used coordinating conjunctions to connect words and groups of words?

____ used correlative conjunctions correctly?

____ used interjections to express strong emotion?

Verbals and Verbal Phrases

Theme: Animals to the Rescue

A Surprising Event!

Look at the photograph and newspaper headline above. We can see that the boy is in the gorilla's living area, but how did he get there? How do you know? *Fallen* clearly conveys that he accidentally tumbled in. Although we often use *fallen* as part of a verb, it works here as an adjective, describing the boy. Verb forms that serve as other parts of speech are called verbals. Using them can add excitement and grace to your writing.

Write Away: Caring and Helping

Think about a time when you received help or comfort from an animal. The animal may have been real, a toy, or a character in a book. Write a paragraph that describes the event. Save the paragraph in your **Working Portfolio.**

Diagnostic Test: What Do You Know?

Choose the letter of the answer that correctly identifies each underlined item.

Brookfield Zoo visitor Eric Allison noticed a small boy climbing the fence at the Tropic World exhibit (1). Eric watched the boy trying to lift himself toward the top (2). He wondered with growing (3) anxiety, is he going to go higher (4)? The boy, losing his balance (5), suddenly tumbled into the gorilla enclosure. A terrified (6) crowd watched a gorilla named Binti approach him. Eric's father, Bob Allison, started to photograph (7) the event. Watching in horror (8) was all anyone could do. Would Binti hurt the boy? Carrying her own baby, (9) Binti came near the boy. Her gentle handling of the boy (10) made newspaper headlines.

1. A. gerund phrase
   B. participial phrase
   C. infinitive phrase
   D. helping verb
2. A. gerund
   B. gerund phrase
   C. infinitive
   D. infinitive phrase
3. A. gerund
   B. present participle
   C. past participle
   D. infinitive
4. A. gerund
   B. gerund phrase
   C. infinitive
   D. infinitive phrase
5. A. gerund
   B. gerund phrase
   C. participle
   D. participial phrase
6. A. gerund
   B. gerund phrase
   C. participle
   D. verb
7. A. gerund
   B. participle
   C. infinitive
   D. helping verb
8. A. infinitive phrase as subject
   B. gerund phrase as subject
   C. participial phrase as adjective
   D. gerund phrase as object of preposition
9. A. gerund
   B. gerund phrase
   C. participial phrase
   D. infinitive phrase
10. A. gerund phrase as subject
    B. gerund phrase as object
    C. participial phrase
    D. infinitive phrase

LESSON 1 Gerunds

1 Here's the Idea

A **verbal** is a word that is formed from a verb and that acts as a noun, an adjective, or an adverb. There are three kinds of verbals: gerunds, participles, and infinitives.

▶ **A gerund is a verbal that ends in *ing* and acts as a noun.** A **gerund phrase** consists of the gerund with its modifiers and complements. Like nouns, gerunds and gerund phrases may be subjects, predicate nouns, direct objects, indirect objects, or objects of prepositions.

GERUND PHRASE

The loud barking of the dogs woke up our neighbors.

GERUND

Using Gerunds	
Subject	**Herding** is something that border collies do well.
Predicate noun	It is their **running** that directs other animals.
Direct object	These dogs like **working.**
Indirect object	They give **herding** their full attention.
Object of a preposition	They are expert at **controlling** sheep and cows.

2 Why It Matters in Writing

Gerunds are good words for describing activities because they imply action. Notice how the writer of the sentence below used gerunds and gerund phrases to discuss the many activities of beavers.

PROFESSIONAL MODEL

Felling timber and ornamental or orchard trees, **damming** ditches and culverts, **digging** and **tunneling,** and **eating** food crops make the beaver an unpopular neighbor.

—Peg Boulay, "Beaver!"

CHAPTER 7

❸ Practice and Apply

A. CONCEPT CHECK: Gerunds

Write the gerunds in these sentences.

The Horse Therapist

1. Horseback riding has many benefits for people with disabilities.
2. People with physical or emotional problems can enjoy moving around.
3. One horse, named Silver, was especially good at walking slowly and carefully.
4. Waiting took patience, but Silver let the teachers lift a woman named Maria onto his back.
5. When Maria started riding, she had never walked in her life.
6. Her activity had been limited to rolling in her wheelchair.
7. From Silver, she learned balancing.
8. After building her strength, she could even walk (with a little help).
9. Silver contributed to Maria's healing.
10. As a result of training with Silver, Maria now lives independently.

Write the entire gerund phrase in each of the sentences above.

➜ **For a SELF-CHECK and more practice, see the EXERCISE BANK, p. 331.**

B. WRITING: Understanding Gerunds

Write about your typical day. Make a list, using gerunds to describe your activities at 9:00 A.M., 12:00 noon, 5:00 P.M., and 8:00 P.M.

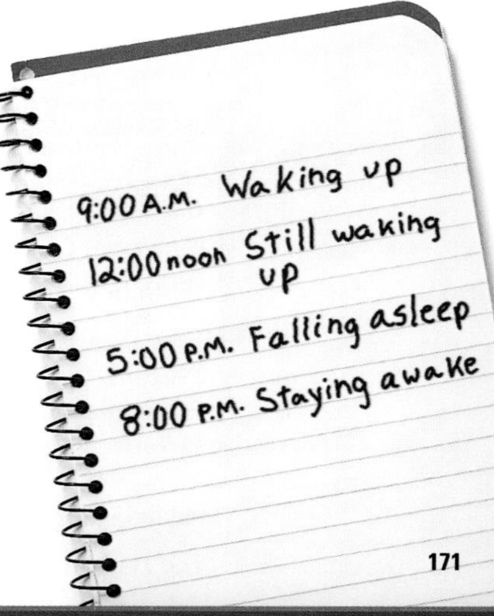

VERBALS

Participles

1 Here's the Idea

A participle is a verb form that acts as an adjective.
A **participial phrase** consists of a participle along with its modifiers and complements. Like other adjectives, participles and participial phrases can modify nouns and pronouns.

MODIFIES MODIFIES

A tired hiker woke a sleeping bear.

PARTICIPLE PARTICIPLE

Present and Past Participles

A **present participle** always ends in *ing.*

MODIFIES

Growling, the bear rose from his slumber.

The **past participle** of a regular verb ends in *ed.* Past participles of irregular verbs, such as *freeze,* are formed in a variety of ways.

MODIFIES

The terrified traveler wanted to run.

MODIFIES

Frozen by fear, he was grateful that the bear only licked him.

A word that ends in *ing* may be a gerund, a participle, or part of a verb phrase. Here's how you can tell the difference.

Words That End in *ing*

	Example	Clue
Gerund	We were annoyed by the moth's **fluttering.**	Could be replaced by a noun
Participle	The moth's **fluttering** wings were white.	Could be replaced by an adjective
Present Participle of Verb	The moth was **fluttering** in the breeze.	Always preceded by a helping verb.

Need help in forming past participles of irregular verbs? See page 102–104.

CHAPTER 7

2 Why It Matters in Writing

If your descriptive writing seems dull, use participles to liven up your sentences. Notice how strongly the participles in the following sentence convey sounds and actions.

LITERARY MODEL

There was a **snarling** growl that seemed to come from the bowels of the earth, **followed** by the sound of **ripping** cloth, screams, and then the **fading** slap of footsteps **running** away.

—Gary Paulsen, "Dirk the Protector"

VERBALS

3 Practice and Apply

MIXED REVIEW: Gerund or Participle?

Write the verbals in these sentences. Identify each verbal as a gerund or participle.

Animal Actors

1. Many TV commercials feature acting animals.
2. There are bell-ringing turkeys and typing chickens.
3. Training any type of animal requires patience.
4. Have you seen the dog-food commercial that shows a dog chasing a chuck wagon?
5. The trainer aroused yearning in the dog by hiding a squeaky toy in a closet.
6. Then the excited dog was let loose.
7. The dog reacted by racing around the corner, dashing across the kitchen, and skidding to a stop.
8. Staring at the door, the dog waited for the trainer to open it.
9. In the finished commercial, the chuck wagon disappears right through the cabinet door.
10. Working comes naturally to most animal actors.

For each participle, write the noun it modifies.

→ **For a SELF-CHECK and more practice, see the EXERCISE BANK, p. 331.**

LESSON 3 Infinitives

CHAPTER 7

1 Here's the Idea

▶ **An infinitive is a verb form that usually begins with the word *to* and that acts as a noun, an adjective, or an adverb.** An **infinitive phrase** consists of an infinitive along with its modifiers and complements.

INFINITIVE
Sam has always wanted to work on his own farm.

Using Infinitives	
Noun	**To run** his farm takes Sam's full energy. (Subject)
	His challenge is **to handle** large animals. (Predicate noun)
	Often, bulls begin **to charge** for no reason. (Direct object)
Adjective	They can be creatures **to fear.**
Adverb	However, the bulls calm down **to receive** food.

How can you tell the difference between an infinitive and a prepositional phrase that begins with *to*? If a verb follows *to*, the words are an infinitive. If a noun or pronoun follows *to*, the words are a prepositional phrase.

INFINITIVE
Sam's dog runs to distract the bulls.
VERB

PREPOSITIONAL PHRASE
The dog runs to the pen.
NOUN

2 Why It Matters in Writing

Infinitives are often used to talk about goals, dreams, and wishes.

Sam hopes to buy more land and to increase his herd.

❸ Practice and Apply

A. CONCEPT CHECK: Infinitives

Write the infinitives in the following sentences. For sentences without an infinitive, write *none*.

The Cat's Meow

1. Ringo the cat liked to nap indoors every morning.
2. To play outside was for afternoons.
3. Yet one morning he was determined to get out.
4. His owners, Carol and Ray, were too sick to let him out.
5. Carol finally managed to open the door.
6. Meowing, the cat went to the gas meter and began to dig.
7. Carol thought he was trying to tell her about a gas leak.
8. She called the gas company, but the technician didn't find anything—until he checked the hole Ringo had been digging.
9. "Your house is about to blow up!" the technician shouted.
10. Ringo's instinct to warn his owners had saved their lives.

For each infinitive, indicate whether it serves as a noun, an adjective, or an adverb.

➜ **For a SELF-CHECK and more practice, see the EXERCISE BANK, p. 332.**

B. REVISING: Using Infinitives

Revise this paragraph by substituting infinitives for the underlined words.

(1) <u>Having</u> a dog or a gerbil was out of the question for Duane Wright. He had trouble breathing whenever he came in contact with animal fur. So he found Goliath, a female iguana. **(2)** She seemed happy <u>while keeping</u> Duane company. One night, Duane had stopped breathing. **(3)** With her sharp claws Goliath started scratching hard <u>with the hope of waking</u> Duane. **(4)** She also began <u>whipping</u> his face with her scaly tail. Eventually, Duane began to breathe again. **(5)** Who would believe that an iguana would come <u>around rescuing</u> a man?

LESSON 4 Verbal Phrases

1 Here's the Idea

A verbal phrase includes a verbal and any modifiers or complements it may have. As you have seen in the preceding lessons, there are three types of verbal phrases: gerund phrases, participial phrases, and infinitive phrases.

A **gerund phrase** consists of a gerund plus its modifiers and complements. Like a gerund itself, the entire phrase is used as a noun.

GERUND PHRASE (subject)

Sunning himself is Silas the snake's favorite activity.

GERUND PHRASE (object of a preposition)

He likes it so much he forgets about eating his dinner.

A **participial phrase** consists of a participle plus its modifiers and complements. The entire phrase modifies a noun or pronoun.

PARTICIPIAL PHRASE

Finishing his run, the horse walked for a few minutes.

His trainer, stunned by his speed, checked her stopwatch.

An **infinitive phrase** consists of an infinitive plus its modifiers and complements. The entire phrase functions as a noun, an adjective, or an adverb.

INFINITIVE PHRASE (subject)

To run free in peace and solitude was Luna's greatest goal.

INFINITIVE PHRASE (adjective)

She took every chance to escape from the house.

2 Why It Matters in Writing

You can use verbals and verbal phrases to make your descriptions flow. Notice how the revised description at the top of the next page flows better and conveys greater excitement than the draft.

STUDENT MODEL

DRAFT

Noble Cause galloped down 46th Street. He was racing after the criminal, hoping to catch him. The police horse panted and snorted. Finally, he stopped the villain in his tracks.

REVISION

Galloping down 46th Street, Noble Cause raced to catch the criminal. Finally, the police horse, **panting and snorting,** stopped the villain in his tracks.

❸ Practice and Apply

VERBALS

A. CONCEPT CHECK: Verbal Phrases

Write the verbal phrase in each sentence, and identify it as a gerund phrase, a participial phrase, or an infinitive phrase.

Priscilla the Piglet

1. Strolling around the neighborhood pleased Priscilla, a three-month-old piglet.
2. Her owner, Victoria Herberta, would walk the slightly spoiled piglet on a purple leash.
3. Victoria taught Priscilla to swim with the family dogs.
4. One day a friend, Carol, took Priscilla to the lake to swim with her son Anthony.
5. Carol told Anthony to stay in the shallow water.
6. He decided to follow Carol and the pig into the deep water.
7. Unfortunately, Anthony felt himself sinking fast.
8. Rescuing Anthony was now necessary.
9. Grabbing Priscilla's leash, the boy held on tightly.
10. The 45-pound piglet began pulling the 90-pound boy back to shore.

➜ **For a SELF-CHECK and more practice, see the EXERCISE BANK, p. 332.**

B. REVISING: Understanding Verbal Phrases

Return to the paragraph your wrote for the **Write Away** on page 168. Add three verbal phrases to make your writing more interesting and fluent.

Grammar in Literature

Using Verbals to Write About Action

Because verbals are formed from verbs, writers often find them especially helpful in writing about action. Notice the way Kipling's use of gerunds, infinitives, and participles adds life to this description. As we enter the story, a tailor bird named Darzee has just warned Rikki-Tikki-Tavi, the story's mongoose hero, that the cobra Nagaina is about to pounce.

CHAPTER 7

Rikki-tikki-tavi

by Rudyard Kipling

Rikki-Tikki knew better than to waste time in staring. He jumped up in the air as high as he could go, and just under him whizzed by the head of Nagaina, Nag's wicked wife. She had crept up behind him as he was talking, to make an end of him; and he heard her savage hiss as the stroke missed. He came down almost across her back, and if he had been an old mongoose, he would have known that then was the time to break her back with one bite; but he was afraid of the terrible lashing return stroke of the cobra. He bit, indeed, but did not bite long enough; and he jumped clear of the whisking tail, leaving Nagaina torn and angry.

"Wicked, wicked Darzee!" said Nag, lashing up as high as he could reach toward the nest in the thorn bush; but Darzee had built it out of reach of snakes, and it only swayed to and fro.

GERUND
names an activity. What gerund names the activity Rikki-Tikki actually does?

INFINITIVE PHRASES
explain Rikki's and Nagaina's behaviors.

PARTICIPLES
describe the rapid movements of the animals as they fight.

Practice and Apply

Using Verbals in Writing

Follow the directions to write your own action story about animals. You can write about the animals in Rikki Tikki Tavi, or you can write about more familiar animals, like cats, dogs, or birds.

1. List four gerunds naming the activities that the animals might do.
2. List four participles you might use as adjectives to describe each of the animals.
3. Briefly explain what would happen. Use at least one infinitive phrase as you describe the action.
4. Evaluate your work. How would your writing be different if you hadn't used participles? Put your writing and your evaluation in your **Working Portfolio.**

1. Gerunds	2. Participles
1. hissing	1. fallen
2.	2. defeated
3.	3.
4.	4.

3. The hissing of the cat startled the fallen bird.

Mixed Review

A. Gerunds, Participles, and Infinitives Identify each underlined verbal as a gerund, a participle, or an infinitive.

(1) Many animals seem <u>to be able</u> to sense natural disasters before they happen. **(2)** There are stories about bears <u>coming</u> out of hibernation early, just before an earthquake. **(3)** At other times, <u>frightened</u> animals have warned of tornadoes and floods. **(4)** One woman told of her cat's <u>stopping</u> a car accident. **(5)** The cat, Missey, usually didn't mind <u>riding</u> in the car. **(6)** But one day, she refused <u>to go</u>. **(7)** <u>Hiding</u> under the car was his way of avoiding the trip. **(8)** As the woman tried to coax Missey out, she saw a car <u>coming</u> around the corner. **(9)** <u>Crashing</u> through a row of mailboxes, it landed in the lake. **(10)** If the cat hadn't stopped his owner from leaving, they would have been in the path of the <u>sinking</u> car.

B. Verbal Phrases

Look at the cartoon on this page. Then write a paragraph telling what will happen next. Let your imagination run wild. Use a variety of verbals and verbal phrases in your sentences.

Examples:

Taunted by the evil fish, the fisherman gritted his teeth.

Taking revenge would be sweet.

Mastery Test: What Did You Learn?

Choose the letter of the answer that correctly identifies each underlined item.

> Bruno was a dog living in Northern Ireland (1). Having been injured by an exploding (2) car bomb, Bruno was frightened of explosives. Seeing some thugs with firecrackers near his backyard (3), Bruno barked furiously. One day his owner, Brian McMullan, was working (4) on his damaged (5) car in the backyard. McMullan's one-year-old daughter, Anne Marie, sat playing nearby. The thugs threw a firecracker into the yard. When Anne Marie started to reach (6) for it, Bruno reacted by jumping (7) in front of her. The firecracker exploded, sending Bruno to the ground (8). Fearing that Bruno was dead, McMullan rushed to him (9). Bruno was scarred, but he survived. Saving Anne Marie (10) made Bruno a hero.

1. A. gerund
   B. gerund phrase
   C. participle
   D. participial phrase

2. A. gerund
   B. present participle
   C. past participle
   D. infinitive

3. A. gerund
   B. gerund phrase
   C. participle
   D. participial phrase

4. A. gerund
   B. participle
   C. infinitive
   D. verb

5. A. gerund
   B. participle
   C. participial phrase
   D. infinitive

6. A. infinitive
   B. participle
   C. gerund
   D. gerund phrase

7. A. gerund
   B. participle
   C. infinitive
   D. verb

8. A. infinitive used as adjective
   B. infinitive phrase
   C. participial phrase
   D. verb

9. A. infinitive
   B. gerund phrase
   C. participle
   D. prepositional phrase

10. A. gerund phrase
    B. verb
    C. participial phrase
    D. infinitive phrase

Student Help Desk

Verbals and Verbal Phrases at a Glance

Kind of Verbal	Job	Example
Gerund Phrase	Noun	**Rescuing** hikers is the job of Saint Bernards.
Participial Phrase	Adjective	These dogs, carefully **trained,** brave storms.
Infinitive Phrase	Noun	They have been taught **to search** thoroughly.
	Adjective	They are the dogs **to trust.**
	Adverb	They are always quick **to respond.**

Gerund, Participle, or Verb?

Lending a Hand

	Example	Clue
Gerund	**Swimming** was Sue's only hope for survival.	Could be replaced by a noun
Participle	Her **swimming** movements attracted a sea turtle.	Could be replaced by an adjective
Verb	The turtle that **was swimming** next to her helped her stay afloat.	Always preceded by a helping verb

To Build a Fire

Infinitive or Prepositional Phrase?

	Example	Clue
Infinitive	Hal built a fire **to keep** warm. (VERB: keep)	A verb follows *to.*
Prepositional phrase	Hal's dog snuggled up **to him.** (PRONOUN: him)	A noun or pronoun follows *to*.

Infinitive Phrases

Noun

SUBJECT
To own a parrot was Joan's dream.

PREDICATE NOUN
The parrot's favorite activity was **to talk.**

DIRECT OBJECT
Soon, the parrot began **to imitate** voices heard on television.

Adjective

Once, an intruder thought the bird was something **to fear.**

Adverb

For the burglar, the bird's sounds became too strange **to bear.**

VERBALS

The Bottom Line

Checklist for Verbals and Verbal Phrases

Have I . . .

____ used gerund phrases to express actions?

____ used participial phrases to modify nouns and pronouns?

____ understood the functions of different kinds of words that end in *ing*?

____ understood the difference between infinitives and prepositional phrases beginning with *to*?

____ used infinitive phrases as nouns, adjectives, and adverbs?

____ used verbals and verbal phrases to add fluency and excitement to my writing?

Sentence Structure

Theme: Get Involved

Give It a Try

Have you ever gotten incomplete or confusing directions? Then you might understand why these volunteers were frustrated by their "to do" list. Often you can use compound and complex sentences to communicate clearly. What clear directions can you build from the sentences and fragments in the list?

Write Away: No Big Deal

It's not always a big deal to help other people or improve the environment. However, little things can mean a lot. Write about a time when someone did a small thing that helped you. Put your writing in your **Working Portfolio.**

Diagnostic Test: What Do You Know?

Choose the letter that correctly identifies each underlined section.

There are many ways to volunteer, since there are so many worthy causes. (1) Right now young people are feeding the homeless. (2) They are also working as assistant camp counselors for needy children, and they are restoring the environment. (3) Although (4) these ways of volunteering sound very different, each reflects a desire to serve others. (5) People who volunteer (6) not only help those in need, but they help themselves as well. (7) Whatever these people choose to do, volunteering can make them feel good, and it can change their outlook on life. (8) It can give them exciting experiences that they would not have otherwise. (9) Because volunteering can be a lot of fun, (10) many people work long and hard for their favorite causes.

1. A. independent clause
   B. dependent clause
   C. compound sentence
   D. simple sentence
2. A. independent clause
   B. dependent clause
   C. compound sentence
   D. complex sentence
3. A. part of a compound sentence
   B. sentence fragment
   C. part of a complex sentence
   D. simple sentence
4. A. coordinating conjunction
   B. subordinating conjunction
   C. adverb clause
   D. relative pronoun
5. A. independent clause
   B. dependent clause
   C. compound sentence
   D. simple sentence
6. A. noun clause
   B. adjective clause
   C. adverb clause
   D. independent clause
7. A. coordinating conjunction
   B. subordinating conjunction
   C. relative pronoun
   D. independent clause
8. A. simple sentence
   B. compound sentence
   C. complex sentence
   D. compound-complex sentence
9. A. noun clause
   B. adjective clause
   C. adverb clause
   D. independent clause
10. A. noun clause
    B. adjective clause
    C. adverb clause
    D. independent clause

LESSON 1
What Is a Clause?

1 Here's the Idea

▶ **A clause is a group of words that contains a subject and a verb.** For example, the following sentence contains two clauses.

SUBJECT ↓ ↓ VERB
Some students work in the food pantry
because they care about helping hungry people.
SUBJECT ↑ ↑ VERB

There are two kinds of clauses, independent and dependent.

Independent and Dependent Clauses

CHAPTER 8

▶ **An independent clause expresses a complete thought and can stand alone as a sentence.**

Some students work in the food pantry
INDEPENDENT CLAUSE

▶ **A dependent clause does not express a complete thought and cannot stand alone as a sentence.** Most dependent clauses are introduced by words like *because, when, if, while,* and *that.*

because they care about helping hungry people
DEPENDENT CLAUSE

A dependent clause can be joined to an independent clause to add to the complete thought that the independent clause expresses.

Some students work in the food pantry because they care about helping hungry people.

Students also make bag lunches that are distributed at a shelter.

Dependent clauses are also known as **subordinate clauses.** These clauses cannot stand alone and are dependent on the main clause.

❷ Why It Matters in Writing

By itself, a dependent clause is a sentence fragment. Notice how connecting the dependent clause to the preceding sentence in the model below makes a sentence that expresses a complete thought.

STUDENT MODEL

Students will organize a coat-and-hat drive this winter. Because homeless people often do not have warm clothes.

INDEPENDENT CLAUSE

DEPENDENT CLAUSE

SENTENCES

❸ Practice and Apply

A. CONCEPT CHECK: What Is a Clause?

Identify each underlined group of words as an independent clause or a dependent clause.

Helping People Who Are Homeless

1. When Amber Lynn Coffman was only nine years old, she wrote a book report about a biography of Mother Teresa.
2. The book inspired her to volunteer at a shelter for the homeless when she was ten years old.
3. Because Amber wanted to do more, she started an organization.
4. Amber and 14 other student volunteers prepared 600 bag lunches each week.
5. They did this so that homeless people in their town of Glen Burnie, Maryland, could have a good meal.

6. <u>While Amber prepared lunches each week</u>, she thought about doing something special for the holiday season.
7. <u>She organized a huge gift drive</u>, which was very successful.
8. People donated small, useful gifts <u>that were wrapped by volunteers</u>.
9. <u>Amber's work inspired other students around the country</u> because they saw the power of one student to help others.
10. <u>Now Amber's organization exists in about 30 states</u>, and her efforts have been recognized nationally.

➜ **For a SELF-CHECK and more practice, see the EXERCISE BANK, p. 333.**

B. EDITING: Fixing Fragments

Read the following first draft of a student's paragraph. Rewrite the paragraph to eliminate sentence fragments. Combine dependent clauses with independent clauses.

STUDENT MODEL

My friend Cara had a great idea for her last birthday party. She made it a "wish list" party. So that homeless people could get some of the items they needed. Cara called a shelter to get a wish list. When she sent out her invitations. She sent along copies of the list. Cara asked her friends to bring things from the list instead of gifts. While we had fun at her party. We were also helping others.

C. WRITING: Creating a Caption

This photograph shows Amber Lynn Coffman and some of her fellow volunteers at work. On a separate sheet of paper, write a caption for the photo, describing what is happening. Use at least one independent clause and one dependent clause.

CHAPTER 8

LESSON 2 Simple and Compound Sentences

1 Here's the Idea

Simple Sentences

▶ **A simple sentence contains one independent clause and no dependent clauses.** Remember that even a simple sentence can be quite elaborate. Each of the following sentences has only a single independent clause.

Shawn tutors.
INDEPENDENT CLAUSE

Benita teaches young children acrobatics after school.

Compound Sentences

▶ **A compound sentence contains two or more independent clauses and no dependent clauses.** The clauses in a compound sentence must be closely related in thought.

Shawn tutors, and he helps students learn math.
INDEPENDENT CLAUSE — INDEPENDENT CLAUSE

Independent clauses can be joined by a comma and a coordinating conjunction or by a semicolon.

Some children have no books, and volunteers can hold book drives for them.

Some children have no toys; volunteers can collect donated toys for them.

Coordinating Conjunctions
for and nor or but so yet

Don't mistake a simple sentence with a compound predicate for a compound sentence. No punctuation should separate the parts of a compound predicate.

The Newcomers' Club wrote a clever script, and then filmed it.

❷ Why It Matters in Writing

You can avoid short, choppy sentences in your writing by using compound sentences. Notice how the writer of the model below combined related ideas to form compound sentences.

STUDENT MODEL

The park in my neighborhood has a lot of garbage all over the place. My friends and I want to clean it up, so we wrote to the park district for permission. We just got the OK, and we can start this weekend.

Related thoughts combined

❸ Practice and Apply

A. CONCEPT CHECK: Simple and Compound Sentences

Identify each sentence as simple or compound.

Help for a Little Girl

1. The vice-principal of Alex Moore's school had a 16-month-old daughter with leukemia.
2. Alex wanted to help; he started making arrangements for a benefit auction to raise money for the girl's treatment.
3. Alex's younger brother, Cameron, and two other friends also became interested in the benefit.
4. They would charge people for a dinner and hold the auction at the dinner.
5. The group continued planning the benefit, but not many people would buy the $25 tickets for the dinner.
6. Cameron, a fifth grader, had an idea.
7. They should get Mark Eaton of the Utah Jazz basketball team at the dinner.
8. Mark Eaton lived in their hometown—Park City, Utah—and he was happy to help them out.
9. The boys called 80 sponsors, and all contributed goods.

10. More than 200 people bought tickets to the benefit, so the group raised several thousand dollars.

➜ **For a SELF-CHECK and more practice, see the EXERCISE BANK, p. 334.**

B. REVISING: Combining Sentences

Combine each pair of sentences to form a compound sentence, using one of the coordinating conjunctions *and, but, for, or, nor, so,* or *yet.* Remember to use a comma before the coordinating conjunction.

Helping Out During a Hurricane

1. Tropical storms often hit Florida. People from this state know how to prepare.
2. Windows are easily broken by fierce winds. The people cover them with plywood.
3. Not only do they board up windows in their own homes. They volunteer to help their neighbors board up too.
4. Volunteers also put sandbags around buildings near the shore. The bags help prevent damage from high waves.
5. Schools are shut down. County and state offices are closed.
6. People on low-lying islands near the shore may need to evacuate. They can go to emergency shelters.
7. Volunteers at the shelters help prepare food. They organize games and other activities for children.
8. After a hurricane there may be a lot of damage to homes. Fallen trees and other debris may be scattered about.
9. Volunteers repair buildings. They also clean up.
10. A hurricane is a great trial for a community. It can awaken the community's volunteer spirit.

Working Portfolio Reread what you wrote for the **Write Away** on page 184. Check to see if any short sentences can be combined to form compound sentences.

Complex Sentences

CHAPTER 8

1 Here's the Idea

A complex sentence contains one independent clause and one or more dependent clauses.

Most dependent clauses start with words like *when, until, who, where, because,* and *so that.* Such a clause might tell when something happened, which person was involved, or where the event took place.

DEPENDENT CLAUSE — INDEPENDENT CLAUSE

When we visited, Mrs. Brodsky shared her memories of working in a shipyard during World War II.

Mr. Ruiz was a photographer until he was drafted.

Mr. Liuzzo, who is a retired pilot, talked to us about his experiences in enemy territory, where he was a prisoner of war.

2 Why It Matters in Writing

You can use complex sentences to clarify relationships between ideas. First read the passage below without the changes. Then read it as it has been revised. Notice how the revisions clarify why Nick does what he does.

STUDENT MODEL

My friend Nick really enjoys visiting people at the Pines Nursing Home. because They have many moving stories of life in our town during World War II. Nick records their memories. so that he can share ~~He shares~~ them with his social studies class.

Tells why Nick enjoys visiting

Tells why he records memories

3 Practice and Apply

A. CONCEPT CHECK: Complex Sentences

Write these sentences on a sheet of paper. Underline each independent clause once and each dependent clause twice.

Foster Grandparents

1. Although the Foster Grandparent Program is more than 40 years old, many people do not know about it.
2. This program was established so that children with special needs could get extra attention.
3. Anyone can volunteer who is at least 60 years old and meets other requirements.
4. After a volunteer is trained, he or she works 15 to 40 hours a week.
5. Because foster grandparents need to be involved in the lives of their "grandchildren," they maintain a close relationship for a year or longer.
6. Foster grandparents often help with homework so that the children can improve in school.
7. Although foster grandparents are volunteers, they are paid.
8. They also receive travel expenses while they serve.
9. Since this government program was founded in 1965, there have been foster grandparent projects in all 50 states.
10. Because more than 31,000 volunteers served in 2005, more than 262,000 children benefited that year.

→ **For a SELF-CHECK and more practice, see the EXERCISE BANK, p. 334.**

B. REVISING: Varying Sentence Structure

Rewrite the following paragraph to make the ideas clearer. Combine simple sentences 1 and 2 to make a complex sentence. Combine sentences 3 and 4 to eliminate repetition. Combine sentences 5 and 6 to show how ideas connect.

STUDENT MODEL

(1) Children establish a relationship with a foster grandparent. **(2)** Their grades and school attendance improve. **(3)** Children report that they feel better about themselves. **(4)** They also report that they feel more positive about their future. **(5)** They stay out of trouble more often. **(6)** Their foster grandparents care about them and reinforce important values.

SENTENCES

Kinds of Dependent Clauses

1 Here's the Idea

Adjective Clauses

▶ **An adjective clause is a dependent clause used as an adjective.** An adjective clause modifies a noun or a pronoun. It tells what kind, which one, how many, or how much.

Student volunteers read stories to the children who were in the daycare center.
MODIFIES NOUN
ADJECTIVE CLAUSE

Adjective clauses are usually introduced by relative pronouns.

Relative Pronouns
who whom whose that which

The story, which made them laugh, is about a monkey.

Notice that a clause that begins with *which* is set off with commas.

Adverb Clauses

▶ **An adverb clause is a dependent clause used as an adverb.** It modifies a verb, an adjective, or an adverb. An adverb clause might tell where, when, how, why, to what extent, or under what conditions.

Adverb clauses are introduced by subordinating conjunctions such as *if, because, even though, than, so that, while, where, when, as if,* and *since.*

They were happy because they were going to the zoo.
MODIFIES ADJECTIVE
ADVERB CLAUSE

MODIFIES ADVERB

The zoo closed earlier than they expected.

An adverb clause should be followed by a comma when it comes before an independent clause. When an adverb clause comes after an independent clause, a comma may or may not be needed before it.

When the field trip ended, the volunteers took the children back to the daycare center.

The volunteers took the children back to the daycare center when the field trip ended.

For more about adjectives and adverbs, see Chapter 5, pp. 124–149.

Noun Clauses

SENTENCES

A noun clause is a dependent clause used as a noun. Like a noun, a noun clause can serve as a subject, a direct object, an indirect object, an object of a preposition, or a predicate noun. In the caption below, the noun clause is the subject of the sentence.

NOUN CLAUSE SERVING AS SUBJECT

What frustrates many physically challenged people is the problem of getting around.

Volunteers know that physically challenged people do not want special treatment.
NOUN CLAUSE SERVING AS DIRECT OBJECT

NOUN CLAUSE SERVING AS INDIRECT OBJECT
Christopher will tell whoever is volunteering the locations of the elevators.

Noun clauses are introduced by words such as those shown in the following chart.

Words That Introduce Noun Clauses				
that	how	when	where	whether
why	what	whatever	who	whom
whoever	whomever	which	whichever	

If you can substitute the word *something* or *someone* for a clause in a sentence, it is a noun clause. (Volunteers know *something*. Christopher will tell *someone*.)

For more about nouns, see Chapter 2, pp. 34–55.

CHAPTER 8

2 Why It Matters in Writing

You can use dependent clauses to add detail to your writing. They allow you to express important ideas in a few words.

LITERARY MODEL

One of the young men who worked at the group home—a college student named Jack—grew a large garden in the back of the house. . . .

Jack tried to explain to Ernie that the seeds would grow into vegetables, but Ernie could not believe this until he saw it come true.

—Cynthia Rylant, "A Crush"

Adjective clause tells which young men.

Noun clause tells what Jack tried to explain.

Adverb clause tells when Ernie could believe.

3 Practice and Apply

A. CONCEPT CHECK: Kinds of Dependent Clauses

Write these sentences on a sheet of paper. Underline each dependent clause, and identify it as an adjective clause, an adverb clause, or a noun clause.

Raising a Guide Dog

1. Some people who are visually challenged have guide dogs.
2. These dogs are important because they help the people get around in daily life.
3. A guide dog that completes its training can lead a visually challenged person across busy streets.
4. In fact, a visually challenged person can handle most traveling situations if a guide dog is with him or her.
5. There are organizations that raise puppies to be guide dogs.
6. Each puppy is given to a family who cares for it for a year.
7. They treat the puppy as if it were their own.
8. When the year is over, they give the dog back for special training.
9. All family members know why the dog must leave.
10. They realize that the dog will become a visually challenged person's constant companion.

➜ **For a SELF-CHECK and more practice, see the EXERCISE BANK, p. 335.**

SENTENCES

B. WRITING: Using Clauses

Complete the sentence below by adding clauses of the types indicated in parentheses.

(1) Some students (adjective clause) volunteer at animal shelters. **(2)** They help take care of dogs and cats (adverb clause). **(3)** (noun clause) is appreciated by animal lovers everywhere.

Compound-Complex Sentences

1 Here's the Idea

A compound-complex sentence contains two or more independent clauses and one or more dependent clauses.

DEPENDENT CLAUSE — INDEPENDENT CLAUSE

When our school celebrates Earth Day, we sign up for environmental projects, and we try to complete them all in one day.

INDEPENDENT CLAUSE

Students have cleaned up the beaches, and they have planted flowers in the parks so that the shore looks inviting to visitors.

CHAPTER 8

2 Why It Matters in Writing

You can use compound-complex sentences in your writing to show complicated relationships between events and ideas. Notice how Joan Aiken used such sentences in a detailed description of what a boy sees in a magical garden.

LITERARY MODEL

The gate grew again above him, and when he opened it and ran across the lawn through the yew arch, he found himself in a flagged garden full of flowers like huge blue cabbages. . . .

The orchard was most wonderful, for instead of mere apples its trees bore oranges, lemons, limes and all sorts of tropical fruits whose names he did not know, and there were melons and pineapples growing, and plantains and avocados.

—Joan Aiken, "The Serial Garden"

INDEPENDENT CLAUSES

DEPENDENT CLAUSES

3 Practice and Apply

A. CONCEPT CHECK: Compound-Complex Sentences

Identify each sentence as compound, complex, or compound-complex.

Helping Disaster Victims

1. In 1998 a hurricane swept through Central America, where it hit Honduras and Nicaragua especially hard.
2. Hurricane Mitch was one of the strongest storms ever in this region; it caused great destruction.
3. People on the coast tried to flee to higher ground, but flooding and mudslides made escape difficult.
4. More than 9,000 people were killed, and crops and roads were wiped out.
5. TV images of homeless and hungry people touched many Americans, who responded generously.
6. They donated money and supplies, which were flown to the region.
7. Volunteers helped clear roads so that supplies could get to villages that needed them.
8. Charity groups distributed food and safe drinking water, and they handed out sleeping bags and mosquito nets, which were needed in the tropical climate.
9. Medical volunteers treated people who desperately needed care.
10. Other volunteers rebuilt homes, and they helped restore the farm economy so that people could earn a living again.

➜ **For a SELF-CHECK and more practice, see the EXERCISE BANK, p. 335**

B. WRITING: Creating Compound-Complex Sentences

Combine the following sentences to create a compound-complex sentence. Use *when* and *and* in your new sentence.

It rains. Rivers overflow. Neighborhoods near the rivers flood.

Grammar in Literature

Using Compound and Complex Sentences

How do you write a description that allows you to create a vivid picture of a person? In the following excerpt, author William Jay Jacobs brings Eleanor Roosevelt to life by using compound and complex sentences. Such sentences allow him to vary the sentence structure and to add important details about Mrs. Roosevelt.

CHAPTER 8

from **Eleanor Roosevelt**

by William Jay Jacobs

UPI/Bettmann

After becoming interested in the problems of working women, she [Eleanor] gave time to the Women's Trade Union League (WTUL). . . . It was through the WTUL that she met a group of remarkable women. . . .They awakened her hopes that something could be done to improve the condition of the poor. . . .

Eleanor helped the Red Cross raise money. She gave blood, sold war bonds. . . . In 1943, for example, she visited barracks and hospitals on islands throughout the South Pacific. When she visited a hospital, she stopped at every bed. . . . Often, after she left, even battle-hardened men had tears in their eyes. . . .

In December 1945 President Harry S. Truman invited her to be one of the American delegates going to London to begin the work of the United Nations. Eleanor hesitated, but the president insisted. He said that the nation needed her; it was her duty.

COMPLEX SENTENCE with adjective clause explaining Eleanor's hopes.

COMPLEX SENTENCE with adverb clauses explains how Eleanor acted and how she was affected by her visits to the hospitals.

COMPOUND SENTENCE with coordinating conjunction explains how Eleanor came to her position at the United Nations.

Practice and Apply

Using Clauses to Create Interesting Sentences

Follow the instructions below to revise this passage by creating compound and complex sentences that add variety and interest to the writing.

(1) Eleanor Roosevelt had a very unhappy childhood. **(2)** She did enjoy visits to see her uncle, Theodore Roosevelt. **(3)** Uncle Ted would read to the children. **(4)** The children had a day of romping outside and swimming. **(5)** Hearing his stories was very comforting to Eleanor and the other children. **(6)** Today volunteers often read to children to comfort them. **(7)** Who are hospitalized. **(8)** The volunteers make sure they choose books that each child will understand. **(9)** They also choose books that are funny. **(10)** They leave the book with the sick child. Until the next time they come.

1. Combine sentences 1 and 2 to make a compound sentence. Use the conjunction **but** to join the sentences.
2. Combine sentences 3 and 4 into a complex sentence. Begin sentence 4 with the subordinating conjunction *after.*
3. Combine sentence 6 with fragment 7, which is an adjective clause, to make a complex sentence.
4. Combine sentences 8 and 9 to make a compound-complex sentence.
5. Combine sentence 10 with the adverb clause after it to make a complex sentence.

You write it. Explain how your revisions affect the quality of the draft. Which version explains more about Eleanor's actions? Which version is easier to read? Put your paragraph in your **Working Portfolio.**

Mixed Review

A. Sentence Structure Read the model about a student volunteer. Then write the answers to the questions below it.

PROFESSIONAL MODEL

(1) Rebecca is a seventh-grader who volunteers in a tutoring program for first-graders at her school. **(2)** The tutors in the program help the younger students with their reading. **(3)** They read stories to the students, and then the younger students read to the tutors. **(4)** Rebecca teaches her student Megan. **(5)** She herself struggled when she was in first grade, and she is thrilled that she can help teach someone else.

—Martin McNamara

CHAPTER 8

1. Is sentence 1 simple or complex?
2. Does sentence 1 have an adjective, adverb, or noun clause?
3. Is sentence 2 simple or complex?
4. Is sentence 3 compound or complex?
5. What is the coordinating conjunction in sentence 3?
6. Is sentence 4 simple or complex?
7. Is sentence 5 compound or compound-complex?
8. Name the independent clauses in sentence 5.
9. Name the dependent clauses in sentence 5.
10. Does sentence 5 have an adjective, adverb, or noun clause?

B. Combining Clauses Rewrite the following paragraph, combining clauses to eliminate sentence fragments and to connect related ideas.

Reading Is Fundamental is a national organization. It promotes literacy. Students can participate. Who are interested. They can teach adults. Who may not have had a chance to learn. When they were young. After people learn to read. They lead more successful lives.

Mastery Test: What Did You Learn?

Choose the letter of the term that correctly identifies each underlined section.

Do you know <u>that free "volunteer vacations" are available through national and state parks</u> (1)? The parks have many types of volunteer positions <u>that need to be filled</u> (2). <u>Although</u> (3) some of the positions require experience, others do not, <u>and</u> (4) newcomers are welcomed. <u>Volunteers have the chance to spend time in beautiful natural settings, and they can combine work with pleasure.</u> (5) Their housing, <u>which</u> (6) can be campsites, and their meals are usually provided <u>while they are volunteering</u> (7). <u>What benefits are available</u> (8) depends on individual circumstances. <u>There is usually plenty of free time for volunteers to explore the parks on their own, so a volunteer vacation can be quite interesting.</u> (9) Among the most popular parks are those in Alaska and Hawaii, <u>which often have waiting lists</u> (10).

1. A. independent clause
   B. dependent clause
   C. compound sentence
   D. simple sentence

2. A. adjective clause
   B. noun clause
   C. simple sentence
   D. adverb clause

3. A. subordinating conjunction
   B. coordinating conjunction
   C. relative pronoun
   D. noun clause

4. A. subordinating conjunction
   B. coordinating conjunction
   C. relative pronoun
   D. noun clause

5. A. simple sentence
   B. compound sentence
   C. complex sentence
   D. compound-complex sentence

6. A. relative pronoun
   B. adjective clause
   C. adverb clause
   D. independent clause

7. A. adjective clause
   B. adverb clause
   C. noun clause
   D. independent clause

8. A. noun clause
   B. adjective clause
   C. adverb clause
   D. independent clause

9. A. simple sentence
   B. compound sentence
   C. complex sentence
   D. sentence fragment

10. A. adjective clause
    B. adverb clause
    C. noun clause
    D. independent clause

Student Help Desk

Sentence Structure at a Glance

SIMPLE SENTENCE = independent clause

Olivia is running in a 5K race.

COMPOUND SENTENCE = independent clause + independent clause(s)

Nick is also running, but Greg isn't.

COMPLEX SENTENCE = independent clause + dependent clause(s)

Greg can't, because he is officiating.

COMPOUND–COMPLEX SENTENCE =

independent clauses + dependent clauses

Patti will find sponsors, and Jed will collect donations when we are ready.

CHAPTER 8

Punctuating Compound and Complex Sentences

Join Up!

Use commas . . .	Example
to join independent clauses with coordinating conjunctions	She ran to the finish, **but** he dropped out.
after adverb clauses that begin sentences	After the race was over, they rested.
to set off adjective clauses that begin with *which*	His injury, **which was painful**, seemed rather severe.
Use semicolons . . .	
to join independent clauses without conjunctions	She was sympathetic; he was disappointed.

Avoiding Clause Confusion

Dependent Clause	Function	Example
Adjective clause	• modifies noun or pronoun • tells what kind, which one, how many, or how much	The **students** **who participated** enjoyed the race.
Adverb clause	• modifies verb, adjective, or adverb • tells where, when, how, why, to what extent, or under what conditions	They felt **proud** **because they had done something worthwhile.**
Noun clause	• acts as subject, direct object, indirect object, object of preposition, or predicate noun	**What helps others** can be rewarding for volunteers too.

SENTENCES

The Bottom Line

Checklist for Sentence Structure

Can I improve my writing by . . .

____ eliminating sentence fragments?

____ creating compound sentences to link closely related ideas?

____ using dependent clauses to show how ideas are related?

____ using dependent clauses to add details?

____ punctuating compound and complex sentences correctly?

Chapter 9

Subject-Verb Agreement

Theme: It's an Art

What's the Message?

What decisions do you think these artists had to make before beginning their mural? When working on a collaborative project, artists must discuss matters such as subject, style, and composition. If they fail to agree, they probably won't succeed in producing a harmonious artwork.

In the art of writing, subject-verb agreement is important for effective communication. Mistakes in agreement may confuse and frustrate readers. This chapter will help you use subjects and verbs correctly.

Write Away: Public Art

Draw a sketch of a public work of art, such as a statue or mural, in your town or neighborhood. Then write a description of the artwork and discuss why someone might have wanted to display it in public. Save your writing in your **Working Portfolio.**

Diagnostic Test: What Do You Know?

Choose the letter of the best revision for each underlined group of words.

Diego Rivera were one of Mexico's greatest artists. (1) His murals and paintings have influenced (2) artists around the world. Many portrays (3) historical subjects. For example, *The History of Mexico* illustrates (4) about 500 years of Mexican history. Within this mural is several groups (5) of images. The first group show (6) life in Mexico before the arrival of the Spaniards. Others portrays (7) the Spanish conquest of Mexico and the cruelty of colonialism. The images reflects Rivera's deep concern (8) for the suffering of common people.

1. A. Diego Rivera are one of Mexico's greatest artists.
   B. Diego Rivera have been one of Mexico's greatest artists.
   C. Diego Rivera was one of Mexico's greatest artists.
   D. Correct as is
2. A. His murals and paintings has influenced
   B. His murals and paintings has been influencing
   C. His murals and paintings is influencing
   D. Correct as is
3. A. Many portray
   B. Many is portraying
   C. Many has portrayed
   D. Correct as is
4. A. *The History of Mexico* illustrate
   B. *The History of Mexico* do illustrate
   C. *The History of Mexico* have illustrated
   D. Correct as is
5. A. Within this mural was several groups
   B. Within this mural are several groups
   C. Within this mural appears several groups
   D. Correct as is
6. A. The first group shows
   B. The first group are showing
   C. The first group is showing
   D. Correct as is
7. A. Others portray
   B. Others does portray
   C. Others has portrayed
   D. Correct as is
8. A. The images was reflecting Rivera's deep concern
   B. The images reflect Rivera's deep concern
   C. The images has reflected Rivera's deep concern
   D. Correct as is

Agreement in Number

1 Here's the Idea

A verb must agree with its subject in number.

Number refers to whether a word is singular or plural. A word that refers to one person, place, thing, idea, action, or condition is singular. A word that refers to more than one is plural.

Singular and Plural Subjects

Singular subjects take singular verbs.

AGREE

The new museum displays works by local artists.

SINGULAR SUBJECT ↑ ↑ SINGULAR VERB

She enjoys the towering sculptures at the art center.

CHAPTER 9

Plural subjects take plural verbs.

AGREE

Chicago's art museums display priceless paintings.

PLURAL SUBJECT ↑ ↑ PLURAL VERB

We enjoy the peaceful outdoor sculpture garden.

Most nouns that end in *s* or *es* are plural. For example, *artists* and *brushes* are plural nouns. However, most verbs that end in *s* are singular. *Paints* and *draws* are singular verb forms.

Verb Phrases

In a verb phrase, it is the first helping verb that agrees with the subject. A verb phrase is made up of a main verb and one or more helping verbs.

AGREE

Theresa has collected ceramic figurines.

↑ SINGULAR HELPING VERB

She is building a large collection.

AGREE

Friends have admired her interesting collection.

PLURAL HELPING VERB

They have been finding new figurines for her collection.

Doesn't and *Don't*

Two common contractions are *doesn't* and *don't.* Use *doesn't* with all singular subjects except *I* and *you*. Use *don't* with all plural subjects and with the pronouns *I* and *you*.

Samuel doesn't use computer clip art.
SINGULAR VERB: does + not = doesn't

We don't like slick and professional illustrations.
PLURAL VERB: do + not = don't

I don't like these pictures.
WITH PRONOUN I: do + not = don't

S-V AGREEMENT

2 Why It Matters in Writing

Errors in subject-verb agreement can occur when you revise your work. If you change a subject from singular to plural or vice versa, be sure to change the verb as well.

STUDENT MODEL

DRAFT

Three statues have been purchased for the park. Residents **want** to beautify the neighborhood.

REVISION

Three statues have been purchased for the park. An important resident **wants** to beautify the neighborhood.

③ Practice and Apply

A. CONCEPT CHECK: Agreement in Number

For each sentence, write the verb form that agrees in number with the subject.

African *Kente* Cloth

1. The Ashanti people of Ghana (has, have) been making *kente* cloth for centuries.
2. *Kente* weavers (creates, create) complex designs with bright colors and geometric patterns.
3. The designs (doesn't, don't) just provide visual pleasure.
4. Each element (has, have) a precise meaning.
5. For example, the color gold (suggests, suggest) mineral wealth.
6. A shield pattern (suggests, suggest) a defense against hostile forces.
7. Weavers often (takes, take) months to complete *kente* garments.
8. The Ashanti people (wears, wear) *kente* cloth on important occasions.
9. Some designs (is, are) reserved for royalty.
10. *Kente* garments (appears, appear) in many museum collections.

➜ **For a SELF-CHECK and more practice, see the EXERCISE BANK, p. 336.**

B. WRITING: Completing a Caption

Choose the correct verb forms to complete the caption for the photograph.

The color gold in this piece of *kente* cloth (symbolizes, symbolize) mineral wealth. These fabrics (is, are) made by the Ashanti people of Ghana.

Compound Subjects

❶ Here's the Idea

A **compound subject** is made up of two or more subjects joined by a conjunction such as *and, or,* or *nor.*

Subjects Containing *And*

▶ **A compound subject whose parts are joined by *and* usually takes a plural verb.**

Georgia and Louise paint exceptionally well.

Sometimes a subject containing *and* refers to a single thing or idea, so a singular verb is used.

War and peace is the theme of the mural.

S-V AGREEMENT

Subjects Containing *Or* or *Nor*

▶ **When the parts of a compound subject are joined by *or* or *nor,* the verb should agree with the part closest to it.**

AGREE

Either ticket stubs or a photo completes your collage.

AGREE

Either a photo or ticket stubs complete your collage.

❷ Why It Matters in Writing

Writers sometimes reverse the order of compound subjects to make them sound more natural. If you do this, you may need to change the verb to make it agree with the new order.

The students or the teacher is attending the show.

The teacher or the students are attending the show.

❸ Practice and Apply

A. CONCEPT CHECK: Compound Subjects

Identify the sentences containing mistakes in subject-verb agreement, and rewrite them correctly. If a sentence contains no error, write *Correct*.

Crafty Arts

1. Arts and crafts are often hard to tell apart.
2. A basket or pot serve a practical function, such as food storage.
3. Yet collectors and museum curators prizes these objects for their beauty.
4. Many pots and jars display high levels of artistry.
5. Even forks and spoons appears in museum collections.
6. Arms and armor occupies special halls in some museums.
7. Neither dirt nor blood stains remains on their shiny surfaces.
8. Adults and children find these tools of warfare appealing.
9. Antique beds, couches, or a rug seem enticing to the weary museum patron.
10. Fortunately, signs and watchful guards reminds us not to rest on them.

➜ **For a SELF-CHECK and more practice, see the EXERCISE BANK, p. 337.**

B. REVISING: Making Verbs Agree with Compound Subjects

Rewrite this article for a school newspaper so that verbs agree with compound subjects. There are five errors.

In My Opinion . . .

Many ideas and opinions is expressed visually in editorial cartoons. Familiar symbols and caricatures communicate the cartoonists' messages. For example, a torn flag or a battered Uncle Sam suggest trouble in the nation. Politicians and celebrities are often criticized by exaggerating their physical appearance. Pompous leaders and corrupt people makes good targets. Sometimes neither caricatures nor a visual symbol bring across a cartoonist's point clearly. In such a case, a speech balloon or a caption help readers understand the cartoon.

Agreement Problems in Sentences

1 Here's the Idea

Some sentences—ones with subjects in unusual positions, ones containing predicate nouns, ones in which prepositional phrases separate subjects and verbs—can be tricky. Here are some tips for choosing the correct verb forms in these situations.

Subjects in Unusual Positions

A subject can follow a verb or part of a verb phrase in a question, a sentence beginning with *here* or *there*, or a sentence in which an adjective, an adverb, or a phrase is placed first.

Subjects in Unusual Positions

Type of Sentence	Example
Question	**Does** this **music video contain** interesting computer graphics?
Sentence beginning with *here* or *there*	Here **is** an on-air **announcer** with an enjoyable play list.
Sentence beginning with adverb, adjective, or phrase	Around the nation is **heard** the **sound.**

The following tips can help you to find the subject in one of these kinds of sentences.

Here's How **Choosing a Correct Verb Form**

(Is, Are) the visual effects better than the song recording?

1. Rephrase the sentence so that the subject precedes the verb.
   The visual **effects** (**is, are**) better than the song recording.
2. Determine whether the subject is singular or plural.
   effects (plural)
3. Choose the verb form that agrees with the subject.
   The visual **effects are** better than the song recording.
4. Add correct verb to the original sentence.
   Are the visual **effects** better than the song recording?

S-V AGREEMENT

Predicate Nouns

In a sentence containing a predicate noun, the verb should agree with the subject, not the predicate noun.

AGREE

Nechita's works have been a topic of magazine articles.

Her inspiration is abstract paintings by Pablo Picasso.

Prepositional Phrases

The subject of a verb is never found in a prepositional phrase. Don't be fooled by words that come between a subject and a verb. Mentally block out those words. Then it will be easy to tell whether the subject is singular or plural.

AGREE

The colors ~~of a Javanese batik garment~~ indicate where it came from.

Traditionally, the pattern ~~of symbols~~ represents things found in nature.

CHAPTER 9

❷ Why It Matters in Writing

Writers sometimes place verbs before subjects to make their writing more interesting. When you do this, make sure that the verbs agree with their subjects.

LITERARY MODEL

Between two pieces of cardboard were a **letter** and a large color **photograph.**

The photograph showed John Wilson down on his right knee before a glistening dark wall. . . . Leaning against the wall to his right was Zebra's **drawing** of the helicopter and the zebra racing together across a facelike landscape.

—Chaim Potok, "Zebra"

❸ Practice and Apply

A. CONCEPT CHECK: Agreement Problems in Sentences

Rewrite these sentences, correcting agreement errors. If a sentence contains no error, write *Correct*.

Poster Power

1. Does your classmates collect posters?
2. On the walls of many teenagers' rooms hang pictures of favorite singers, actors, and athletes.
3. An effective tool for advertising or announcing events is posters.
4. Vibrant colors in a poster attracts the public's attention.
5. Among the greatest of poster artists were Henri de Toulouse-Lautrec.
6. Has you ever seen Toulouse-Lautrec's bold, striking posters?
7. Japanese prints were the source of his inspiration.
8. There is few posters more famous than *I Want You!*
9. On that World War I recruitment poster is a portrait of Uncle Sam.
10. There is also patriotic posters from World War II.

➜ **For a SELF-CHECK and more practice, see the EXERCISE BANK, p. 337.**

B. MIXED REVIEW: Proofreading and Editing

Find the five errors in subject-verb agreement in this paragraph. In each case, write the correct verb form.

Roll the Videotape

Does you ever record family celebrations with a video camera? Then you probably has the basic skills to create a work of video art. Video artists combine technology with artistic expression. Just as painters apply paint to canvas, video artists record images for television monitors. There is works of video art that tell stories, just like feature films. Others are more like sculptures or paintings. For example, the artist Nam June Paik has created a pyramid out of 40 television sets. On all of the sets play a video of a dancing man. Paik are one of the most prominent artists working with video.

Indefinite Pronouns as Subjects

1 Here's the Idea

▶ **When used as subjects, some indefinite pronouns are always singular, some are always plural, and some can be singular or plural, depending on how they're used.** Remember, an indefinite pronoun is a pronoun that does not refer to a specific person, place, thing, or idea.

Indefinite Pronouns					
Singular	another anybody anyone anything each either	everybody everyone everything neither nobody no one	nothing one somebody someone something		
Plural	both	few	many	several	
Singular or Plural	all	any	most	none	some

CHAPTER 9

Singular indefinite pronouns take singular verbs.

Everyone enjoys Alexander Calder's mobiles.

Something about them reminds people of childhood.

Plural indefinite pronouns take plural verbs.

Few of the mobiles have electric motors.

Many consist of metal, wood, and wire.

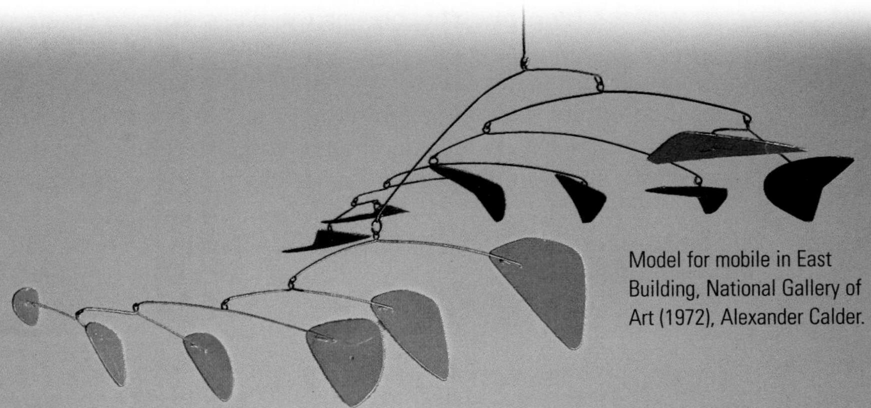

Model for mobile in East Building, National Gallery of Art (1972), Alexander Calder.

Singular or Plural?

The indefinite pronouns *all, any, most, none,* and *some* can be either singular or plural. When you use one of these words as a subject, think about the noun it refers to. If the noun is singular, use a singular verb; if it is plural, use a plural verb.

REFERS TO

All of the mobiles move in a breeze.

REFERS TO

Most of the design is ingenious.

Sometimes an indefinite pronoun refers to a noun in a previous sentence.

PLURAL NOUN

Many people attended the exhibition. Most were astonished.

INDEFINITE PRONOUN PLURAL VERB

S-V AGREEMENT

2 Why It Matters in Writing

When you write about events for an assignment or a school newspaper, you will probably need to use indefinite pronouns as subjects. To help readers understand your writing, use correct subject-verb agreement.

PROFESSIONAL MODEL

A fascinating art show has opened this weekend in Biloxi. **Each** of the paintings portrays a different blues musician. **Many** are painted in a realistic style. **Some** of the art depicts older musicians who play acoustic instruments.

—Chris Bayard

3 Practice and Apply

A. CONCEPT CHECK: Indefinite Pronouns as Subjects

Rewrite correctly each sentence in which the verb does not agree with the subject. If a sentence is correct, write *Correct*.

In Black and White

1. Many knows the saying "A picture's worth a thousand words."
2. One remembers the fascinating images in photo essays.
3. Few merely entertains people.
4. Most addresses important real-life issues.
5. For example, both *Let Us Now Praise Famous Men* and *How the Other Half Lives* tell powerful stories.
6. Some of the photographs reveals poverty.
7. Others portrays nature's fury.
8. Everyone are touched by pictures that capture human suffering.
9. No one ignores such strong evidence of problems in society.
10. All of this photography motivate people to take a stand.

Mother and two children on road at Tule Lake City, September 1939. Photo by Dorothea Lange.

➜ **For a SELF-CHECK and more practice, see the EXERCISE BANK, p. 218.**

B. WRITING: Agreement with Indefinite Pronouns

For each sentence, choose the verb form that agrees with the subject.

(1) Everybody (enjoys, enjoy) our school's art fairs. **(2)** Most of the artworks (is, are) quite good. **(3)** Something always (makes, make) the students smile because it is so ridiculous. **(4)** Yet one (has, have) no need to fear humiliation. **(5)** None of the artists (gets, get) upset. **(6)** None of the criticism (is, are) mean-spirited. **(7)** Everyone (understands, understand) that artists should be encouraged. **(8)** Some (takes, take) longer to develop their talent. **(9)** Each of us (has, have) the right to express himself or herself in art. **(10)** All of the fairs (is, are) conducted in this spirit.

LESSON 5

Problem Subjects

1 Here's the Idea

When collective nouns, nouns ending in s, titles, and numerical expressions are used as subjects, it can be difficult to tell whether they take singular or plural verbs.

Collective Nouns

Collective nouns name groups of people or things.

Common Collective Nouns					
group	crew	flock	family	class	team
crowd	herd	public	club	faculty	choir

Many collective nouns can take singular or plural verbs, depending on how they are used. When a collective noun refers to people or things acting as a group, it takes a singular verb.

The faculty sponsors an art exhibit each year.
(THE FACULTY MEMBERS ARE ACTING AS A GROUP.)

When a collective noun refers to people or things acting as individuals, it takes a plural verb.

The faculty disagree on the rules of the exhibit.
(THE FACULTY MEMBERS ARE ACTING AS INDIVIDUALS.)

Singular Nouns Ending in *S*

Some nouns that end in *s* or *ics* look plural but actually refer to singular concepts. When used as subjects, they take singular verbs.

Singular Nouns with Plural Forms			
measles	linguistics	news	pediatrics
politics	forensics	civics	mathematics
genetics	mechanics	physics	economics
ceramics	molasses	mumps	

S-V AGREEMENT

AGREE

Ceramics is the art of making objects from clay.

AGREE

The news includes information about several exhibits.

Titles

▶ **Titles of works of art, literature, and music are singular.** Even a title consisting of a plural noun takes a singular verb.

***Sunflowers* is a famous painting by Vincent van Gogh.**

Amounts and Time

▶ **Words and phrases that express weights, measures, numbers, and lengths of time are often treated as singular.** They take singular verbs when they refer to amounts rather than numbers of individual items.

Measures and Amounts		
Measures	seven pounds two cups	**Two hundred twenty-five tons is** the weight of the Statue of Liberty.
Amounts	three hours nine dollars	**Four years seems** a long time to work on a single portrait.

CHAPTER 9

A fraction can take a singular or plural verb, depending on whether it refers to a single part or to a number of items.

Five-sixths of the canvas is blank.

(THE FRACTION REFERS TO ONE PART OF THE CANVAS.)

Two-thirds of the paintings are abstract.

(THE FRACTION REFERS TO A NUMBER OF PAINTINGS.)

❷ Why It Matters in Writing

When you write about science or math, you need to use numbers, weights, and measures. Show your readers that you know your stuff by using the correct verb forms with them.

Six-tenths of the human body is water.

3 Practice and Apply

A. CONCEPT CHECK: Problem Subjects

Rewrite the underlined words in the following sentences to correct the mistake in subject-verb agreement. If a sentence contains no error, write *Correct*.

Memorial Wall

1. *In Country* describe a girl's effort to learn more about her father, who was killed in Vietnam.
2. Her family travel to Washington, D.C., to visit the Vietnam Veterans Memorial.
3. Many spend time at the wall designed by Maya Lin.
4. Each of the wall's halves are about 250 feet long.
5. Three days are how long it takes to read all 58,209 names of soldiers killed or missing in the war.
6. Mathematics fails to explain the wall's dramatic effect.
7. The public also views other sculptures at the memorial.
8. *Three Servicemen* by Frederick Hart stand near the wall.
9. Our class have looked at an exhibit of objects left at the wall.
10. A group of photos show a young man with family and friends.

→ **For a SELF-CHECK and more practice, see the EXERCISE BANK, p. 338.**

B. WRITING: Using Fractions Correctly

Choose the correct verb form to complete each sentence about the bar graph. Then write a sentence explaining how you chose the correct form.

1. Two-thirds of the class (is, are) going on the trip to Washington, D.C.
2. One-half of the students (has, have) seen the Statue of Liberty.

Numbers of Students Who Have Visited Two Sites
(class size = 30)

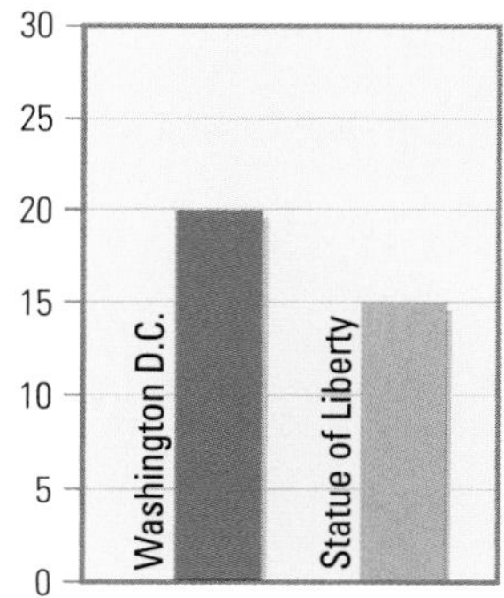

S-V AGREEMENT

Grammar in Math

Word Problems

When you write and solve word problems, you need to pay attention to grammar. Subject-verb agreement can be tricky—especially if you're using fractions. In the following word problem, the subjects and the verbs that agree with them are highlighted.

240 **Section 6** Multiplication of Fractions

42 **Theater** Northern Illinois University has a collection of scale models of stage sets. These models show sets that were built for Early American performances of operas. The models are built to a scale of 1/48 of the actual size. The model shown is a set representing a public square in nineteenth century Bohemia, a region of the Czech Republic.

Exploration:

A door on one of the buildings in the model is 11/16 in. wide and 1 3/4 in. tall. Explain how you would find the actual dimensions of the door on the stage set.

The word *is* agrees with the subject *door,* not with the plural word *buildings.*

EXAMPLE

Describe how you would find the width of the actual door on the stage set.

ANSWER

11/16 in. is multiplied by 48 to find the width of the door on the stage set.

Singular subject *11/16 in.* agrees with the singular verb *is.*

CHAPTER 9

Practice and Apply

A. Use the information on the photograph of the model to write and answer a word problem. Figure out how many poles could be cut from a dowel that is 1 foot long.

B. Write and solve a word problem in which you find the size of the pole on the actual stage set. Be sure you explain the proportion of the model to the set. Remember—if you are using fractions as subjects, you should use a singular verb.

Mixed Review

A. Agreement in Number, Compound Subjects, and Indefinite Pronouns Write the verb form that agrees with the subject of each sentence.

1. Curators and conservators (is, are) important employees in museums.
2. Each of these people (has, have) specific responsibilities.
3. A curator (arranges, arrange) artworks in museum galleries.
4. Curators also (looks, look) for artworks to add to museums' collections.
5. Major museums (has, have) a curator for each department.
6. A conservator (cleans, clean) artworks.
7. Conservators also (performs, perform) scientific tests on them.
8. The tests (reveals, reveal) how old the artworks are and how they were made.
9. A conservator or a curator (needs, need) extensive training.
10. Most (has, have) advanced degrees in art history.

B. Additional Agreement Problems Rewrite the following advertisement, correcting six errors in subject-verb agreement.

CHAPTER 9

Mastery Test: What Did You Learn?

Choose the letter of the best revision for each underlined group of words.

<u>There are</u> (1) a remarkable example of folk art in Los Angeles, called the Watts Towers. This <u>group of sculptures were</u> (2) created by Simon Rodia. <u>The group contain</u> (3) nine sculptures. <u>Some are</u> (4) nearly 100 feet tall. Rodia gave them names such as *Ship of Marco Polo* and *Santa Maria Tower*. These <u>names remind</u> (5) us of Rodia's Italian heritage. <u>Each of the sculptures are made</u> (6) of steel rods, wire mesh, and mortar. <u>Bottle caps, seashells, and other found objects is imbedded</u> (7) in the mortar for decoration. Tourists from around the world <u>comes</u> (8) to view the Watts Towers.

1. A. There have been
   B. There is
   C. There were
   D. Correct as is
2. A. group of sculptures are
   B. group of sculpture is
   C. group of sculptures was
   D. Correct as is
3. A. The group contains
   B. The group have contained
   C. The group are containing
   D. Correct as is
4. A. Some is
   B. Some stands
   C. Some was
   D. Correct as is
5. A. names does remind
   B. names has reminded
   C. names is reminding
   D. Correct as is
6. A. Each of the sculptures were made
   B. Each of the sculptures have been made
   C. Each of the sculptures is made
   D. Correct as is
7. A. Bottle caps, seashells, and other found objects was imbedded
   B. Bottle caps, seashells, and other found objects are imbedded
   C. Bottle caps, seashells, and other found objects has been imbedded
   D. Correct as is
8. A. come
   B. has come
   C. is coming
   D. Correct as is

Student Help Desk

Subject-Verb Agreement at a Glance

A singular subject takes a singular verb.

The artist paints dancers.

A plural subject takes a plural verb.

Dancers pose in her studio.

Subjects and Verbs

Tricky Cases

Verb phrase The first helping verb should agree with the subject.	**Folk art is getting** expensive. **Collectors are raising** prices.
Prepositional phrase between subject and verb Block out the phrase when deciding which verb form to use.	The **vases** ~~in this museum~~ **are** priceless.
Compound subject containing *and* Always use a plural verb.	The **artist and** his **work arouse** controversy.
Compound subject containing *or* or *nor* The verb should agree with the part of the subject closest to it.	Neither the **critics nor** the **average citizen likes** this exhibit.
Indefinite pronoun A singular pronoun takes a singular verb; a plural pronoun takes a plural verb. Some pronouns can be singular or plural.	**Everyone admires** this masterpiece. **Few understand** it. **Some** of the paint **is** peeling. **Some** of the critics **want** the museum to restore it.
Collective noun Use a singular verb if it refers to a whole, a plural verb if it refers to individuals.	The **staff selects** the paintings. The **staff are arguing** among themselves.
Singular noun ending in s Use a singular verb.	**Politics is** an art.
Title or expression of amount Use a singular verb.	**Three ounces** of gold **was** used in the sculpture.

CHAPTER 9

Other Agreement Problems

Slippery Subjects

Predicate noun Make sure the verb agrees with the subject.	**Animals** **are** the subject of his photo series. The **subject** of his photo series **is** animals.
Question Change the question to a statement to find the subject.	(**Is, are**) the tapestries on the wall? The **tapestries** **are** on the wall.
Statement in which subject follows verb Turn the sentence parts around before deciding on a verb form.	Here (**is, are**) the expressionist paintings. The expressionist **paintings** **are** here. Beneath each painting (**is, are**) a title and a date. A **title** and a **date** **are** beneath each painting.

S-V AGREEMENT

The Bottom Line

Checklist for Subject-Verb Agreement

Have I . . .

____ used singular verbs with singular subjects?

____ used plural verbs with plural subjects?

____ made the first helping verbs in verb phrases agree with the verbs' subjects?

____ used plural verbs with compound subjects containing *and?*

____ made verbs agree with the closest parts of compound subjects containing *or* or *nor?*

____ used correct verb forms with indefinite-pronoun subjects?

____ used singular verbs to agree with titles and some numerical expressions?

____ used verbs that agree with subjects in unusual positions?

Chapter 10

Capitalization

Theme: Let the Games Begin!

Here's the Ticket

Congratulations! You are one of the lucky spectators who has a ticket to the opening ceremony of the Olympic Games. What is the date and the time of the ceremony? Where is it scheduled to take place? On the ticket above, capitalized words such as *July* and *Congress Center* provide you with the answers. We use capitalization as a way to make certain words—such as names, titles, and dates—stand out from others.

Write Away: Olympic Favorites

Write a paragraph describing your favorite Olympic event or competitor. Save the paragraph in your **Working Portfolio.**

Diagnostic Test: What Do You Know?

For each underlined passage, choose the letter of the correct revision.

Baron Pierre de coubertin (1), a french educator (2), was responsible for creating the modern Olympic Games. He (3) thought that an International sports (4) competition would promote World peace (5). According to Dave Anderson in *The story of the Olympics,* (6) Coubertin said, "The revival of the Olympic Games will bring athletism to a high state of perfection."

The first modern Olympic Games took place in 1896 in athens, Greece (7). This site was East (8) of the place where the ancient Olympics had been held. The track-and-field events were held at the Panathenaic stadium (9). The Games (10) were a huge success and set the groundwork for many more Olympic competitions.

1. A. baron
   B. pierre
   C. Coubertin
   D. Correct as is

2. A. French
   B. Educator
   C. A
   D. Correct as is

3. A. olympic
   B. games
   C. he
   D. Correct as is

4. A. International Sports
   B. international sports
   C. international Sports
   D. Correct as is

5. A. World Peace
   B. world Peace
   C. world peace
   D. Correct as is

6. A. *the*
   B. *Story*
   C. *olympics*
   D. Correct as is

7. A. athens, greece
   B. Athens, Greece
   C. Athens, greece
   D. Correct as is

8. A. This site was east
   B. this site was east
   C. this site was East
   D. Correct as is

9. A. panathenaic stadium
   B. panathenaic Stadium
   C. Panathenaic Stadium
   D. Correct as is

10. A. the Games
    B. the games
    C. The games
    D. Correct as is

People and Cultures

Here's the Idea

Names and Initials

▶ **Capitalize people's names and initials.**

Michelle **K**wan **J**ackie **J**oyner-**K**ersee

Robert **D.** **B**allard **W. P.** **K**insella

Personal Titles and Abbreviations

▶ **Capitalize titles and abbreviations of titles that are used before names or in direct address.**

Mr. Carl Lewis **D**r. Dot Richardson

General Colin Powell **M**s. Jenny Thompson

Did you write a book about the Olympics, **P**rofessor?

Capitalize abbreviations of some titles when they follow a name.

Todd Owens, **J**r. Sylvester Fine, **D.D.S.**

Mary Mueller, **Ph**.**D.**

▶ **Capitalize titles of heads of state, royalty, or nobility only when they are used before persons' names or in place of persons' names.**

Baron Pierre de Coubertin **D**ame Judi Dench

Attorney **G**eneral Janet Reno **E**mperor Hirohito

Do not capitalize these titles when they are used without proper names or after names.

We saw the **q**ueen sitting in the royal box.

Family Relationships

▶ **Capitalize words indicating family relationships only when they are used as names or before names.**

Aunt Carla Cousin Maggie Grandpa Johnson

Both Dad and Uncle Ray love to watch the Olympics on TV.

In general, do **not** capitalize a family-relationship word when it follows a person's name or is used without a proper name.

Lisa Fernandez, my cousin, will compete in the next Olympiad.

The Pronoun *I*

▶ **Always capitalize the pronoun *I*.**

Jo and I learned how to play softball from my cousin.

CAPITALIZATION

Religious Terms

▶ **Capitalize the names of religions, sacred days, sacred writings, and deities.**

Religious Terms	
Religions	Christianity, Buddhism, Islam
Sacred days	Ramadan, Easter, Yom Kippur
Sacred writings	Koran, Torah, Bible
Deities	God, Yahweh, Allah

Do not capitalize the words *god* and *goddess* when they refer to gods of ancient mythology.

The ancient Olympic Games honored the Greek god Zeus.

Nationalities, Languages, and Races

▶ **Capitalize the names of nationalities, languages, races, and most ethnic groups, as well as adjectives formed from these names.**

Kurds	**N**ative **A**merican	**F**rench
Hispanic	**A**frican **A**merican	**K**orean

2 Practice and Apply

CONCEPT CHECK: People and Cultures

Write the 15 words and abbreviations that should be capitalized but are not in the paragraph below. Capitalize each correctly.

An Olympic Legend

(1) When I was in sixth grade, my class studied the history of the ancient Olympic Games. **(2)** My teacher, mr. jones, assigned the books *The Olympic Games* by Theodore knight and *Olympic Games in Ancient Greece* by Shirley glubok and Alfred tamarin. **(3)** Knight tells of a legendary event that is considered the start of the first Olympics. **(4)** According to legend, king oenomaus offered princess hippodamia's hand in matrimony to the man who could find her and escape in a chariot while being pursued by the king. **(5)** After 13 men failed in their attempt to defeat oenomaus, prince pelops determined he would beat the king. **(6)** Somehow while pelops escaped with the princess, the axle in the king's chariot broke. **(7)** Pelops defeated the king and married hippodamia. **(8)** To celebrate his victory, the prince ordered a feast and gave thanks to the god zeus.

➜ **For a SELF-CHECK and more practice, see the EXERCISE BANK, p. 339.**

CHAPTER 10

 First Words and Titles

1 Here's the Idea

Sentences and Poetry

Capitalize the first word of every sentence.

Baseball comes from an English sport called rounders.

In traditional poetry capitalize the first word of every line.

LITERARY MODEL

It looked extremely rocky for the Mudville nine that day;
The score stood two to four, with but an inning left to play.
—Ernest Lawrence Thayer, "Casey at the Bat"

Modern poets sometimes choose not to begin the lines of their poems with capital letters. If you make this choice in your own writing, make sure the meaning of your work is still clear.

Quotations

Capitalize the first word of a direct quotation presented as a complete sentence.

Yogi Berra once asked a player, "How can you think and hit at the same time?"

Babe Ruth once stated that even if a team has "the greatest bunch of individual stars in the world," it won't succeed unless the players play as a team.

In a divided quotation, do not capitalize the first word of the second part unless it starts a new sentence.

"Don't worry," said Nina. "There's always next season."

"Yes," said Fred, "but with us it's always spring training."

CAPITALIZATION

Outlines

Capitalize the first word of each entry in an outline and the letters that introduce major subsections.

I. **T**raditional games
   A. **G**ames played in teams
      1. **B**aseball
      2. **F**ootball
      3. **S**occer
II. **E**xtreme games
   A. **A**ir games
      1. **S**kydiving
      2. **W**indsurfing

Parts of a Letter

Capitalize the first word in the greeting and in the closing of a letter.

Dear Miss Ulasovich:

Yours truly,

CHAPTER 10

Titles of Works

Capitalize the first word, the last word, and all other important words in a title. Don't capitalize articles, coordinating conjunctions, or prepositions of fewer than five letters.

Type of Media	Examples
Books	*The Giver, The Call of the Wild*
Plays and musicals	*Bleacher Bums, Les Misérables*
Short stories	"The **N**oble **E**xperiment," "**T**hank **Y**ou, **M**'am"
Poems	"The **B**at," "**O**de to an **A**rtichoke"
Periodicals	*Sports Illustrated, Teen People*
Musical compositions	"Take **M**e **O**ut to the **B**all **G**ame," "**L**a **B**amba"
Movies	*Hoop Dreams, The Natural*
Television shows	*Weekend Sports, Boy Meets World*
Works of art	*American Gothic, Mona Lisa, The Thinker*

❷ Practice and Apply

A. CONCEPT CHECK: First Words and Titles

Write the words that should be capitalized but are not in these sentences. Capitalize each correctly.

Baseball—America's National Pastime

1. An outline for the game of baseball might begin like this:
I. how the game is played
  A. equipment
    1. baseball
    2. bat

2. A famous scholar and educator, Jacques Barzun, once wrote, "whoever wants to know the heart and mind of America had better learn baseball."

3. There are many movies about baseball, including *field of dreams*.

4. This movie was based on W. P. Kinsella's book *shoeless joe.*

5. Another enormously popular baseball film is *the natural*.

6. The last line of the poem "casey at the bat" is familiar to many people.

7. It runs, "but there is no joy in Mudville: Mighty Casey has struck out."

8. A letter written by a child to his or her favorite home-run hitter might begin "dear mr. Sosa."

9. The closing of the letter might consist of a phrase such as "sincerely yours."

10. Finally, let us not forget this memorable quote by the New York Mets manager Yogi Berra: "it's never over till it's over."

→ **For a SELF-CHECK and more practice, see the EXERCISE BANK, p. 339**

B. WRITING: The Name Game

Identify your favorite short story, magazine, song, movie, and television show. Then for each choice, write a sentence explaining why it's your favorite. Remember to capitalize titles.

CAPITALIZATION

Mixed Review

A. Capitalization in Outlining Rewrite the following portion of an outline, correcting the nine words that should be capitalized.

I. indoor games
   A. board games
   B. word and picture games
      1. charades
      2. twenty questions
II. outdoor games
   A. ball games
      1. baseball
      2. soccer

B. Capitalization in a Business Letter Rewrite the following business letter, correcting the 15 items that should be capitalized.

1399 Maple Street
Wilmette, Illinois 60091
January 2, 2000

Mr. Dominic d. Domenicas, sr.
The Domino Company
333 Congress Parkway
Highland Heights, Ohio 44143

dear mr. domenicas:

I am writing about the set of dominoes made by your company that i recently purchased. unfortunately, my set is incomplete, containing only 27 dominoes rather than the usual 28. since your picture is shown on the box, with the words underneath it stating "your satisfaction is guaranteed or your money will be promptly refunded," i am writing directly to you.

My uncle david and i are very eager to try out the new dominoes. Please let me know what your company can do to correct this matter.

sincerely yours,
Gabe zaharias
Gabe zaharias

CHAPTER 10

LESSON 3 Places and Transportation

1 Here's the Idea

Geographical Names

In geographical names, capitalize each word except articles and prepositions.

Geographical Names	
Divisions of the world	Northern Hemisphere, Arctic Circle
Continents	Africa, North America, Australia
Bodies of water	Lake Erie, Pacific Ocean, Nile River
Islands	Oahu, Philippines, Aleutian Islands
Mountains	Rocky Mountains, Mount Hood, Andes
Other landforms	Niagara Falls, Cape Horn, Gobi Desert
Regions	Latin America, Southeast Asia, Gulf of Mexico
Nations	Monaco, Peru, Canada, Czech Republic
States	Texas, California, Florida
Cities and towns	Chicago, Providence, Olympia
Roads and streets	Pennsylvania Avenue, Interstate 55, Main Street

Bodies of the Universe

Capitalize the names of planets and other specific objects in the universe.

Milky Way   Halley's Comet   Triton

Venus   Alpha Centauri   Pluto

Two moons of Mars were discovered—Phobos and Deimos.

Regions and Sections

Capitalize the words *north, south, east,* and *west* when they name particular regions of the United States or the world or are parts of proper names.

In **S**outh Africa, children use small stones to play a game called *diteko.*

Children who live in the **N**orth might enjoy the snow game known as fox and geese.

Do not capitalize these words when they indicate general directions or locations.

If you go **s**outh on Main Street, you will find Mel's Video Rental.

Buildings, Bridges, and Other Landmarks

CHAPTER 10

Capitalize the names of specific buildings, bridges, monuments, and other landmarks.

World **T**rade **C**enter   **S**tatue of **L**iberty

Golden **G**ate **B**ridge   **V**ietnam **M**emorial

Did you know that **F**ort **S**umter is a national monument?

Planes, Trains, and Other Vehicles

Capitalize the names of specific airplanes, trains, ships, cars, and spacecraft.

Vehicle Names	
Airplanes	*Air Force One, Spirit of St. Louis*
Trains	*Southwest Chief, Orient Express*
Ships	U.S.S. *Arizona, Pinta*
Cars	**M**ustang, **P**relude, **P**athfinder
Spacecraft	*Challenger, Columbia, Apollo V*

2 Practice and Apply

A. CONCEPT CHECK: Places and Transportation

Write the words that should be capitalized but are not in each sentence. Capitalize each correctly.

Just Playing Games

1. Dr. Jane J. Peabody's research for her book took her all over north america.
2. First, she boarded the train called the *cardinal.*
3. In the appalachian mountains she learned about homemade folk games, such as button on a string.
4. Later, in New Orleans, she saw the gulf of mexico for the first time.
5. She rented a Ford taurus for the next leg of her journey.
6. Heading west, she visited the grand canyon.
7. San luis, a town in northern mexico, provided a wealth of information about Native American games, such as *el coyote.*
8. Driving along the Pacific coastline, Dr. Peabody took some time to see the Redwood National forest.
9. She continued north to vancouver, british Columbia, where she observed Canadian children playing games.
10. Dr. Peabody eventually arrived back home in champaign, illinois, with stacks of information to use for her book.

→ **For a SELF-CHECK and more practice, see the EXERCISE BANK, p. 340.**

B. REVISING: Correcting Map Titles

Look at this map of the eastern part of Australia, site of the games of the XXVII Olympiad. Find and correct five capitalization errors.

CAPITALIZATION

Organizations and Other Subjects

1 Here's the Idea

Organizations and Institutions

Capitalize all important words in the names of organizations, institutions, stores, and companies.

Library of Congress — Jefferson Middle School

Harry's Finer Foods — Babe Ruth Baseball League

Historical Events, Periods, and Documents

Capitalize the names of historical events, periods, and documents.

Historical Events, Periods, and Documents	
Events	Civil War, Boston Tea Party, French Revolution
Periods	Great Depression, Bronze Age, Middle Ages
Documents	Bill of Rights, Gettysburg Address, Panama Canal Treaty

Do you have any relatives who were in the Gulf War?

Time Abbreviations and Calendar Items

Capitalize the abbreviations B.C., A.D., A.M., and P.M.

The first recorded Olympic contest took place in 776 B.C.

The volleyball tryouts are at 5:00 P.M. sharp.

Capitalize the names of months, days, and holidays, but not the names of seasons (except when they are part of the names of festivals or celebrations).

April — Saturday — Thanksgiving Day

May — Winter Formal — Fourth of July

This year my birthday, April 7, is on a Sunday.

Memorial Day is the unofficial start of summer.

CHAPTER 10

Special Events, Awards, and Brand Names

▶ **Capitalize the names of special events and awards.**

Heisman **T**rophy **W**orld **C**up

Pulitzer **P**rize **P**an-**A**merican **G**ames

The annual **H**arvest **F**estival is scheduled for next weekend.

▶ **Capitalize the brand name of a product but not a common noun that follows a brand name.**

Spiker volleyballs **E**asy **O**ver hurdles

❷ Practice and Apply

CONCEPT CHECK: Organizations and Other Subjects

Find and correct ten capitalization errors in the school-calendar page below.

north side junior high

september Events

Sunday, Sept. 1	
Monday, Sept. 2:	Labor day
tuesday, Sept. 3:	3:30 P.m. girls' volleyball tryouts
Wednesday, Sept. 4:	Auditions for Thornton Wilder's *Our Town*
Thursday, Sept. 5:	Lions vs. vikings at home football game
Friday, Sept. 6:	District 112 Board of education meeting
Saturday, Sept. 7:	NSJH car wash

Grammar in Physical Education

Making the Most of Capitals

Writing is important in everything—even at sports meets. Although athletes may not write while they're throwing the shot put or sprinting the last 50 meters, they do need to share information about rules, schedules, and events.

The team manager for the Mae Jemison Jets has drafted a reminder memo for the members of his team. Because he was in a rush, he made a few errors in capitalization. Luckily, he had a friend proofread his draft.

Instructions for Round-Robin Track Meet

Where:

South Village Recreation Area, Sauk city

City is a proper noun.

Directions for carpool drivers:

Take Onarga Street west to Route 42. Turn left and go three blocks. (You'll pass Martha's Cafe on the right and a less-for-more gas station on the left.) Park in the section marked with an orange banner.

Less-for-More is a brand name.

When:

wednesday,

October 13, 3:00 P.M.

Wednesday is a proper noun.

What to bring:

bring instruction sheet, track shoes, warm-up suit, and water bottle.

Capitalize the first word in a sentence.

What to do once you get there:

- Go to the area assigned to Mae Jemison junior high.
- Check the schedule.
- do your warm-up exercises.
- Be at the track at least 15 minutes before your race.
- **Relax and do your best!**

Proper noun

For more information, contact michael Warner, 555-3745.

Michael is a proper noun.

CHAPTER 10

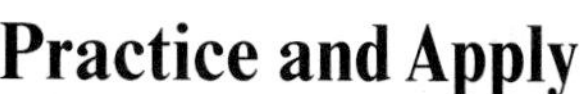

Practice and Apply

Writing: Reporting the Results Use the results in the diagram to write an article about the Jets for your school newspaper. Include the following information in your article:

- when and where the meet was held
- how each team did
- the name of the winning team (You decide.)
- any particularly exciting or unusual events during the meet

Be sure to check your capitalization. Save your paragraph in your **Working Portfolio.**

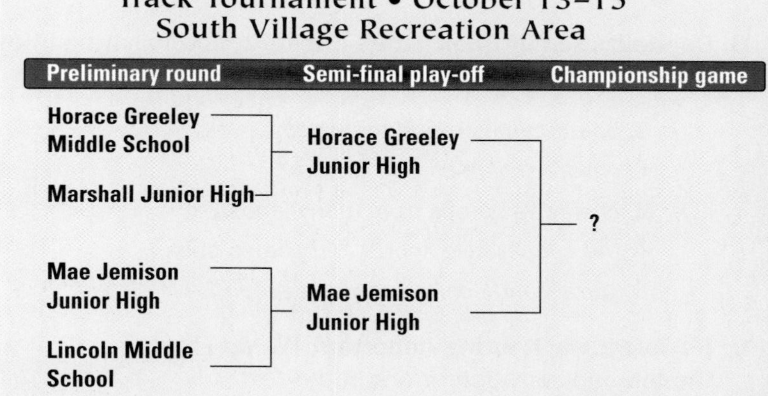

Mixed Review

A. Proofreading: Capitalization Identify and correct the 25 capitalization errors in the following paragraph.

STUDENT MODEL

It takes most people between 10 and 15 minutes to run a mile; only world-class runners can run the mile in less than 4 minutes. On may 6, 1954, in oxford, england, roger bannister broke the 4-minute-mile barrier that many people had failed to surpass. While bannister was a medical student at st. mary's hospital in london, he trained as a runner for britain's amateur athletic association (AAA) team. Bannister's world record of 3 minutes and 59.4 seconds stood for only seven weeks before john landy ran the mile in 3 minutes and 58 seconds in turku, finland. In july 1999 the moroccan runner hicham el guerrouj claimed the world record by running the mile in an astonishing 3 minutes 43:13 seconds in rome, italy.

B. Capitalization of Book Titles Capitalize the following titles of books correctly.

1. *board games round the world*
2. *children's games and rhymes*
3. *children's games from many lands*
4. *the cooperative sports and games book*
5. *games and sports the world around*

C. Revision: Capitalizing Important Words Fix the ten capitalization errors in the text below so that the tickets will be correct when they're printed.

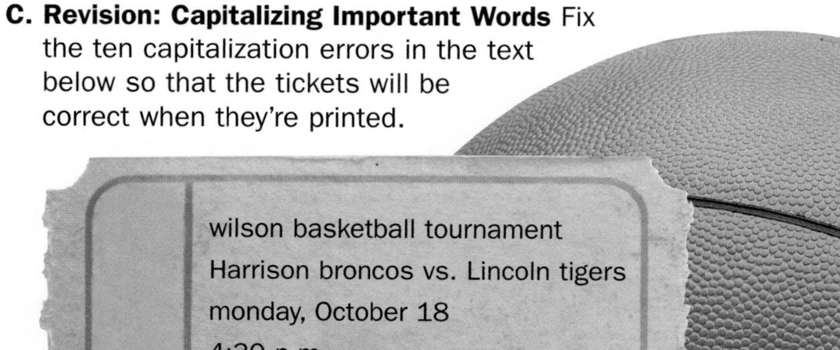

Mastery Test: What Did You Learn?

For each underlined passage, choose the letter of the correct revision.

I received an invitation to a Memorial day party (1) at my friend David corny's house (2). The party was to be on monday, May (3) 27, at 12:30 P.m. The (4) invitation stated that we would be going on a scavenger hunt. I had never before been on a scavenger hunt.

When I got to David's house, his mom, mrs. Corny (5), handed each of us partygoers a list of items that we needed to find during the scavenger hunt. About 20 items were listed, including a native American belt (6), the book *to Kill a Mockingbird* (7), a pink sock, Mr. Suds bubble bath (8), and a roll of candy from the Lions' club (9). Right then and there I knew that we would all be jumping into Mrs. Corny's SUV and driving all over Wisconsin (10) for the rest of our lives to find all of that stuff.

1. A. Day
   B. memorial
   C. Party
   D. Correct as is
2. A. House
   B. david
   C. Corny's
   D. Correct as is
3. A. Monday, May
   B. monday, may
   C. Monday, may
   D. Correct as is
4. A. the
   B. p.m.
   C. P.M.
   D. Correct as is
5. A. Mom
   B. corny
   C. Mrs.
   D. Correct as is
6. A. american
   B. Native
   C. Belt
   D. Correct as is
7. A. *To*
   B. *kill*
   C. *mockingbird*
   D. Correct as is
8. A. mr.
   B. Bubble Bath
   C. suds
   D. Correct as is
9. A. lions'
   B. Club
   C. The
   D. Correct as is
10. A. wisconsin
    B. Suv
    C. suv
    D. Correct as is

CAPITALIZATION

Student Help Desk

Capitalization at a Glance

YOU'RE SAFE!

CHAPTER 10

Do Capitalize

Proper nouns that name particular people, places, or things:

The **F**inn family will visit **S**ydney, **A**ustralia, for the **O**lympic **G**ames.

Family words used with names or in place of names:

Julia watched the hockey game with **U**ncle Tim.

First words of sentences:

Who will win this year's state championship?

First words in lines of traditional poetry:

And somewhere men are laughing, and somewhere children shout,
But there is no joy in Mudville: Mighty Casey has struck out.

—Ernest Lawrence Thayer, "Casey at the Bat"

First words and important words in titles:

__T__he __H__ouse on __M__ango __S__treet

Proper nouns that name particular dates, holidays, events, or awards.

On **J**uly 4, **I**ndependence **D**ay, Gus will compete in the **N**ewport **S**ummer **C**ook-**O**ff.

Don't Capitalize

YOU'RE OUT!

Common nouns referring to people, places, or things:

Our **t**eam is traveling **s**outh through the **d**esert for our next **m**eet.

Family words used as common nouns:

My **c**ousin is the fastest sprinter in the entire state.

First words in lines of some contemporary poems:

the world is not a pleasant place
to be without
someone to hold and be held by

—Nikki Giovanni, "The World Is Not a Pleasant Place to Be"

Articles, conjunctions, and short prepositions in titles:

"Ode **t**o **a**n Artichoke"

Common nouns referring to times, events, or awards:

Jasmine is planning on running the **m**arathon in the **s**pring.

CAPITALIZATION

The Bottom Line

Checklist for Capitalization

Have I capitalized . . .

- ____ people's names and initials?
- ____ personal titles preceding names?
- ____ names of races, languages, and nationalities?
- ____ names of religions and other religious terms?
- ____ names of bodies of the universe?
- ____ names of monuments, bridges, and other landmarks?
- ____ names of particular planes, trains, and other vehicles?
- ____ names of historical events, eras, and documents?
- ____ names of special events, awards, and brands?

Punctuation

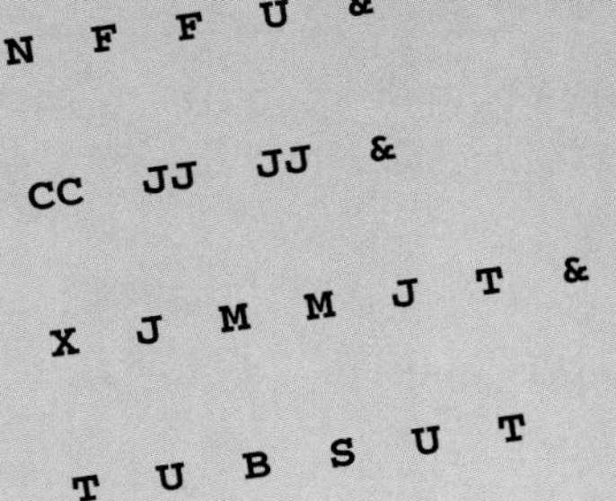

TOP SECRET

SECRET CODE: FOR YOUR EYES ONLY

A=Z	J=I	S=R
B=A	K=J	T=S
C=B	L=K	U=T
D=C	M=L	V=U
E=D	N=M	W=V
F=E	O=N	X=W
G=F	P=O	Y=X
H=G	Q=P	Z=Y
I=H	R=Q	

& = letter space

AA=1	EE=5	II=9
BB=2	FF=6	JJ=0
CC=3	GG=7	
DD=4	HH=8	

Theme: Secret Messages

What's It All About?

You may have figured out the words and numbers in the secret message above, but without punctuation, what do they mean? Are you to meet at 300 Willis Street? Or are you to meet at 3:00 and go to a movie called *Willis*? Maybe the movie starts at 3:00, so you'll need to meet earlier. By now, you see how important punctuation can be!

Write Away: I've Got a Secret

Write a short message to a friend in which you use a simple code of letters, numbers, or nonsense words. Be sure to use punctuation in your message. Keep your message and your code key in your **Working Portfolio.**

Diagnostic Test: What Do You Know?

Choose the letter of the best revision of each underlined item.

Not all secret messages are codes, ciphers are used (1) for secret communication too. A code is a group of words symbols or numbers (2) that has meaning to the receiver. For example, in World War II, the message It is hot in Suez (3) instructed France's (4) resistance to attack railroad lines. In a cipher, by contrast, (5) the letters of a message are scrambled or replaced by other letters or numbers. You could write "I can;t (6) read one half (7) of your cipher" by using a number for each alphabet letter. Would it surprise you that *cipher* comes from a word meaning "to number" (8) Cryptology, the science of code breaking (9) comes from two Greek words meaning "secret wording." To learn more, read "The Secret Code Book" (10) by Helen Huckle.

1. A. codes; ciphers are
   B. codes? Ciphers are
   C. codes! Ciphers are
   D. Correct as is

2. A. words: symbols or numbers
   B. words, symbols or numbers
   C. words, symbols, or numbers
   D. Correct as is

3. A. It is hot in Suez"
   B. "It is hot in Suez"
   C. "It is hot in Suez
   D. Correct as is

4. A. Frances'
   B. Frances
   C. France"s
   D. Correct as is

5. A. In a cipher, by contrast;
   B. In a cipher by contrast,
   C. In a cipher, by contrast
   D. Correct as is

6. A. can,t
   B. can't
   C. cant
   D. Correct as is

7. A. one—half
   B. one-half
   C. one'half
   D. Correct as is

8. A. "to number."
   B. "to number?"
   C. "to number"?
   D. Correct as is

9. A. Cryptology, the science of code breaking,
   B. Cryptology the science of code breaking,
   C. Cryptology; the science of code breaking
   D. Correct as is

10. A. The Secret Code Book
    B. *"The Secret Code Book"*
    C. *The Secret Code Book*
    D. Correct as is

Periods and Other End Marks

Here's the Idea

Periods, question marks, and exclamation points are known as **end marks** because they are used to indicate the end of a sentence. Periods have other uses as well.

Periods

Use a period at the end of a declarative sentence.

A declarative sentence makes a statement.

Our team uses a code to make up plays.

The key is a carefully kept secret.

Use a period at the end of almost every imperative sentence. An imperative sentence gives a command. Some imperative sentences express excitement or emotion and therefore end with exclamation points.

Do not ask me to reveal our code.

Stop! Don't tell the other team!

Use a period at the end of an indirect question. An indirect question reports what a person asked without using the person's exact words.

INDIRECT QUESTION	The coach asked if our team code had been broken.
DIRECT QUESTION	The coach asked, "Has our team code been broken?"

Question Marks

Use a question mark at the end of an interrogative sentence. An interrogative sentence asks a question.

Did the other team break the code?

Have they figured out all our plays?

CHAPTER 11

Exclamation Points

▶ **Use an exclamation point to end an exclamatory sentence.** An exclamatory sentence expresses strong feeling.

What a terrible situation!

▶ **Use an exclamation point after an interjection or any other exclamatory expression.**

Oh! I have an idea!

Wow! Tell us!

Other Uses for Periods

▶ **Use a period at the end of most abbreviations or after an initial.**

Common Abbreviations and Initials

Abbreviations

sec. second	**Thurs.** Thursday	**lb.** pound	**gal.** gallon
min. minute	**Pres.** President	**hr.** hour	**mo.** month
St. Street	**Feb.** February	**yr.** year	**in.** inch

Initials

R.N. registered nurse	**P.M.** *post meridiem* (after noon)
B.A. bachelor of arts	**M.D.** doctor of medicine
P.O. post office	**R.K.S.** Rebecca Kate Simmons

Abbreviations Without Periods

CIA Central Intelligence Agency	**mph** miles per hour
VCR videocassette recorder	**cm** centimeter
CA California	**mm** millimeter

▶ **Use a period after each number or letter in an outline or a list.**

Outline

Uses for Codes
I. Use in wartime
  A. World War I
  B. World War II
II. Industrial uses
  A. To protect new methods
  B. To protect consumers' privacy

List

Communication Codes
1. Braille
2. American Sign Language
3. Egyptian hieroglyphics
4. Mayan hieroglyphics
5. Morse code
6. Semaphore

PUNCTUATION

2 Practice and Apply

A. CONCEPT CHECK: Periods and Other End Marks

Write the proper end mark for each numbered blank below.

Timely Messages

Do you think you are the only one interested in secret writing__1__ Nonsense__2__ For hundreds of years, people have used secret messages__3__ Did you know that the great Roman general Julius Caesar invented a cipher__4__ He used it to communicate with his staff in Rome__5__ Consider also Mary Queen of Scots, who smuggled ciphers out of her household in England__6__ One cipher told of a plot to kill England's queen, Elizabeth I. Poor Mary__7__ Her note was intercepted and read, and she was put to death. During World War II, what do you think the Allies found in sunken German submarines__8__ They found German codebooks. They used the books to decode messages about German naval operations__9__ What do you think happened__10__

→ **For a SELF-CHECK and more practice, see the EXERCISE BANK, p. 341.**

CHAPTER 11

B. WRITING: Punctuating Abbreviations

The notes below were taken by a spy who had forgotten how to punctuate abbreviations. Write the notes, using correct punctuation.

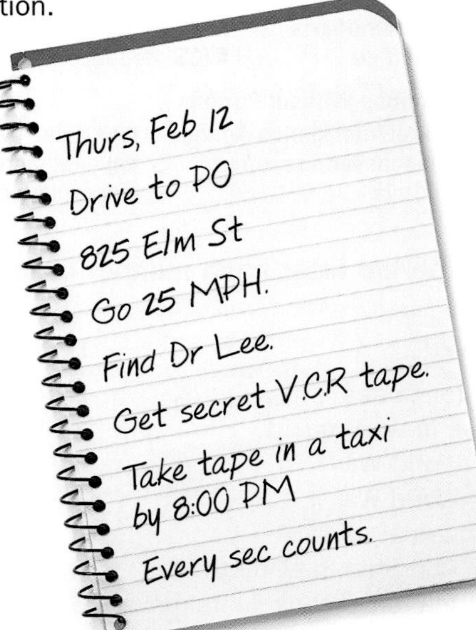

LESSON 2 Commas in Sentences

1 Here's the Idea

Commas are used to make the meanings of sentences clear by separating certain elements of the sentences.

Commas in Compound Sentences

▶ **Use a comma before a conjunction that joins independent clauses in a compound sentence.**

The ancient Egyptians' written language was called hieroglyphics, **and** it was not decoded for many centuries.

In ancient times, scribes could read and write hieroglyphics, **but** most other Egyptians could not.

Scribes passed rigorous examinations, **or** they were rejected as scribes.

WATCH OUT Sometimes a sentence has a two-part compound verb but is not a compound sentence. Do not use a comma in this kind of sentence.

Scribes could **read** and **write** **hieroglyphics.**

PUNCTUATION

Commas with Items in a Series

▶ **Use a comma after every item in a series except the last one.** A series consists of three or more items.

Symbols of **birds**, **lions**, and **snakes** appear in hieroglyphics.

Hieroglyphics could be read **from left to right**, **from right to left**, or **from top to bottom.**

Hieroglyphic writing was used for **business contracts**, **legal documents**, and other **important records.**

▶ **Use a comma between adjectives of equal rank that modify the same noun.**

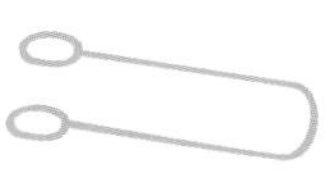

Here's How **Adding Commas Between Adjectives**

To decide whether a comma is needed between two adjectives modifying the same noun, try one of the following tests.

Hieroglyphics used colorful decorative symbols.

1. Place the word *and* between the adjectives.

   Hieroglyphics used colorful and decorative symbols.

2. If the sentence still makes sense, replace *and* with a comma.

   Hieroglyphics used colorful, decorative symbols.

1. **Or** reverse the order of the adjectives.

   Hieroglyphics used decorative and colorful symbols.

2. If the sentence still makes sense, replace *and* with a comma.

   Hieroglyphics used decorative, colorful symbols.

Do not use a comma between adjectives that express a single idea.

The symbols were often painted with brilliant gold paint.

Commas with Introductory Words and Phrases

Use a comma after an introductory phrase that contains a prepositional phrase. Use a comma after introductory words.

Even after 2,000 years of study, no one could read hieroglyphics.

Finally, the Rosetta Stone was found in Egypt.

Commas with Interrupters

Use commas to set off a word or phrase that interrupts the flow of thought in a sentence.

The stone provided**, at long last,** a key to hieroglyphics.

Use commas to set off nouns of direct address. A noun of direct address names the person or group being spoken to.

Alex, your class would be thrilled with this discovery.

Your class**, Alex,** would be thrilled with this discovery.

Commas with Appositives

An **appositive** is a word or phrase that identifies or renames a noun or pronoun that comes right before it. Use commas when the appositive adds extra information; do not use commas when the appositive is needed to make the meaning clear.

Jean Champollion**, a French scholar,** deciphered the Rosetta stone. (The phrase *a French scholar* adds extra information.)

The French scholar **Jean Champollion** deciphered the Rosetta stone. (The phrase *Jean Champollion* tells which French scholar and makes the sentence clear and complete.)

Commas to Avoid Confusion

▶ **Use a comma whenever the reader might otherwise be confused.**

UNCLEAR Before hieroglyphics records were not kept on stone or paper.

CLEAR Before hieroglyphics, records were not kept on stone or paper.

UNCLEAR After we studied hieroglyphics were less mysterious.

CLEAR After we studied, hieroglyphics were less mysterious.

PUNCTUATION

2 Practice and Apply

CONCEPT CHECK: Commas in Sentences

Write the following paragraph, adding commas where they are needed.

A Hairy Story

Think of this readers when you have your next haircut. A Persian king had to get a message to his military leader a Persian general. The king shaved a man's head tattooed a message on his bare scalp and told the man to let the hair grow back. The man then traveled to find the general but no one knew he carried a message. When he reached the general however he delivered his message. Yes as you guessed it he had his head shaved again!

➜ **For a SELF-CHECK and more practice, see the EXERCISE BANK, p. 342.**

Commas: Dates, Addresses, and Letters

CHAPTER 11

1 Here's the Idea

See these rules in action in the letter below.

Commas in Dates, Addresses, and Letters	
Commas in dates	In dates, use a comma between the day and the year. (Use a comma after the year if the sentence continues.)
Commas in addresses	Use a comma between the city or town and the state or country. (Use a comma after the state or country if the sentence continues.)
Commas in letters	Use a comma after the greeting of a casual letter and after the closing of a casual or business letter.

385 Webster Avenue
Hanover, MA 02339
March 26, 2000

Dear Alanna,

Do you remember the code we used to keep secrets from our nosy brothers? Well, some animals have codes too. They understand each other. On February 12, 2000, a scientist from Denver, Colorado, spoke at my school. She told us that bees communicate by the way they move. A bee's dance can tell other bees where to find good flowers for making honey. Isn't that incredible? Come and visit soon.

Your friend,
Regina

Line 2: comma between city and state

Line 3: comma between day and year

Line 4: comma after greeting

Line 9: comma after year

Line 10: comma after state

Line 17: comma after closing

Do not use a comma between the state and the ZIP code.

2 Practice and Apply

A. CONCEPT CHECK: Commas in Dates, Addresses, and Letters

Write the following letter, adding any missing commas.

158 W. 23 Street
New York NY 10010
February 20 2000

Dear Hank

Do you know about Katy Payne? Payne studies elephants in countries like Kenya, Africa. She has found out that elephants' voices are below the human level of hearing! Payne proved this with a special tape recorder. Elephants can call to one another over hundreds of miles. What a terrific hidden code! You could call to me in New York City from Albany New York! Today Katy Payne lives in Ithaca New York where she writes and studies her elephant data. She will speak here on March 19 2000 and I can't wait to hear her.

Take care
Sammy

➜ **For a SELF-CHECK and more practice, see the EXERCISE BANK, p. 342.**

B. WRITING: Dear Friend

Put a letter together, using these parts. Don't forget to add commas where they belong.

210 Oak St.

Hinton IA 51104

May 3 2000

Dear Jon

I'm giving a surprise swimming party for Sara next Friday at the public pool in Moville Iowa. Keep it a secret.

Sincerely

Teresa

PUNCTUATION

Punctuating Quotations

1 Here's the Idea

To punctuate quotations, you need to know where to put quotation marks, commas, and end marks.

Direct Quotations

A direct quotation is a report of a speaker's exact words.

Use quotation marks at the beginning and the ending of a direct quotation.

"Flowers have meaning," said Sophie.

Use commas to set off explanatory words used with direct quotations (whether they occur at the beginning, in the middle, or at the end of the sentences).

Sophie said, "Flowers have meaning."

"Flowers**," said Sophie,** "have meaning."

"Flowers have meaning**," said Sophie.**

If a quotation is a question or an exclamation, place the question mark or exclamation point inside the closing quotation marks.

"What do flowers mean**?"** I asked.

If quoted words are part of a question or exclamation of your own, place the question mark or exclamation point outside the closing quotation marks.

Do flowers tell "secret messages**"?**

Commas and periods always go inside closing quotation marks. They're too little to stay outside.

CHAPTER 11

Indirect Quotations

▶ **Do not use quotation marks to set off an indirect quotation.** An indirect quotation is a restatement, in somewhat different words, of what someone said. An indirect quotation is often introduced by the word *that*. It does not require a comma.

INDIRECT Shakespeare wrote **that** a rose would smell sweet regardless of its name.

DIRECT Shakespeare wrote, "a rose by any other name would smell as sweet."

Divided Quotations

A divided quotation is a direct quotation that is separated into two parts, with explanatory words such as *he said* or *she said* between the parts.

▶ **Use quotation marks to enclose both parts of a divided quotation.**

"A rose," he said, **"means love."**

▶ **Do not capitalize the first word of the second part of a divided quotation unless it begins a new sentence.**

"A rose," he said, **"sometimes** means treachery."

"A rose usually means love," he said. **"Sometimes** it means treachery."

▶ **Use commas to set off the explanatory words used with a divided quotation.**

"A rose **," he summed up,** "can mean treachery or love."

PUNCTUATION

Quotation Marks in Dialogue

In dialogue, a new paragraph and a new set of quotation marks show a change in speakers.

A dialogue is a conversation between two or more speakers.

LITERARY MODEL

"Indeed. That is most interesting. Did the tune, perhaps, go like this?"

The princess hummed a few bars.

"That's it! How did you know?"

"Why, you foolish boy, it was I who put the spell on the garden, to make it come alive when the tune is played or sung."

—Joan Aiken, "The Serial Garden"

CHAPTER 11

Using Quotation Marks

Use this model to review the punctuation in this lesson.

PROFESSIONAL MODEL

Did you know that some call flowers "secret messages"? Sophie told me that each kind of flower means something different.

"What does a rose mean?" I asked.

"It depends on the color," she explained. "In England, a red rose means true love, but a yellow rose suggests that a person has cheated."

"That's a strong message!" I exclaimed. I asked what a man might do if he received a yellow rose from his girlfriend.

"He might send her white violets," said Sophie, "to proclaim his innocence."

—J. Gallagher

Question with quoted words

Indirect quotation

Dialogue

Exclamation

Divided quotation

❷ Practice and Apply

A. CONCEPT CHECK: Quotation Marks

Write the following passage, correcting errors in the use and placement of quotation marks.

The Language of Flowers

"I want to send Megan flowers," Jay said.

"Are you nuts"? asked Dan. "She'll think you like her."

"I do," said Jay, and I want her to know it. Now help me look up in this book which flowers mean what."

Dan agreed that "he would help."

"Look!" said Jay. Irises mean faithfulness and courage."

Dan suggested that "he send pansies," which mean "I'm thinking of you."

"Good," Jay said.

"Geraniums," said Dan, "mean happiness".

Jay decided "he had enough ideas.

➜ **For a SELF-CHECK and more practice, see the EXERCISE BANK, p. 343.**

B. EDITING: Speaking Indirectly

Write as well as Shakespeare. Make these quotations your own by changing them into indirect quotations.

Example: We asked, "Did Shakespeare study flowers?"
Answer: We asked whether Shakespeare studied flowers.

1. Our teacher said, "Shakespeare knew the language of flowers."
2. In *Hamlet,* he has Ophelia say, "There's rosemary, that's for remembrance."
3. Oberon says "I know a bank where the wild thyme blows."
4. "Thyme meant sweetness," according to *The Book of Flowers and Herbs.*
5. A historian tells us, "Shakespeare's audience knew the meanings of the flowers he mentioned."

Semicolons and Colons

1 Here's the Idea

A **semicolon** indicates a break in a sentence. It is stronger than a comma but not as strong as a period. A **colon** indicates an abrupt break. A colon indicates that a list follows. Colons are also used after greetings in business letters and in expressions of time.

Semicolons in Compound Sentences

Use a semicolon to join parts of a compound sentence without a coordinating conjunction.

Enslaved people sang songs with secret messages; the songs told listeners how to escape.

Use a semicolon between the parts of a compound sentence when the clauses are long and complicated or when they contain commas.

Runaways navigated by the stars; and they lived off the land, slept outdoors, and walked hundreds of miles to freedom.

Semicolons with Items in a Series

When there are commas within parts of a series, use semicolons to separate the parts.

The travelers took clues from songs, such as a song about the stars; from quilts, which had special coded designs; and from other people along the way.

Colons

Use a colon to introduce a list of items.

An escapee carried few items: a knife, a flint, and a warm cloak.

Avoid using a colon directly after a verb or a preposition.

INCORRECT The recipients are: Joe, Sam, and Rita.
INCORRECT Send this message to: Joe, Sam, and Rita.
CORRECT Send this message to the following people: Joe, Sam, and Rita.

Use a colon after the formal greeting in a business letter.

Dear Ms. Smith: Dear Sir:

Use a colon between numerals indicating hours and minutes in expressions of time.

Meet me at 8:00 P.M. We'll send the message at 8:30.

2 Practice and Apply

A. CONCEPT CHECK: Semicolons and Colons

Write the following paragraphs, correcting errors in the use of semicolons and colons.

Walking the Underground Railroad

Here are two ways conductors on the Underground Railroad hid messages; in songs and in quilts. "The Drinking Gourd," for example, sounded like a folk song, however, it was a map to freedom. The "gourd" was actually the constellation known as the Big Dipper, it points to the North Star. The lyrics of the song told slaves how to head north; to the free states. The quilts were signal flags, travelers would see them and know where to go. The following quilt designs carried directions; the Bear's Paw, which told people to follow bear tracks in the mountains, the Crossroads, which said to head to Cleveland, Ohio; and the Flying Geese; which said to follow geese to water. Unlike real trains, which might leave at a specific time, say 730 P.M., the "freedom trains" left: anytime after dark.

→ For a SELF-CHECK and more practice, see the EXERCISE BANK, p. 343

B. WRITING: All Business

Write a short business letter to the catalog company in this advertisement, ordering a list of items you would need to make a signal quilt. Choose from the items in the ad. Model your letter on the sample business letter in the Model Bank on page 624.

Hyphens, Dashes, and Parentheses

1 Here's the Idea

Hyphens, dashes, and parentheses help make your writing clear by separating or setting off words or parts of words.

Hyphens

Use a hyphen if part of a word must be carried over from one line to the next.

1. The word must have at least two syllables to be broken.
   RIGHT: num - ber   WRONG: co - de
2. Separate the word between syllables.
   RIGHT: let - ter   WRONG: lette - r
3. You must leave at least two letters on each line.
   RIGHT: twen - ty   WRONG: a - cross

Use hyphens in certain compound words.

half-dollar   great-grandmother

Use hyphens in compound numbers from twenty-one through ninety-nine.

sixty-three   twenty-six

Use hyphens in spelled-out fractions.

two-thirds   three-fourths

Dashes

Use dashes to show an abrupt break in thought.

Louis Braille—who lost his sight at age three—invented an alphabet for blind people.

Parentheses

Use parentheses to set off material that is loosely related to the rest of a sentence.

Each six-dot cell stands for a character (a letter of the alphabet, a number, a punctuation mark, or a contraction).

CHAPTER 11

❷ Practice and Apply

CONCEPT CHECK: Hyphens, Dashes, and Parentheses

Read the following paragraph. Then indicate what punctuation mark—hyphen, dash, or parenthesis—is needed in each numbered blank. If no mark is needed, write *None.*

Braille's Brainstorm

Louis Braille was born in a small town in France nearly two hundred years ago. At age three, he was accidentally blinded. He learned to find his way around by tapping with a cane __(1)__ the sound told him where it was safe to step. Ten __(2)__year-old Louis went to the National Institute for Blind Youth in Paris. He had heard the school had a library full of books __(3)__ he could read __(4)__ but it had only a few. The letters in the books were embossed __(5)__ so the books were large, bulky, and very expensive to produce).

As a student, Louis met Charles Barbier (a retired army captain __(6)__. Barbier had invented a "night-writing" system __(7)__ involving dots and dashes punched into cardboard—that let soldiers write and read orders in the dark. Louis spent the next several years simplifying Barbier's system and __(8)__ another twenty __(9)__ seven years fighting to get the Braille alphabet adopted. He died at the relatively young age of forty __(10)__ three.

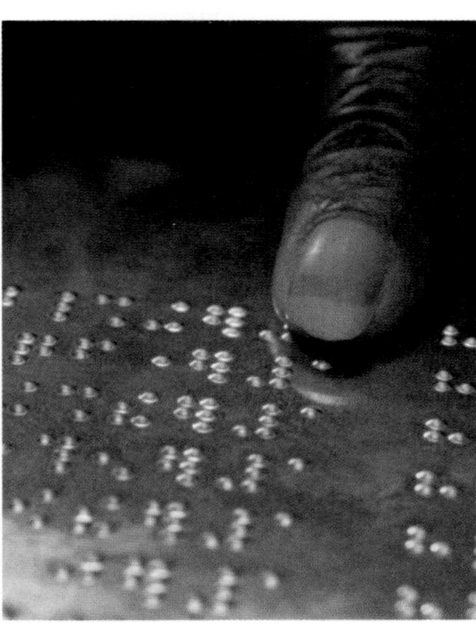

A person reading braille.

→ **For a SELF-CHECK and more practice, see the EXERCISE BANK, p. 344.**

LESSON 7

Apostrophes

1 Here's the Idea

Apostrophes are used in possessive nouns, contractions, and some plurals.

Apostrophes in Possessives

Use an apostrophe to form the possessive of any noun, whether singular or plural.

For a singular noun, add 's even if the word ends in s.

Becky's bike   Louis's alphabet

For plural nouns that end in s, add only an apostrophe.

the girls' code   the pioneers' messages

For plural nouns that do not end in s, add 's.

the children's code   the people's plan

Apostrophes in Contractions

Use apostrophes in contractions.

In a contraction, words are joined and letters are left out. An apostrophe replaces the letter or letters that are missing.

Commonly Used Contractions

I am → I'm	you are → you're	you will → you'll
she is → she's	they have → they've	it is → it's
cannot → can't	they are → they're	was not → wasn't

Don't confuse contractions with possessive pronouns, which do not contain apostrophes.

Contractions Versus Possessive Pronouns

Contraction	Possessive Pronoun
it's (*it is* or *it has*)	its (belonging to it – *its tail*)
who's (*who is*)	whose (belonging to whom – *whose coat*)
you're (*you are*)	your (belonging to you – *your book*)
they're (*they are*)	their (belonging to them – *their house*)

Apostrophes in Plurals

▶ **Use an apostrophe and *s* to form the plural of a letter, a numeral, or a word referred to as a word.**

Cross your *t* **'s**. The speaker used too many *um* **'s**.

How many 5 **'s** are in the answer?

❷ Practice and Apply

A. CONCEPT CHECK: Apostrophes

Write the paragraph, correcting the errors in the use of apostrophes.

Give Me an *E*

One person's code is anothers challenge. Cryptanalyst's are people who break codes. They're most important clue is how often certain letters and word's appear. In English, *e*s and *t*s occur most often, and *the* is the most common word. Code breakers first goal is to identify these frequently occurring letters. Then theyll start to figure out the words the letters appear in. Once they know what the code uses to mean *e* and *t*, theyre able to find the word *the*. Then they'll know what the code uses for *h*. Its a hard job, but it's rewards are many.

➜ **For a SELF-CHECK and more practice, see the EXERCISE BANK, p. 344.**

B. WRITING: Who or What Owns It?

Break the code by writing the correct possessive phrase for each "coded" message below.

Take the car that belongs to you.

Go to the house owned by Janus.

at the end of the day

for the party that belongs to Marty

Bring the gift belonging to the class.

Punctuating Titles

1 Here's the Idea

Use quotation marks and italics correctly in titles to show what kind of work or selection you are writing about.

Quotation Marks

Use quotation marks to set off the titles of short works.

Quotation Marks for Titles	
Book chapter	"Dirk the Protector" from *My Life in Dog Years*
Story	"The Richer, the Poorer"
Essay	"Names/ Nombres"
Article	"Primal Compassion"
Song	"Row, Row, Row Your Boat"
Poem	"I Might, I May, I Must"

CHAPTER 11

Italics and Underlining

In handwriting, you show that something should be in italic type by **underlining** it.

Use italics for titles of longer works and for the names of ships, trains, spacecraft, and airplanes (but not for types of planes). Show that they should be in italic type by underlining them.

Italics or Underlines for Titles			
Book	*The Phantom Tollbooth*	**Epic poem (book length)**	*Beowulf*
Play	*Rent*	**Painting**	*Mona Lisa*
Magazine	*Spin*	**Ship**	*Titanic*
Movie	*Star Wars*	**Train**	*Broadway Limited*
TV series	*60 Minutes*	**Spacecraft**	*Voyager 1*
Long musical composition or CD	*Surfacing*	**Airplane (specific plane, not type)**	*Spirit of St. Louis* (but not DC-10)

❷ Practice and Apply

A. CONCEPT CHECK: Punctuating Titles

Write the titles in the following paragraph correctly by using quotation marks or underlines.

Surrounded by Codes and Ciphers

The first book on secret writing, or cryptography, was Polygraphia, written in 1499. Today there are several magazines on the subject, including The Journal of Cryptology. An article titled New Directions in Cryptography was published not long ago. When Russians captured the German ship Magdeburg during World War I, they found a German naval codebook. To learn how to create and break codes, read the book Codes and Secret Writing by Herbert S. Zim. The hero of Edgar Allan Poe's short story The Gold Bug finds a cipher that directs him to pirate treasure. The old TV series The Avengers had plots dealing with secret codes; the recent movie The Avengers did not. Even some songs, such as the 1970 single Knock Three Times, have referred to codes. Some paintings such as Paul Klee's *Garden Signs* have symbols that may seem to be codes.

Garden Signs by Paul Klee

➜ **For a SELF-CHECK and more practice, see the EXERCISE BANK, p. 345.**

B. WRITING: Favorite Titles

Write down the titles of your favorite book, poem, movie, TV show, and song. Then, with a partner, take turns giving clues about each other's favorite titles and write down your guesses. Be sure to use underlines and quotation marks correctly.

Grammar in Literature

Punctuation and Poetry

Without punctuation, poetry may seem like it's written in a secret code. The first word of every line is often capitalized and sentences may not end at the end of a line. For these reasons, punctuation marks are especially important in helping you understand and enjoy reading poetry—and writing it too.

by Ted Hughes

The goofy Moose, the walking house-frame
Is lost
In the forest. He bumps, he blunders, he stands.

With massy bony thoughts sticking out near his ears—
Reaching out palm upwards, to catch whatever might be
falling from heaven—
He tries to think,
Leaning their huge weight
On the lectern of his front legs.

He can't find the world!
Where did it go? What does a world look like?
The Moose
Crashes on, and crashes into a lake, and stares at the
mountain and cries
"Where do I belong? This is no place!"

He turns and drags half the lake out after him
And charges the cackling underbrush—

He meets another Moose.
He stares, he thinks "It's only a mirror!"

"Where is the world?" he groans, "O my lost world!
And why am I so ugly?
And why am I so far away from my feet?"

He weeps.
Hopeless drops drip from his droopy lips.

The other Moose just stands there doing the same.

Two dopes of the deep woods.

Missing periods indicate that sentences continue.

Quotation marks indicate the moose's exact thoughts.

A dash tells you that the sentence runs into the next stanza.

Here, the author deliberately uses a sentence fragment.

Practice and Apply

Using Punctuation in Poetry

Write your own poem about one of the strange animals in the pictures. Your poem can stress the humor of the animal's appearance as the model does. It could describe a viewer's response to the animal or the animal's response to the viewer. Even more exciting would be to present two animals reacting to one another. Be sure to use correct punctuation to help readers understand and appreciate your verse. Save your poem in your **Working Portfolio.**

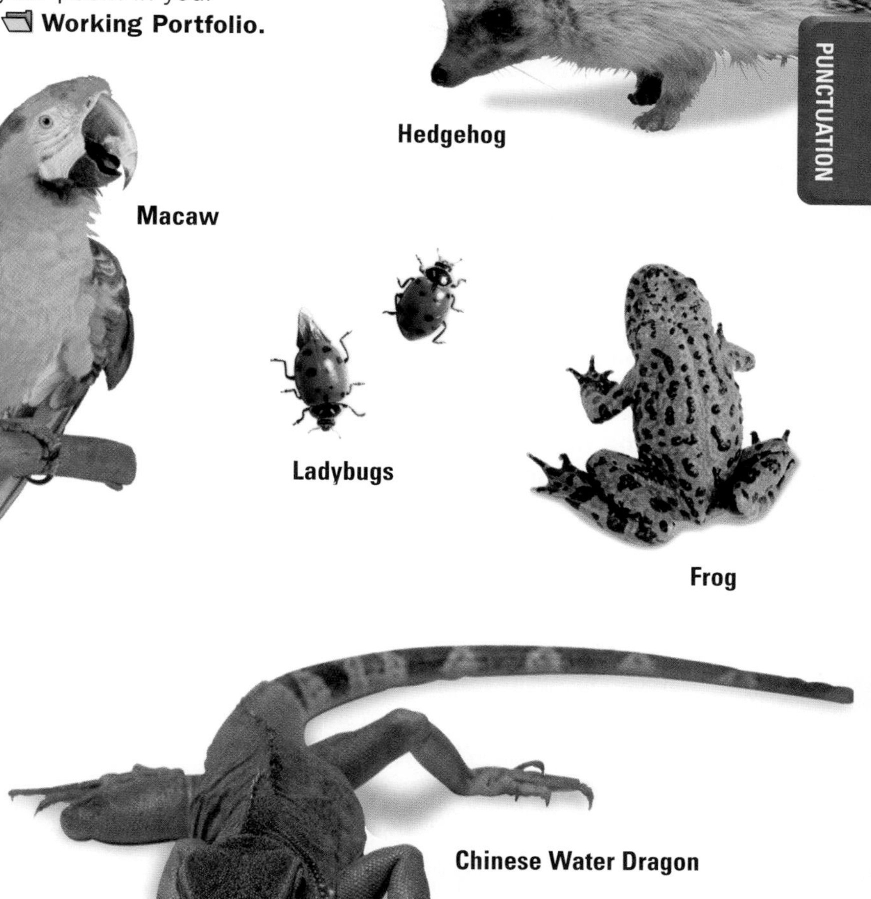

Hedgehog

Macaw

Ladybugs

Frog

Chinese Water Dragon

Mixed Review

A. Proofreading Rewrite the passage below, adding any missing punctuation.

The Secret of the Navajo Code Talkers

During World War II the United States was looking for ways to ensure that its secret messages could not be decoded by the enemy. Philip Johnston who had grown up on the Navajo Indian Reservation and had become fluent in the Navajo language suggested recruiting Navajo soldiers to speak their native language. The language had no written form or alphabet very few people spoke it.

Navajo code talkers Preston Toledo and Frank Toledo

More than 400 Navajos went to the South Pacific. There they sent and received messages in an unbreakable code, their native tongue. They took part in all the Marines assaults on Pacific islands, from Guadalcanal in 1942 to Okinawa in 1945. Japans surrender occurred on August 14 1945.

"When I was going to boarding school, exclaimed code talker Teddy Draper Sr., "the U S government told us not to speak Navajo but during the war, they *wanted* us to speak it!

In 1969 nearly twenty five years after World War II had ended), the code talkers were nationally recognized. A book called *Warriors: Navajo Code Talkers* tells their story.

B. Revising Read the passage below. Then rewrite the passage, putting the punctuation marks where they belong. Add paragraph breaks. Then see if you can add one mark that is not given.

PROFESSIONAL MODEL

Punctuation 'R Easy

Hi Mr Johnson exclaimed Bob Where do you want me to put these punctuation marks Oh just stick them there at the end of the following sentence answered Mr Johnson OK said Bob ".!"."?"",,".."!".

—Dave Barry, *Dave Barry Is Not Making This Up*

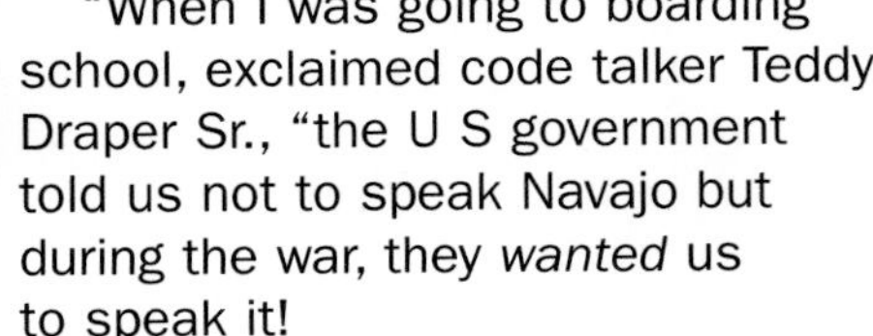

Mastery Test: What Did You Learn?

Choose the letter of the best revision of each underlined item.

People sometimes joke that the initials for the National Security Agency—NSA—(1) stand for Never Say Anything. Its (2) not really a joke, though. The NSA is the largest; most hidden (3) intelligence organization in the United States. Those who work for it must learn to keep quiet about what they do, how they do it and (4) what they learn. The NSA constructs and oversees all the codes used by US (5) intelligence services. Of course— (6) the agency also is involved in decoding other countries (7) messages. I can hear you saying, This is the job for me! (8) But the NSA hires only one of every six people who apply, (9) competition is very tough. However, if you study science or engineering, you could be considered. Do you still want a job as a code maker or a code breaker. (10)

1. A. Agency, NSA—
   B. Agency—NSA;
   C. Agency NSA—
   D. Correct as is

2. A. Its'
   B. It's
   C. It(s)
   D. Correct as is

3. A. largest: most hidden
   B. largest most hidden
   C. largest, most hidden
   D. Correct as is

4. A. do, how they do it, and
   B. do; how they do it; and
   C. do: how they do it, and
   D. Correct as is

5. A. U-S
   B. U,S,
   C. U.S.
   D. Correct as is

6. A. Of course;
   B. Of course
   C. Of course,
   D. Correct as is

7. A. countries'
   B. countrie's
   C. countries's
   D. Correct as is

8. A. This is the job for me!"
   B. "This is the job for me!"
   C. "This is the job for me!
   D. Correct as is

9. A. apply
   B. apply:
   C. apply;
   D. Correct as is

10. A. code breaker!
    B. code breaker?
    C. code breaker—
    D. Correct as is

Student Help Desk

Punctuation at a Glance

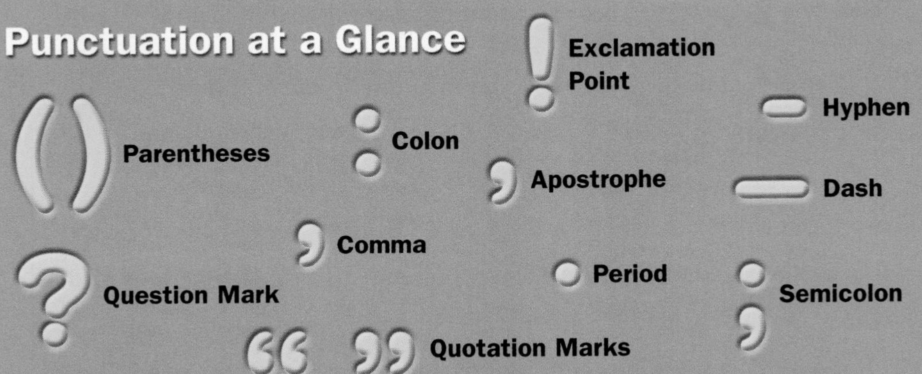

Punctuating Titles

Italics Versus "Quotation Marks"

Italics (longer works)

Books, Movies, Magazines, Plays, TV series, Paintings, Long musical works, Epic poems

Quotation Marks (shorter works)

Stories, Essays, Songs, Poems, Book chapters, Episodes in a TV series, Magazine articles

Punctuation with Commas

	Use commas. . .	Examples
Items in a series	to separate items in a series	secrets, messages, and codes
Introductory words	after introductory words	Believe me, you must try.
Interrupters	to set off interrupters	It is, of course, your decision.
Nouns of direct address	to set off nouns of direct address	Are you, Jenny, prepared to try?

Punctuation with Quotation Marks

The Inside Report

Always Inside	(no matter what)
Period	Sly said, "We'll break their code."
Comma	"We'll learn their secrets," said Guy.
Sometimes Inside	(if they punctuate the quoted words)
Question mark	"What's the secret word?" asked Jack.
Exclamation point	"What a horrible shock!" cried the spy.
Sometimes Outside	(if they punctuate a sentence containing quoted words)
Question mark	Did you tell Jack to read "The Spy Who Cried"?
Exclamation point	I hated the story "Three Spies and Me"!

PUNCTUATION

The Bottom Line

Checklist for Punctuation

Have I . . .

____ ended every sentence with an appropriate end mark?

____ used commas before the conjunctions in compound sentences?

____ used commas to separate items in a series?

____ used commas correctly in dates, addresses, and letters?

____ used quotation marks before and after a speaker's words?

____ used a semicolon instead of a conjunction in long compound sentences?

____ used apostrophes to form contractions and possessives?

____ used italics and quotation marks correctly for titles?

Diagramming: Sentence Parts

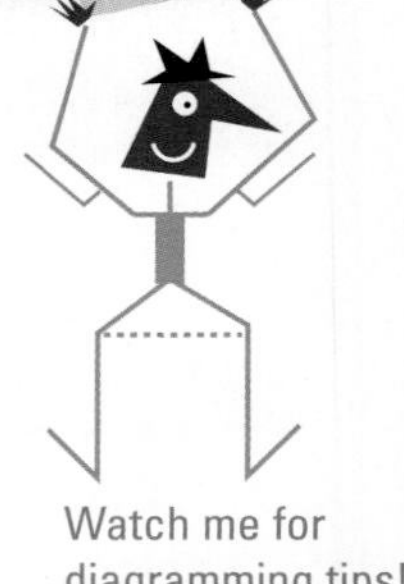

Watch me for diagramming tips!

Here's the Idea

Diagramming is a way of showing the structure of a sentence. Drawing a diagram can help you see how the parts of a sentence work together to form a complete thought.

Simple Subjects and Verbs

Write the simple subject and verb on one line. Separate them with a vertical line that crosses the main line.

Campers hiked.

Campers | hiked

Compound Subjects and Verbs

For a compound subject or verb, split the main line. Put the conjunction on a dotted line connecting the compound parts.

Compound Subject

Campers and counselors hiked.

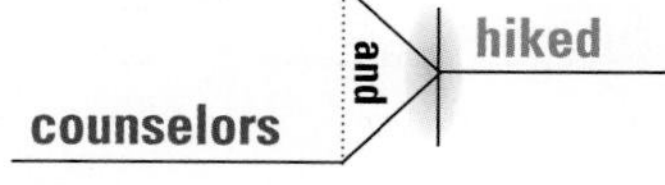

Because there are two subjects, the left side of the main line is split into two parts.

Compound Verb

Campers hiked and chatted.

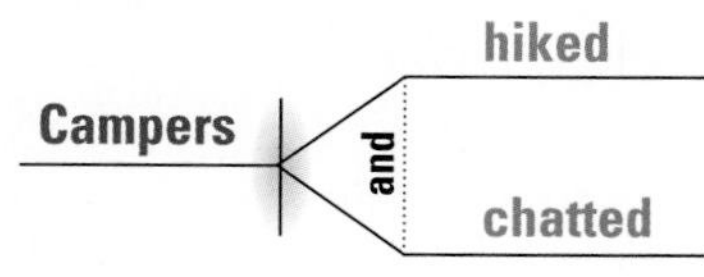

Compound Subject and Compound Verb

Campers and counselors hiked and chatted.

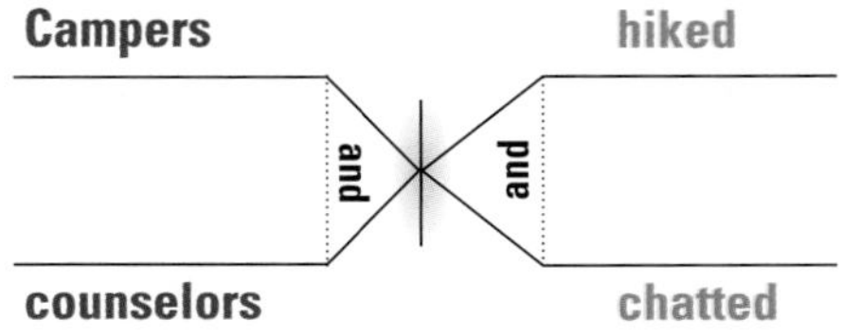

Because there are two subjects and two verbs, both sides of the main line are split into two parts.

A. CONCEPT CHECK: Subjects and Verbs

Diagram these sentences, using what you have learned.

1. Bears appeared.
2. Trees creaked and swayed.
3. Bees and butterflies fluttered and swarmed.

Adjectives and Adverbs

Write adjectives and adverbs on slanted lines below the words they modify.

A steep mountain suddenly loomed ahead.

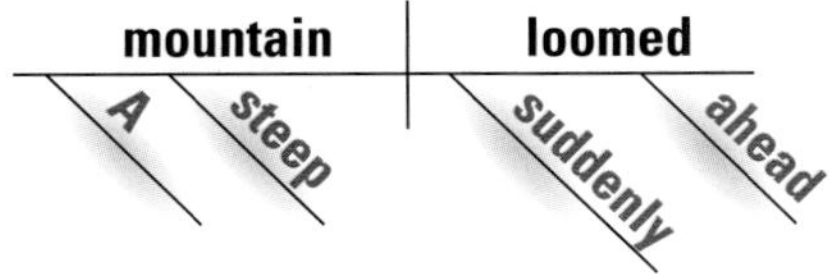

B. CONCEPT CHECK: Adjectives and Adverbs

Diagram these sentences, using what you have learned.

1. Dry, brown leaves rustled constantly.
2. Gloomy, gray clouds floated soundlessly overhead.
3. Sleepy campers rested peacefully.

Subject Complements

- Write a predicate noun or a predicate adjective on the main line after the verb.
- Separate the subject complement from the verb with a slanted line that does not cross the main line.

Predicate Noun

Cave explorers are spelunkers.

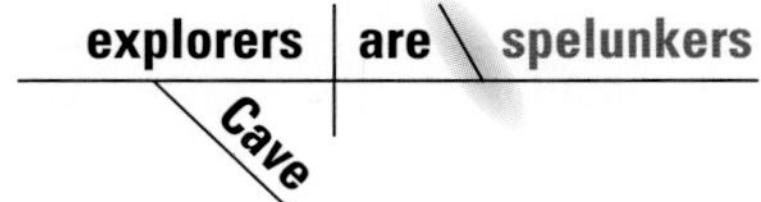

Predicate Adjective

Damp, dark caves can be scary.

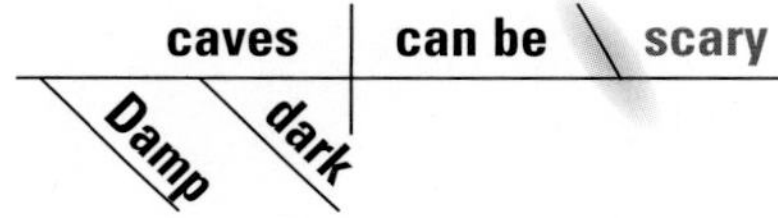

DIAGRAMMING

Direct Objects

A direct object follows the verb on the main line.

Brave spelunkers explore mysterious caves.

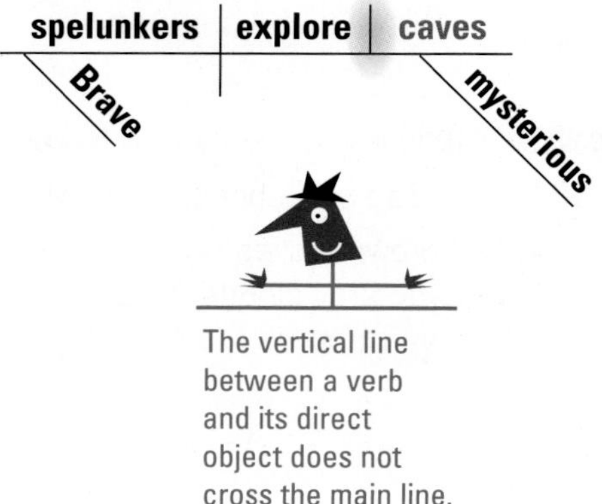

The vertical line between a verb and its direct object does not cross the main line.

Write compound direct objects on parallel lines that branch from the main line.

Cave explorers wear sturdy clothing and hard hats.

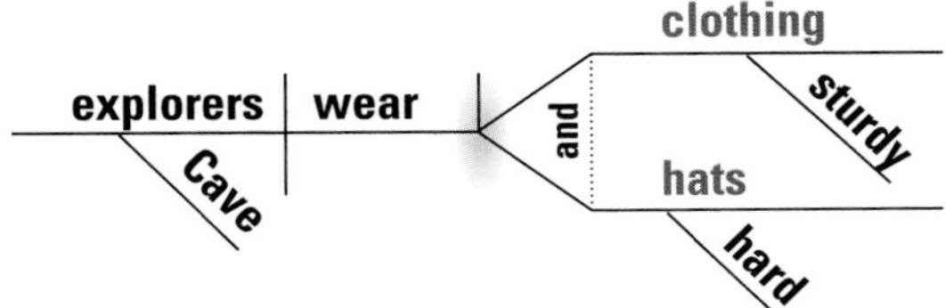

Indirect Objects

Write an indirect object below the verb, on a horizontal line connected to the verb with a slanted line.

Serious explorers give safety their careful consideration.

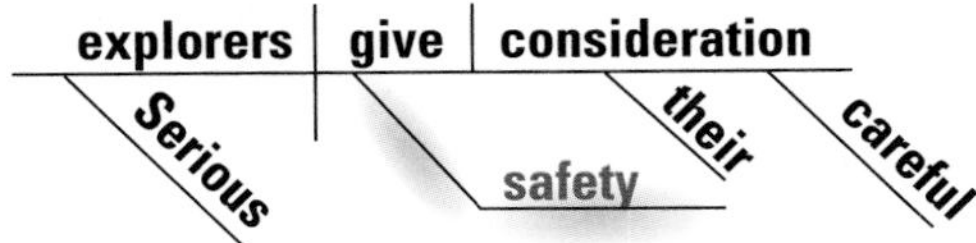

DIAGRAMMING

C. CONCEPT CHECK: Subject Complements and Objects

Diagram these sentences, using what you have learned.

1. Some caves are gigantic.
2. Spelunkers are courageous people.
3. Caves often contain long stalactites and tall stalagmites.

D. MIXED REVIEW: Diagramming

Diagram the following sentences.

1. Jewel Cave is gigantic.
2. It is an unusual underground world.
3. Shiny calcite crystals line the walls.
4. Strange, colorful formations fill the underground rooms.
5. The underground temperature is cool.
6. Visitors wear sturdy shoes and light jackets.
7. Knowledgeable guides give the visitors a lengthy tour.
8. Tourists and guides see shiny crystals and dark pools.
9. Brave visitors can take a candlelight tour.
10. They may encounter many bats!

Diagramming: Phrases and Clauses

Prepositional Phrases

- Write the preposition on a slanted line below the word the prepositional phrase modifies.
- Write the object of the preposition on a horizontal line attached to the slanted line and parallel to the main line.
- Write words that modify the object of the preposition on slanted lines below it.

Adjective Prepositional Phrase

Natural forces may cause cracks in solid rocks.

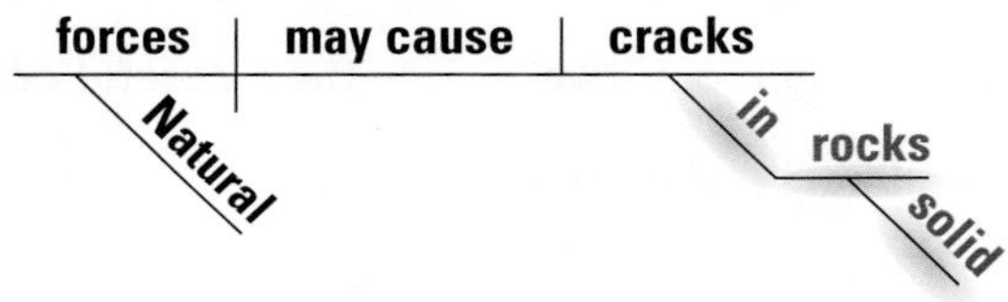

This adjective phrase modifies a noun. Adjective phrases can also modify pronouns and other prepositional phrases.

Adverb Prepositional Phrase

Glaciers move loose rocks down the valley.

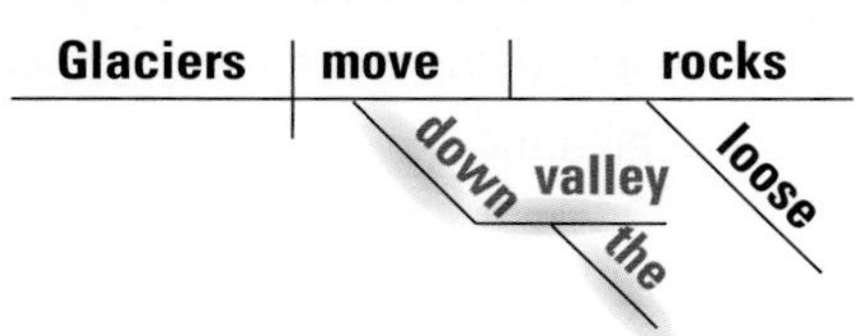

This adverb phrase modifies a verb. Adverb phrases can also modify adjectives and adverbs.

E. CONCEPT CHECK: Prepositional Phrases

Diagram these sentences, using what you have learned.

1. A glacier is a river of ice.

2. The flow of a heavy glacier carves a valley in a mountainside.

3. Inside their houses, people hear the eerie sounds of the ice outside.

DIAGRAMMING

Compound Sentences

- Diagram the independent clauses on parallel horizontal lines.
- Connect the verbs in the two clauses by a dotted line with a step in it.
- Write the coordinating conjunction on the step.

Birds fly naturally, but humans fly in balloons.

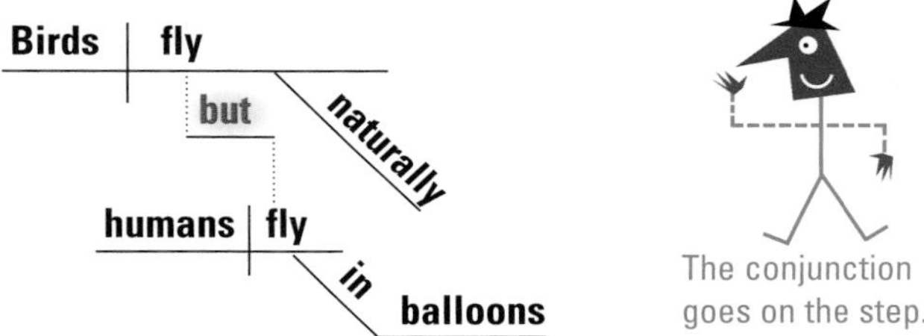

The conjunction goes on the step.

DIAGRAMMING

F. CONCEPT CHECK: Compound Sentences

Diagram these sentences, using what you have learned.

1. Balloons travel slowly, and they are blown by the wind.
2. Many have tried around-the-world flights, but few have succeeded.

Complex Sentences

Adjective and Adverb Clauses

- Diagram the main clause first. Diagram the subordinate clause on its own horizontal line below the main line.
- Use a dotted line to connect the word introducing the clause to the word it modifies.

Adjective Clause

The pilot is the person who controls a hot-air balloon.

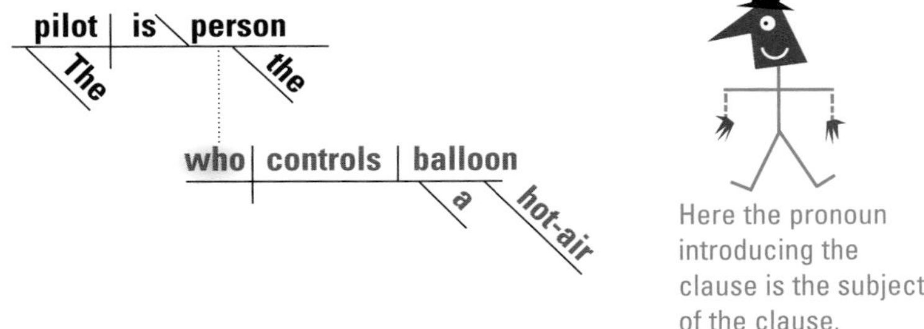

Here the pronoun introducing the clause is the subject of the clause.

Adverb Clause

After the balloon lands, the pilot releases the air.

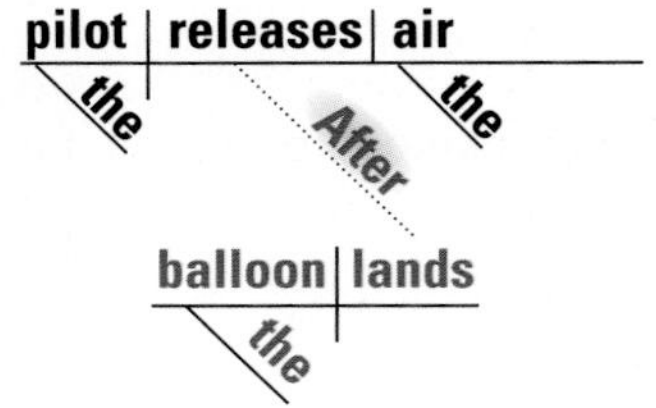

The conjunction goes on the dotted line, which connects the verbs in the two clauses.

Noun Clause

- Diagram the main clause first.
- Figure out what role the subordinate clause plays in the sentence.
- Diagram the subordinate clause on a separate line that is attached to the main line with a vertical forked line.
- Place the forked line in the diagram according to the role of the noun clause in the sentence.
- Diagram the word introducing the noun clause according to its function in the clause.

You may wonder how balloons come down.

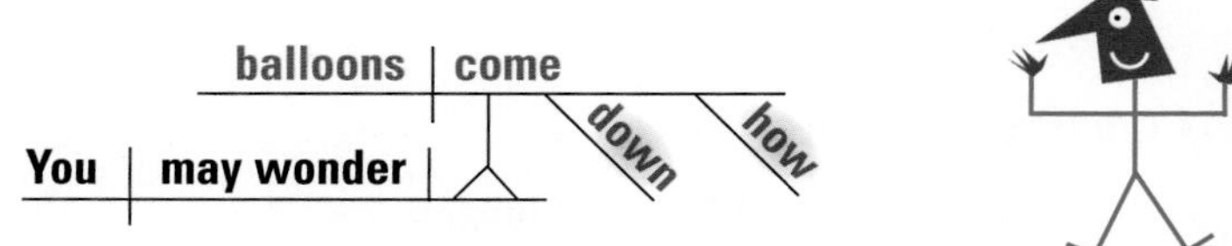

The noun clause functions as the direct object in this sentence.

DIAGRAMMING

G. CONCEPT CHECK: Complex Sentences

Diagram these sentences, using what you have learned.

1. Someone who plans trips is a navigator.
2. While the trip continues, the navigator gives directions.
3. The navigator may tell the driver where he should turn.

H. MIXED REVIEW: Diagramming

Diagram the following sentences.

1. The campers planned a canoe trip, and they packed their duffels.
2. They drove for three hours before they put their canoes in the water.
3. When they reached their destination, they were very tired.
4. Some of the campers pitched their tents where they could find shelter.
5. They frowned at the other campers who did not help.
6. They asked why the others had come.
7. The campers who had been resting soon got busy.
8. They unpacked pots and pans, and they searched the duffels for food.
9. Because they could not find the food, they looked for edible plants.
10. What they finally prepared was dandelion greens.

A+

Quick-Fix Editing Machine

You've worked hard on your assignment. Don't let misplaced commas, sentence fragments, and missing details lower your grade. Use this Quick-Fix Editing Guide to help you detect grammatical errors and make your writing more precise.

Fixing Errors

Improving Style

QUICK FIX

1 Sentence Fragments

What's the problem? Part of a sentence has been left out.

Why does it matter? A fragment can be confusing because it does not express a complete thought.

What should you do about it? Find out what is missing and add it.

What's the Problem?	Quick Fix
A. A subject is missing. Feature four wheels in a row.	**Add a subject.** **In-line skates** feature four wheels in a row.
B. A predicate is missing. In-line skates first in the 1700s.	**Add a predicate.** In-line skates first **appeared** in the 1700s.
C. Both a subject and a predicate are missing. Probably the world's first roller skates.	**Add a subject and a predicate to make an independent clause.** **They were** probably the world's first roller skates.
D. A dependent clause is treated as if it were a sentence. Because they were much faster than traditional roller skates.	**Combine the fragment with an independent clause.** **They became popular** because they were much faster than traditional roller skates. **OR** **Delete the conjunction.** ~~Because~~ they were much faster than traditional roller skates.

For more help, see Chapter 1, pp. 25–27.

QUICK FIX

2 Run-On Sentences

What's the problem? Two or more sentences have been written as though they were a single sentence.

Why does it matter? A run-on sentence doesn't show where one idea ends and another begins.

What should you do about it? Find the best way to separate the ideas or to show the proper relationship between them.

What's the Problem?	Quick Fix
A. The end mark separating two sentences is missing. The computer store is a popular spot many kids visit it.	**Add an end mark and start a new sentence.** The computer store is a popular spot**.** **M**any kids visit it.
B. Two sentences are separated only by a comma. My sister wanted an inexpensive game, she rummaged through the sale bins.	**Add a coordinating conjunction.** My sister wanted an inexpensive game, **so** she rummaged through the sale bins. **OR** **Change the comma to a semicolon.** My sister wanted an inexpensive game**;** she rummaged through the sale bins. **OR** **Replace the comma with an end mark and start a new sentence.** My sister wanted an inexpensive game**.** **S**he rummaged through the sale bins. **OR** **Change one of the independent clauses to a dependent clause.** **Because my sister wanted an inexpensive game,** she rummaged through the sale bins.

For more help, see Chapter 1, pp. 25–27.

QUICK FIX

3 Subject-Verb Agreement

What's the problem? A verb does not agree with its subject in number.

Why does it matter? Readers may think your work is careless.

What should you do about it? Identify the subject and use a verb that matches it in number.

What's the Problem?	Quick Fix
A. The first helping verb in a verb phrase does not agree with the subject. **We has** been practicing our strokes for several weeks.	**Decide whether the subject is singular or plural, and make the helping verb agree with it.** **We have** been practicing our strokes for several weeks.
B. The contraction doesn't agree with its subject. The other **students doesn't** know how scared I am.	**Use a contraction that agrees with the subject.** The other **students don't** know how scared I am.
C. A singular verb is used with a compound subject containing *and.* **Reina and the instructor plunges** into the water first.	**Use a plural verb with a compound subject joined by *and.*** **Reina and the instructor plunge** into the water first.
D. A verb doesn't agree with the nearer part of a compound subject containing *or* or *nor.* Neither the instructor nor the **students uses** the diving board.	**Make the verb agree with the nearer part of the compound subject.** Neither the instructor nor the **students use** the diving board.
E. A verb doesn't agree with an indefinite-pronoun subject. **Each** of my friends **hope** to pass this class.	**Decide whether the pronoun is singular or plural, and make the verb agree with it.** **Each** of my friends **hopes** to pass this class.

For more help, see Chapter 9, pp. 206–227.

QUICK FIX

What's the Problem?	Quick Fix
F. A collective noun referring to a single unit is treated as plural. The **class are** using this time to practice.	**If the collective noun refers to a single unit, use a singular verb.** The **class is** using this time to practice.
G. A singular subject ending in *s* or *ics* is mistaken for a plural. Like swimming, **mathematics are** fun.	**Watch out for these nouns and use singular verbs with them.** Like swimming, **mathematics is** fun.
H. A verb doesn't agree with the true subject of a sentence beginning with *here* or *there.* **There is** encouraging words from my classmates.	**Mentally turn the sentence around so that the subject comes first, and make the verb agree with it.** **There are** encouraging **words** from my classmates.
I. A verb agrees with the object of a preposition rather than with its subject. The sound of their **voices give** me confidence.	**Mentally block out the prepositional phrase and make the verb agree with the subject.** The **sound** ~~of their voices~~ **gives** me confidence.
J. A plural verb is used with a period of time or an amount. **Four weeks are** all it took for me to pass the test! **Thirty dollars are** what it cost!	**Use a singular verb.** **Four weeks is** all it took for me to pass the test! **Thirty dollars is** what it cost.

For more help, see Chapter 9, pp. 206–227.

4 Pronoun Reference Problems

What's the problem? A pronoun does not agree in number, person, or gender with its antecedent, or an antecedent is unclear.

Why does it matter? Lack of agreement or unclear antecedents can confuse your reader.

What should you do about it? Find the antecedent and make the pronoun agree with it, or rewrite the sentence to make the antecedent clear.

What's the Problem?	Quick Fix
A. A pronoun doesn't agree in number with its antecedent. Every **town** has **their** deserted house.	**Make the pronoun agree in number with the antecedent.** Every **town** has **its** deserted house.
B. A pronoun doesn't agree in person or in gender with its antecedent. **Kids** know **you** should stay away from a deserted house.	**Make the pronoun agree with the antecedent.** **Kids** know **they** should stay away from a deserted house.
C. A pronoun doesn't agree with an indefinite-pronoun antecedent. **Anyone** can claim that **they** saw something extraordinary.	**Decide whether the indefinite pronoun is singular or plural, and make the pronoun agree with it.** **Anyone** can claim that **he or she** saw something extraordinary.
D. A pronoun could refer to more than one noun. **Roberto** and **Ishi** went into a deserted house. **He** saw something strange.	**Substitute a noun for the pronoun to make the reference clear.** Roberto and Ishi went into a deserted house. **Ishi** saw something strange.
E. A pronoun agrees with a noun in a phrase rather than with its antecedent. Ishi, like many **people,** let **their** imagination run wild.	**Mentally block out the phrase and make the pronoun agree with its antecedent.** **Ishi,** ~~like many people~~, let **his** imagination run wild.

For more help, see Chapter 3, pp. 76–83.

QUICK FIX

5 Incorrect Pronoun Case

What's the problem? A pronoun is in the wrong case.

Why does it matter? Readers may think your work is careless, especially if you are writing a school paper or formal letter.

What should you do about it? Identify how the pronoun is being used, and replace it with the correct form.

What's the Problem?	Quick Fix
A. A pronoun that follows a linking verb is not in the subject case. The best all-around player **is her**.	**Always use the subject case after a linking verb.** The best all-around player **is she.**
B. A pronoun used as an object is not in the objective case. Andrea **asked** Inez and **I** to practice.	**A pronoun takes the objective case when it is used as an indirect object, a direct object, or the object of a preposition.** Andrea **asked** Inez and **me** to practice.
C. A pronoun in a compound subject is in the wrong case. **Ben and me** will start the game.	**Always use the subject case when a pronoun is part of a compound subject.** **Ben and I** will start the game.
D. A pronoun followed by an identifying noun is in the wrong case. **Us players** are ready to play. They told **we fans** to yell louder.	**Mentally drop the noun and decide whether the pronoun is a subject or an object.** **We** ~~players~~ are ready to play. They told **us** ~~fans~~ to yell louder.
E. A contraction is used instead of a possessive pronoun. **You're game** has really improved!	**A possessive pronoun never has an apostrophe.** **Your game** has really improved!

For more help, see Chapter 3, pp. 61–64.

6 *Who* and *Whom*

What's the problem? The pronoun *who* or *whom* is used incorrectly.

Why does it matter? When writers use *who* and *whom* correctly, readers are more likely to take their ideas seriously.

What should you do about it? Decide how the pronoun functions in the sentence, and then choose the correct form.

What's the Problem?	Quick Fix
A. ***Whom*** **is incorrectly used as the subject pronoun.** **Whom is knocking** at our door?	**Use** ***who*** **as the subject pronoun.** **Who is knocking** at the door?
B. ***Whom*** **is incorrectly used as a predicate pronoun.** The visitor **is whom?**	**Use** ***who*** **as the predicate pronoun.** The visitor **is who?**
C. ***Who*** **is incorrectly used as a direct object.** **Who can** we **send** to answer the door?	**Use** ***whom*** **as a direct object.** **Whom can** we **send** to answer the door?
D. ***Who*** **is incorrectly used as the object of a preposition.** A basket was left **by who?**	**Use** ***whom*** **as the object of a preposition.** A basket was left **by whom?**
E. ***Who*** **is incorrectly used as an indirect object.** You **gave who** our address?	**Use** ***whom*** **as an indirect object.** You **gave whom** our address?
F. ***Who's*** **is confused with the possessive pronoun** ***whose.*** **Who's puppy** is in this basket?	**Always use** ***whose*** **to show possession.** **Whose puppy** is in this basket?

For more help, see Chapter 3, pp. 70–71.

QUICK FIX

 Confusing Comparisons

What's the problem? The wrong form of an adjective or adverb is used when making a comparison.

Why does it matter? Comparisons that are not worded correctly can be confusing.

What should you do about it? Use a form that makes the comparison clear.

What's the Problem?	Quick Fix
A. Both *-er* and *more* or *-est* and *most* are used in making a comparison. In the 1920s, cosmetics manufacturers used some of the **most strangest** ingredients in lipstick.	**Delete one of the forms from the sentence.** In the 1920s, cosmetics manufacturers used some of the ~~most~~ **strangest** ingredients in lipstick.
B. A comparative form is used where a superlative form is needed. In fact, dangerous ingredients made lipstick one of the **more** unhealthy cosmetics of that time.	**When comparing more than two things, use the superlative form.** In fact, dangerous ingredients made lipstick one of the **most** unhealthy cosmetics of that time.
C. A superlative form is used where a comparative form is needed. I'm not sure which ingredient was **worst**—spoiled olive oil or dried and crushed insects.	**When comparing two things, use the comparative form.** I'm not sure which ingredient was **worse**—spoiled olive oil or dried and crushed insects.

For more help, see Chapter 5, pp. 137–139.

8 Verb Forms and Tenses

What's the problem? The wrong form or tense of a verb is used.

Why does it matter? Readers may regard your work as careless or find it confusing.

What should you do about it? Change the verb to the correct form or tense.

What's the Problem?	Quick Fix
A. The wrong form of a verb is used with a helping verb. Soft drinks **have rose** in popularity over the past several decades.	**Always use a participle form with a helping verb.** Soft drinks **have risen** in popularity over the past several decades.
B. A helping verb is missing. One consumer group **spoken** out against this trend.	**Add a helping verb.** One consumer group **has spoken** out against this trend.
C. A past participle is used incorrectly. Several decades ago, teens **drunk** twice as much milk as soda pop.	**To write about the past, use the past form of a verb.** Several decades ago, teens **drank** twice as much milk as soda pop. **OR** **Change the verb to the past perfect form by adding a helping verb.** Several decades ago, teens **had drunk** twice as much milk as soda pop.
D. Different tenses are used in the same sentence even though no change in time has occurred. Some heavy soda drinkers **drink** as many as five cans a day and **got** one fourth of their calories from these beverages.	**Use the same tense throughout the sentence.** Some heavy soda drinkers **drink** as many as five cans a day and **get** one fourth of their calories from these beverages.

For more help, see Chapter 4, pp. 100–114.

Missing or Misplaced Commas

What's the problem? Commas are missing or are used incorrectly.

Why does it matter? The incorrect use of commas can make sentences hard to follow.

What should you do about it? Figure out where commas are needed, and add them as necessary.

What's the Problem?	Quick Fix
A. A comma is missing from a compound sentence. Certain plants capture insects and they use them for food.	**Add a comma before the coordinating conjunction.** Certain plants capture insects, and they use them for food.
B. A comma is incorrectly placed after a closing quotation mark. "One such plant is a Venus flytrap"**,** remarked our teacher.	**Always put a comma before a closing quotation mark.** "One such plant is a Venus flytrap," remarked our teacher.
C. A comma is missing before the conjunction in a series. Reggie, Shayna and I hurriedly took notes on the exhibit.	**Add a comma.** Reggie, Shayna, and I hurriedly took notes on the exhibit.
D. A comma is missing after an introductory word, phrase, or clause. After an insect touches the sensitive hairs on a leaf the plant closes like a jaw.	**Add a comma after the introductory word, phrase, or clause.** After an insect touches the sensitive hairs on a leaf, the plant closes like a jaw.
E. Commas are missing around an appositive or a clause that is not essential to the meaning of the sentence. The Venus flytrap which is a fascinating plant takes ten days to digest its prey.	**Add commas to set off the nonessential appositive or clause. Remember that a clause beginning with *which* is preceded by a comma.** The Venus flytrap, which is a fascinating plant, takes ten days to digest its prey.

For more help, see Chapter 11, pp. 253–255.

QUICK FIX

10 Improving Weak Sentences

What's the problem? A sentence repeats ideas or contains too many ideas.

Why does it matter? Repetitive or overloaded sentences can bore readers and weaken the message.

What should you do about it? Make sure that every sentence contains a clearly focused idea.

What's the Problem?	Quick Fix
A. An idea is repeated.	**Eliminate the repeated idea.**
We recently read a news story about bugs **that was in the newspaper.**	We recently read a news story about bugs~~ that was in the newspaper.~~
B. A single sentence contains too many loosely connected ideas.	**Divide the sentence into two or more sentences, using conjunctions such as *and, but, when,* and *because* to show relationships between ideas.**
Radioactive flies and gnats were discovered at a nuclear site in Washington, and officials insisted there was no danger to the public, and one spokesperson said that these insects won't leave the area and they don't fly very far.	**When** radioactive flies and gnats were discovered at a nuclear site in Washington, officials insisted there was no danger to the public**. O**ne spokesperson said that these insects won't ever leave the area **because** they don't fly very far.
C. Too much information about a topic is crammed into one sentence.	**Divide the sentence into two or more sentences, using conjunctions such as *and, but, when,* and *although* to show relationships between ideas.**
The nuclear plant is working to get rid of the insects, but authorities insist that the bugs are no threat to people since according to one expert, a person would have to stand on a contaminated spot for an hour to get exposure equal to a dental x-ray.	**Although** the nuclear plant is working to get rid of the insects, authorities insist that the bugs are no threat to people**. A**ccording to one expert, a person would have to stand on a contaminated spot for an hour to get exposure equal to a dental x-ray.

QUICK FIX

Avoiding Wordiness

What's the problem? A sentence contains unnecessary words.

Why does it matter? The meaning of wordy sentences can be unclear to readers.

What should you do about it? Use words that are precise and eliminate extra words.

What's the Problem?	Quick Fix
A. A single idea is unnecessarily expressed in two ways.	**Delete the unnecessary words.**
At 7:30 A.M. **in the morning,** Marissa has to walk two miles to her summer job.	At 7:30 A.M. ~~in the morning,~~ Marissa has to walk two miles to her summer job.
She has a job that doesn't pay well, **and she doesn't make much money.**	She has a job that doesn't pay well. ~~and she doesn't make much money.~~
B. A simple idea is expressed in too many words.	**Simplify the expression.**
I **am of the opinion** that Marissa needs a bike.	I **think** that Marissa needs a bike.
She should ride a bike to work **on account of the fact** she can get there quickly.	She should ride a bike to work **so** she can get there quickly.
C. A sentence contains words that do not add to its meaning.	**Delete the unnecessary words.**
What I mean to say is Marissa should save her money to buy a bike.	~~What I mean to say is~~ Marissa should save her money to buy a bike.
I have to tell you that Marissa could save the money in just three months.	~~I have to tell you that~~ Marissa could save the money in just three months.

12 Varying Sentence Structure

What's the problem? Too many sentences begin the same way, or too many sentences of one kind are used.

Why does it matter? Lack of variety in sentences makes writing dull and choppy.

What should you do about it? Rearrange the phrases in some of your sentences, and use different types of sentences for variety and impact.

What's the Problem?	Quick Fix
A. Too many sentences in a paragraph begin the same way. **The fans** crowded the sidewalks and waited for the stars to arrive at the premiere. **The fans** screamed and watched their favorite actors enter the theater. The stars waved to their adoring public.	**Rearrange words or phrases in some of the sentences.** **Crowding the sidewalks,** the fans waited for the stars to arrive at the premiere. **As their favorite actors entered the theater,** the fans screamed. The stars waved to their adoring public.
B. Too many declarative sentences are used. There's the camera crew. My friend waves frantically. The crew hardly notice, because they're searching only for famous faces. They don't find any, since all the stars are already inside the theater.	**Add variety by rewriting one sentence as a command, question, or exclamation.** **Is that the camera crew?** My friend waves frantically. The crew hardly notice, because they're searching only for famous faces. They don't find any, since all the stars are already inside the theater.

13 Varying Sentence Length

What's the problem? A piece of writing contains too many short, repetitive sentences.

Why does it matter? The use of too many short, repetitive sentences makes writing choppy and monotonous.

What should you do about it? Combine or reword sentences to create sentences of varying lengths.

What's the Problem?

Too many short, repetitive sentences are used.

The flea market promised many bargains. The flea market was huge. It was outdoors. Bargain hunters explored every table. They were cheerful. One teen sold used video games. A man sold floral arrangements. One group enjoyed the antics of a clown. At the same time others sampled many different foods. The flea market is held every year. People save their treasures all year long. They can sell them at the market.

For more help, see Chapter 8, pp. 189–199.

Quick Fix

Eliminate repetitive sentences that add only one detail about the subject. Insert those details into other sentences.

The **huge outdoor** flea market promised many bargains. **Cheerful** bargain hunters explored every table.

OR

Use a conjunction such as *or, and,* or *but* to combine related sentences.

One teen sold used video games, **and** a man sold floral arrangements.

OR

Form a complex sentence, using a word such as *because, while,* or *although* to combine ideas.

While one group enjoyed the antics of a clown, others sampled many different foods.

OR

Combine the sentences to form a compound-complex sentence.

The flea market is held every year, **and** people save their treasures all year long **so** they can sell them at the market.

QUICK FIX

14 Adding Supporting Details

What's the problem? Not enough details are given for readers to fully understand the topic.

Why does it matter? Questions that aren't answered or opinions that aren't supported weaken a piece of writing.

What should you do about it? Add information and details that will make words and statements clear.

What's the Problem?	Quick Fix
A. An important word is not explained. In 1925, **diphtheria** threatened the town of Nome, Alaska.	**Explain or define the word.** In 1925, diphtheria, **a serious and sometimes fatal disease,** threatened the town of Nome, Alaska.
B. No details are given. Dog-sled teams delivered medical supplies.	**Add details that would help readers understand the significance of an event.** **Twenty** dog-sled teams relayed **almost 700 miles from Anchorage, Alaska, in five days** to deliver **desperately needed** medical supplies.
C. No supporting facts are given. The Iditarod Sled Dog Race is held every year.	**Add supporting facts.** Every year, the Iditarod Sled Dog Race is held **to honor the people and dogs who participated in that rescue mission.**
D. No reason is given for an opinion. There is probably no competitive sport in the world more grueling than this one.	**Add a reason.** There is probably no competitive sport in the world more grueling than this one. **The drivers and dog teams race more than 1,000 miles in high winds and frigid temperatures. They take two to three weeks to reach the finish line.**

15 Avoiding Clichés and Slang

What's the problem? A piece of formal writing contains clichés or slang expressions.

Why does it matter? Clichés do not convey fresh images to readers. Slang is not appropriate in formal writing.

What should you do about it? Reword sentences, replacing the clichés and slang with clear, fresh expressions.

What's the Problem?	Quick Fix
A. A sentence contains a cliché.	**Replace the cliché with a fresh description or explanation.**
The workers were **as busy as bees.**	The workers **bounced from one task to another.**
One person, though, was **as slow as molasses.**	One person, though, was **as slow as leaves falling from a tree.**
B. A sentence contains inappropriate slang.	**Replace the slang with more appropriate language.**
The new gymnastics equipment was **the bomb.**	The new gymnastics equipment **would help us prepare for the state meet.**

QUICK FIX

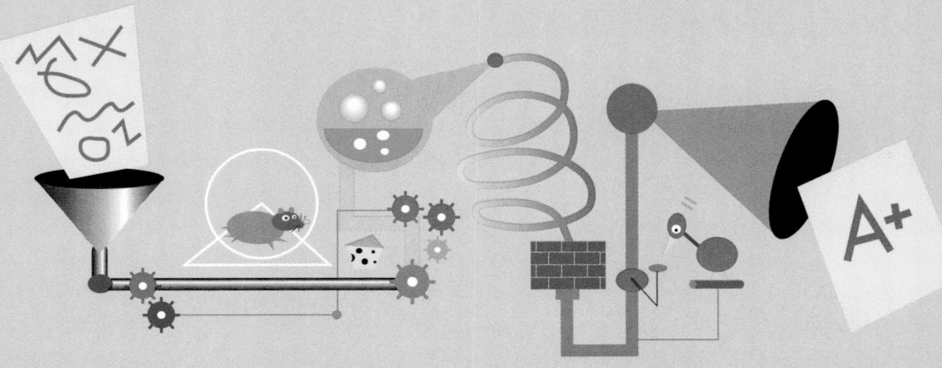

16 Using Precise Words

What's the problem? Nouns, modifiers, and verbs are not precise.

Why does it matter? Writers who use vague or general words don't give readers an accurate picture of their topic.

What should you do about it? Replace vague words with precise and vivid ones.

What's the Problem?	Quick Fix
A. Nouns are too general. The **people** strapped on their **equipment** and moved into the **street.**	**Use specific nouns.** The **anxious skaters** strapped on their **helmets and protective pads** and moved to the **starting line.**
B. Modifiers are too general. **Soon** they would be able to show off their **great** skills on **city** streets.	**Use vivid adjectives and adverbs.** **Immediately,** they would show off their **impressive** skills on **winding** city streets.
C. Verbs tell about the action rather than showing it. The wind **is** against the contestants as they **go** down a steep driveway. The racers **go** around the statue in the park. A barricade forces the skaters to **go** onto the grass.	**Use vivid verbs to show the action.** The wind **slaps** the contestants as they **zoom** down a steep driveway. The racers **orbit** the statue in the park. An unexpected barricade forces the skaters to **swerve** onto the grass.

17 Using Figurative Language

What's the problem? A piece of writing is dull or unimaginative.

Why does it matter? Dull writing bores readers because it doesn't help them form mental pictures of what is being described.

What should you do about it? Add figures of speech to make writing lively and to create pictures in readers' minds.

QUICK FIX

What's the Problem?	Quick Fix
A description is dull and lifeless.	**Add a simile.**
Hopelessly bored, we left the house in search of excitement. We trudged down a narrow path toward the park.	Hopelessly bored, we left the house in search of excitement. We trudged down a narrow path toward the park **like an army of defeated soldiers.**
	OR
	Add a metaphor.
All around us the snow was gray.	All around us the snow was **a gray carpet in need of a cleaning.**
	OR
	Use personification.
We stopped at a yard with snow that looked like whipped cream. The gate was half open.	We stopped at a yard with snow that looked like whipped cream. **The half-open gate invited us to enter.**

18 Paragraphing

What's the problem? A paragraph contains too many ideas.

Why does it matter? A long paragraph discourages readers from continuing.

What should you do about it? Break the paragraph into smaller paragraphs. Start a new paragraph whenever a new idea is presented or the time, place, or speaker changes.

What's the Problem?

Too many ideas are contained in one paragraph.

Although Aunt Leona isn't known for her cooking ability, she offered to help me bake a birthday cake for my mom's party. I accepted her offer because I'm not known for my cooking ability either. After spending the whole morning in the kitchen, we got something into the oven, but what a mess we had afterward. The kitchen looked like the scene of a science experiment gone awry. Then real disaster struck. The cake broke into chunks when we took it out of the oven. "Oh, Aunt Leona!" I groaned. "How can we fix this mess?" "I have an idea," she said. Later that day we served the cake chunks with strawberries and chocolate sauce. Mom and the guests were quite impressed. Aunt Leona had turned disaster into success.

Quick Fix

Although Aunt Leona isn't known for her cooking ability, she offered to help me bake a birthday cake for my mom's party. I accepted her offer because I'm not known for my cooking ability either.

Start a new paragraph to introduce a new idea.

After spending the whole morning in the kitchen, we got something into the oven, but what a mess we had afterward. The kitchen looked like the scene of a science experiment gone awry. Then real disaster struck. The cake broke into chunks when we took it out of the oven.

Start a new paragraph whenever the speaker changes.

"Oh, Aunt Leona!" I groaned. "How can we fix this mess?"

"I have an idea," she said.

Start a new paragraph when the time or place changes.

Later that day we served the cake chunks with strawberries and chocolate sauce. Mom and the guests were quite impressed. Aunt Leona had turned disaster into success.

What's the Problem?

An essay is treated as one long paragraph.

Scary, gigantic beasts are often the subject of today's horror films. However, tales of scary monsters have been told for centuries. One monster that appears in many tales is the fire-breathing dragon. Is it possible that the storytellers were referring to the Komodo dragon? Although it's no monster, the Komodo dragon is the world's largest lizard. It lives on Komodo Island in Indonesia and was discovered in 1912. Before scientists visited the island, rumors about giant dragons persisted. Today we know many facts about this remarkable animal. The Komodo dragon can be as long as 12 feet and weigh as much as 300 pounds. This lizard has strong claws and sharp, sawlike teeth. It eats dead animals as well as live prey. The Komodo dragon does not breathe fire, but it is fearsome. Unlike the dragons in old tales, however, Komodo dragons are protected from hunters, who nearly caused the lizards' extinction.

Quick Fix

Scary, gigantic beasts are often the subject of today's horror films. However, tales of scary monsters have been told for centuries.

Start a new paragraph to introduce the first main idea.

One monster that appears in many tales is the fire-breathing dragon. Is it possible that the storytellers were referring to the Komodo dragon? Although it's no monster, the Komodo dragon is the world's largest lizard. It lives on Komodo Island in Indonesia and was discovered in 1912. Before scientists visited the island, rumors about giant dragons persisted.

Start a new paragraph to introduce another main idea.

Today we know many facts about this remarkable animal. The Komodo dragon can be as long as 12 feet and weigh as much as 300 pounds. This lizard has strong claws and sharp, sawlike teeth. It eats dead animals as well as live prey.

Start a new paragraph to give the conclusion.

The Komodo dragon does not breathe fire, but it is fearsome. Unlike the dragons in old tales, however, Komodo dragons are protected from hunters, who nearly caused the lizards' extinction.

Student Resources

Exercise Bank

Boost your grammar fitness! Use the circled arrows ➜ to find the answers to the Self-Check items. In addition, you can complete exercises in this section to get extra practice in a skill you've just learned.

1 The Sentence and Its Parts

1. Complete Subjects and Predicates (links to exercise on p. 7)

➜ **1.** Complete subject: *Frank Lloyd Wright;* complete predicate: *designed an unusual home in the Pennsylvania woods*
2. Complete subject: *The owners;* complete predicate: *called the house Fallingwater*

In separate columns on a sheet of paper, write the complete subjects and complete predicates of these sentences.

1. Albert Frey was a world-famous architect.
2. The talented Mr. Frey was 94 years old in 1998.
3. He lived modestly in a 16-by-32-foot house on a mountain in southern California.
4. The architect built his desert house in 1964.
5. This amazing house is a rectangular glass-walled shed with a corrugated aluminum roof.
6. A large boulder is in the center of the house!
7. The unusual house has a single room for dining, living, and sleeping.
8. Mr. Frey deliberately built his house with low-maintenance materials.
9. Aluminum was one of the materials he used.
10. This durable material does not need to be repainted or repaired.

2. Simple Subjects (links to exercise A, p. 9)

➜ **2.** Lodges **5.** rodents

Write the simple subject of each sentence.

1. Arctic seals spend most of their lives in water.
2. In the winter, they live under the ice.
3. The female digs out a lair, or den, in a snowbank.
4. The lair is on top of the ice but under the snow.
5. The seal creates a hole down to the ocean below.
6. First she breathes on the ice from underneath.

7. Next, the female nibbles on the softened ice.
8. Then, with her flippers, she scoops out the ice.
9. She also makes air holes through the ice.
10. Her "igloo" will have a wide floor for her and her cub.

3. Simple Predicates, or Verbs (links to exercise A, p. 11)

➜ **1.** lived **2.** traveled

Write the simple predicate, or verb, in each sentence.

1. In the 1800s four sisters claimed 1,920 acres of land on the Great Plains.
2. Settlers dug wells as soon as possible.
3. Many families built windmills.
4. These windmills pumped water from the wells.
5. Some families had no wells.
6. Women carried water several miles to their sod houses.
7. Farmers often used dried buffalo droppings for fuel!
8. Many homesteaders came from Europe.
9. Hundreds of African-American families settled on the plains.
10. These "exodusters" were former slaves.

4. Verb Phrases (links to exercise A, p. 13)

➜ **1.** was developed **2.** could communicate

Write the verb or verb phrase in each sentence below.

1. Using a kit, you can build a house like the graceful Japanese country houses of the 16th century.
2. Large-diameter poles support your finished house.
3. Each house is surrounded by a large veranda.
4. The veranda should provide a pleasing view of nature.
5. Glazed tiles from Japan are supplied for the roof.
6. Only wood from replaceable trees has been chosen for the kits.
7. These graceful houses can be built in all climates.
8. They have been constructed in the United States, the Caribbean, Europe, and Southeast Asia.
9. Such houses have recently survived hurricanes in the West Indies.
10. They have also been winning architectural awards.

5. Compound Sentence Parts (links to exercise A, p. 15)

➜ **1.** *Space stations* and *platforms*
2. *may design* and *build*

Write and identify the compound subject (CS) or compound verb (CV) in each sentence.

1. Since the 1950s, pesticides and pollution have almost wiped out the peregrine falcon.
2. Peregrines and some other birds of prey live high up in cliffs.
3. They swoop down and eat smaller birds and rodents.
4. In the 1980s scientists and researchers introduced falcon pairs to skyscrapers.
5. The birds now nest and breed on ledges of tall buildings.
6. There they have no natural predators and can see lots of prey on the ground below.
7. City falcons hunt and eat pigeons and starlings.
8. They kill and consume mice as well.
9. Some peregrines have been attacked by other falcons or even eaten by them.
10. Office workers and apartment dwellers can now watch the birds from their high-rise windows.

6. Kinds of Sentences (links to exercise A, p. 17)

➜ **1.** INT **2.** D

Identify each of the following sentences as declarative (D), interrogative (INT), exclamatory (EXC), or imperative (IMP).

1. Look at that big yellow and black bee.
2. That's a bumblebee!
3. Did you know they can live as far north as the Arctic Circle?
4. The buzzing sound is a bumblebee fanning its wings.
5. Tell me how they build their nests.
6. The queen constructs a pot of wax and fills it with honey.
7. She lays her eggs in another pot of wax.
8. What happens to the eggs?
9. They hatch and become worker bees.
10. Some hives are a foot wide and have up to 700 workers!

7. Subjects in Unusual Order (links to exercise A, p. 20)

➜ **1.** Subject: *benefits;* verb: *are*
2. Subject: *fans;* verb: *sit*

In separate columns on a sheet of paper, write the subjects and the verbs or verb phrases in these sentences.

1. There are the two skiers in the starting gates.
2. Give the signal for the giant slalom race to begin.
3. Down the steep slope race the athletes.
4. From their skis sprays snow.
5. Watch the next one jump off the top of that ridge.
6. Did the one on the right miss a gate?
7. Across the hill tumbles the first skier.
8. There is the winner of the giant slalom.
9. Are you skiing in this event?
10. Avoid that icy turn near the third gate.

8. Complements: Subject Complements (links to exercise A, p. 22)

➜ **1.** highways, PN **2.** difficult, PA

Write the underlined word in each sentence, and identify it as a predicate noun (PN) or a predicate adjective (PA).

1. The Arctic National Wildlife Refuge is an <u>area</u> in northeastern Alaska.
2. It is among the largest <u>refuges</u> in the United States.
3. Half of the Arctic National Wildlife Refuge is a <u>tundra</u>, or treeless plain.
4. The tundra is so <u>cold</u> that the ground never thaws completely.
5. The refuge is <u>home</u> to many animals, including caribou, polar bears, snowy owls, and lemmings.
6. Lemmings are mouselike <u>creatures</u> that live on the tundra.
7. The arctic fox is a <u>predator</u> that hunts lemmings.
8. Caribou are <u>migratory,</u> traveling more than 1,000 miles each spring to the coastal plain in the refuge.
9. The snowy owl is a large <u>bird</u> that lives in the Arctic during the entire year.
10. Environmentalists are <u>protective</u> of the land and creatures of the Arctic National Wildlife Refuge.

9. Complements: Objects of Verbs (links to exercise on p. 24)

➜ **1.** house, DO **2.** inhabitants, IO; level, DO

Write the objects in these sentences, identifying each as a direct object (DO) or an indirect object (IO).

1. The United States, Russia, and 14 other nations are building a space station.

2. This space station will orbit the earth at 17,500 miles per hour.
3. It will give astronauts a place to live and work in space.
4. Scientific and medical experiments aboard the space station will offer people new insights into life in space.
5. Engineers are constructing the modules of the space station.
6. Rockets and space shuttles are giving these modules a lift into space.
7. During space walks, astronauts will connect the various parts of the space station.
8. A Russian rocket lifted the first section, Zarya, into orbit in November 1998.
9. In December 1998 the crew of the U.S. space shuttle *Endeavour* connected the Unity module to Zarya.
10. Solar panels will give astronauts power for the space station.

10. Fragments and Run-Ons (links to exercise A, p. 27)

➜ **1.** CS **2.** F

Identify each of the following groups of words as a fragment (F), a run-on (RO), or a complete sentence (CS).

1. The Anasazi, a Native American people.
2. Represented by present-day Pueblo people.
3. *Anasazi* is a Navajo word.
4. It may mean "ancient ones" it may also mean "enemy ancestors."
5. Anasazi groups have lived in the Southwest for at least 1,800 years.
6. Built huge dwellings in sandstone cliffs.
7. These dwellings are impressive, you can still see them today.
8. One cliff palace has 150 rooms!
9. Around 1300 A.D. these dwellings were abandoned, nobody knows why.
10. Mysterious but true.

2 Nouns

1. Kinds of Nouns (links to exercise A, p. 38)

➜ **1.** *things,* C; *planet,* C; *sequoias,* C
2. *Sequoya,* P; *scholar,* C; *leader,* C

Write the nouns in these sentences, identifying each as common or proper. Then identify three collective nouns in your list.

1. The Gateway Arch soars high above St. Louis, Missouri.
2. It is made of stainless steel.
3. A competition was held, and the architect Eero Saarinen was chosen to build the landmark.
4. His idea was to construct a giant arch like those built in ancient Rome.
5. The span was constructed by raising sections with cranes.
6. The two sides of the curving arch rose beside the Mississippi River.
7. Safety was an important concern, and no one in the crew was injured during the construction.
8. Unfortunately, the steel expanded in the sun, and the two sides did not meet at the top.
9. A team sprayed cool water on the structure until it shrank to the right size.
10. The population of St. Louis watched on television as the Gateway Arch was completed.

2. Singular and Plural Nouns (links to exercise A, p. 40)

➜ **1.** engineers **4.** rays

Write the plural forms of the underlined nouns.

1. The Statue of Liberty was a gift from the citizen of France.
2. France wanted to symbolize the similar belief of the two country.
3. The statue was designed to be 151 foot (15 story) high.
4. The iron frame was covered with sheet of copper.
5. Different part were made in design studio throughout Paris.
6. The statue was loaded into a ship in section.
7. Many New Yorker—man and woman, boy and girl—had raised money to build a base for the statue to stand on.
8. Seventy-five worker took six month to put Liberty together.
9. Many workers hung from rope to fit the frame and the copper plate together.
10. Visitor were able to climb step into Liberty's torch.

3. Possessive Nouns (links to exercise A, p. 43)

➜ **1.** *Missouri's,* singular **3.** *country's,* singular

Write the possessive form of each underlined noun. Label it as singular or plural.

1. Stonehenge is a circle of stone monuments on England Salisbury Plain.

2. This monument of an unknown people religion is believed to be more than 5,000 years old.
3. America Stonehenge copies are younger and smaller.
4. Sam Hill Stonehenge sits overlooking Washington Columbia River.
5. Hill built the monument in World War I soldiers honor.
6. Georgia Stonehenge copy, called the Georgia Guidestones, has six granite slabs.
7. The slabs carvings are in 12 languages and suggest that readers lives will be better if they "avoid useless officials."
8. Carhenge, an arrangement of cars in Alliance, Nebraska, forms that town tribute to Stonehenge.
9. With some standing upright and others lying across them, the cars reproduce the stones arrangement in the real Stonehenge.
10. In Alliance, residents pride in Carhenge is suggested by their gift shop sign: "We sell Carhenge souvenirs."

4. Compound Nouns (links to exercise A, p. 46)

➜ **1.** *foodstuffs,* plural; *South Dakota,* singular
2. *cornstalks,* plural

Write the compound nouns in the sentences below. Identify each compound as singular or plural.

1. In 1968 the Lorraine Motel in Memphis, Tennessee, became the backdrop of a tragedy.
2. Dr. Martin Luther King, Jr., a gifted public speaker, was killed on the motel's balcony.
3. The site is now a landmark, a museum of the struggle for civil rights.
4. In one exhibit schoolchildren can view a burned-out bus.
5. Rosa Parks rode such a bus in the Montgomery bus boycott.
6. Another exhibit celebrates college students who participated in a sit-in.
7. They quietly demanded their rights at a lunchroom in a department store and were arrested and locked up in the jailhouse.
8. Similar displays honor those who fought segregation at public schools, swimming pools, and drinking fountains.
9. Sightseers hear stories of courageous acts that helped to change public policy across the United States.
10. They leave with vivid mental snapshots of those who struggled for freedom.

5. Nouns and Their Jobs (links to exercise A, p. 48)

→ **1.** *Vietnam War,* subject; *country,* complement; *sorrow,* complement

3. *Veterans,* subject; *war,* object of a preposition

Identify each underlined noun as a subject, a complement, or an object of a preposition.

1. Francis Johnson began wrapping a twine ball in 1950.
2. Johnson added twine for four hours each day until his death in 1989.
3. A crane lifted the huge ball off the ground as it grew larger.
4. The finished object is roughly 38 feet around.
5. The huge sphere brought Darwin, Minnesota, fame.
6. Johnson's ball of twine was a challenge to Frank Stoeber.
7. He rolled his own creation of over 1.6 million feet of material.
8. Stoeber's huge ball grew to be only slightly smaller than Johnson's.
9. But death brought an end to Stoeber's project.
10. Stoeber's Kansas neighbors set up the huge object as a roadside attraction, anyway.

3 Pronouns

1. What Is a Pronoun? (links to exercise A, p. 59)

→ **1.** its **3.** their, them

Write the personal pronouns used in these sentences. Identify each as a subject, an object, or a possessive form.

1. The discovery of King Tutankamen's tomb and its treasures was a great event in the history of archaeology.
2. The archaeologist Howard Carter discovered the tomb. At the time, he was searching Egypt's Valley of the Kings.
3. The ancient Egyptians built fabulous tombs for their dead kings and queens.
4. Carter knew that many sites had been robbed, but he was not discouraged.
5. We know that in 1922 Carter's crew uncovered a set of stairs in the sand.
6. The stairs led them to King Tut's treasure rooms.
7. They found more than 5,000 objects, many made of solid gold.
8. You may have seen pictures of the magnificent gold mask that covered the mummy's head and shoulders.

9. King Tut's tomb is unique because its treasures were undisturbed by robbers.
10. Carter's discovery gave us new knowledge about ancient Egypt.

2. Subject Pronouns (links to exercise on p. 62)

➜ **1.** I **2.** they

Write the correct pronoun form to complete each sentence.

1. When Howard Carter's workers uncovered King Tut's tomb, (they, them) also uncovered a mystery.
2. The first in my family to read about Carter was (I, me).
3. Carter began working in Egypt when (him, he) was only 17.
4. (Him, He) met a British lord, the earl of Carnarvon, who gave him money to explore Egypt's past.
5. Medical researchers found that Tut had died at the age of 18, and (they, them) suggested that he may have been murdered.
6. (Him, He) had many powerful enemies who may have wanted a new king.
7. The circumstances of King Tut's death are suspicious, but (us, we) may never know the truth.
8. If people want to find out more about King Tut's life and death, (they, them) can read several good books.
9. (Me, I) have read an especially good one, called *Gods, Graves, and Scholars,* by C. W. Ceram.
10. My friend Kyra wants to explore too. (Her, She) and I plan to go to Egypt someday.

3. Object Pronouns (links to exercise on p. 64)

➜ **1.** *him,* object **2.** *He,* subject

Write the correct pronoun form to complete each sentence. Identify each as a subject pronoun (SP) or an object pronoun (OP).

1. The mystery surrounding the disappearance of Amelia Earhart makes (I, me) wonder if her fate will ever be known.
2. In 1932 (she, her) became the first woman to fly alone across the Atlantic Ocean.
3. Because of her daring adventures, newspapers gave (she, her) the name First Lady of the Air.
4. It was (she, her) who wanted to be the first woman to fly around the world.
5. Earhart would take with (she, her) a navigator, Fred Noonan.
6. The one who would plan the route was (him, he).

7. In 1937 Earhart and (he, him) set out on the historic round-the-world flight.
8. Earhart's plane disappeared in the Pacific Ocean. Time has given (us, we) few clues about what happened.
9. The disappearance of Amelia Earhart has mystified (us, we) ever since.
10. Earhart's husband, the publisher G. P. Putnam, wrote a biography of (she, her), called *Soaring Wings.*

4. Possessive Pronouns (links to exercise A, p. 67)

➜ **1.** you're **2.** their

Write the correct pronoun or contraction for each sentence.

1. Why would anybody want to study (your, you're) garbage?
2. (It's, Its) an odd fact, but archaeologists are able to learn a lot about a society from the rubbish it leaves behind.
3. In fact, (you're, your) probably not aware that some scientists make a career of analyzing ancient refuse.
4. Recently, however, some scholars have turned (they're, their) attention to modern garbage.
5. (They're, Their) working in a new field called garbage archaeology, or garbology for short.
6. This new field had (it's, its) beginning in 1973, when William Rathje began the Garbage Project at the University of Arizona.
7. Rathje has used the garbage of some households in Tucson to study what (they're, their) buying and eating.
8. Since then the project has expanded (its, it's) scope to include dozens of other cities as well.
9. Scientists have learned a lot about how (you're, your) spending your money.
10. They know about (your, you're) eating and buying habits, and, of course, about the amount of garbage you throw out!

5. Reflexive and Intensive Pronouns (links to exercise on p. 69)

➜ **1.** *himself,* reflexive **2.** *itself,* intensive

Write the reflexive or intensive pronoun in each sentence, labeling it *reflexive* or *intensive*.

1. We like to entertain ourselves by doing yo-yo tricks.
2. Have you yourself ever tried tricks like "walk the dog," "around the world," and "lunar loops"?
3. I myself did not know much about the history of the yo-yo until Beth told me about it.

4. The word itself may come from a Philippine word meaning "to return."
5. Beth likes to keep herself informed on all kinds of subjects.
6. She told me that the toy itself was developed in prehistoric times in the jungles of the Philippines.
7. People taught themselves how to make a type of weapon by tying a piece of cord around a grooved rock.
8. They used these early yo-yos to hunt animals and to protect themselves.
9. I taught myself how to do yo-yo tricks.
10. Beth herself practices yo-yo tricks a little every day.

6. Interrogatives and Demonstratives (links to exercise A, p. 72)

➜ **1.** what **4.** Who

Write the correct demonstrative or interrogative pronoun to complete each sentence.

1. From (who, whom) did you get this book, *The Atlas of Mysterious Places?*
2. (This, These) are the most amazing pictures I've seen!
3. One photograph shows stone statues on Easter Island in the Pacific Ocean. (That, Those) look like ancient guardians of the land.
4. (That, Those) are the cylinder-shaped stones that rest on some of the statues' heads like hats.
5. (Who, Whom) carved these 15-foot-tall human busts?
6. (Who, Whom) would spend the time and energy needed to create them?
7. (Whose, Who's) was the face depicted on the giant figures?
8. (Who, Whom) do the statues honor?
9. (Whom, What) caused the sculptors to abandon their work and leave many statues unfinished?
10. (This, These) are some of the questions that have yet to be answered about the mysterious statues.

7. Pronoun Agreement (links to exercise on p. 75)

➜ **1.** She, Agatha Christie; them, mysteries
3. them, trips

Write the pronouns in these sentences, along with their antecedents.

1. Imagine over a hundred people completely vanishing from their village.

2. Such a disappearance occurred in Virginia in the late 1500s. It still has not been explained.
3. In 1587 John White sailed for Virginia with his fellow passengers—116 men, women, and children.
4. White's daughter and her husband were among the people aboard the ship.
5. A baby girl named Virginia Dare was born in Virginia. She was the first English child to be born in North America.
6. The child was born on Roanoke Island, the place where White and his group landed.
7. White sailed back to England for supplies, but he didn't return until three years later.
8. White searched for the English colonists but did not find them.
9. The colonists may have died, or they may have decided to live among a group of Native Americans.
10. The mystery has baffled many researchers. It remains unsolved.

8. Indefinite-Pronoun Agreement (links to exercise on p. 78)

➜ **1.** their **3.** her

Choose the pronouns that agree with the indefinite-pronoun antecedents.

1. Do you know anyone who has made (their, his or her) own Möbius strip?
2. Many have created this amazing object by first cutting a narrow strip of paper. (He or she, They) then gave one end a half twist before taping the two ends together.
3. Most who experiment with a Möbius strip will be astonished by (his or her, their) experience.
4. Few will fail to notice that the strip's behavior does not meet (his or her, their) expectations.
5. Ask someone to draw a pencil line around the "outside" of the strip. (He or she, They) will discover that the line also goes around the "inside" of the strip.
6. Nobody who cuts a Möbius strip in two lengthwise will end up with two rings. (He or she, They) will have only one ring!
7. Anyone who tries to color one edge of the strip will discover to (his or her, their) surprise that both edges wind up being colored.
8. Many find the Möbius strip mysterious. However, (his or her, their) questions could easily be answered by a topologist.
9. That is the name for someone who studies the properties of shapes. Using (his or her, their) mathematical skills, a

topologist can explain why a Möbius strip has only one side.

10. Everyone has seen a Möbius strip, whether (he or she, they) knows it or not. It is a symbol that appears on many recyclable products.

9. Pronoun Problems (links to exercise A, p. 80)

→ **1.** us

Write the correct pronoun form to complete each sentence.

1. (We, Us) mystery fans have started a club at our school.
2. The name Rue Morgue Society appealed to (we, us) club members, since the first American detective story was *The Murders in the Rue Morgue* by Edgar Allan Poe.
3. If anyone loves solving crime puzzles, it is (we, us) amateur detectives.
4. Sometimes, (we, us) students even talk about trying to help the local police solve real crimes.
5. People who listen to (we, us) mystery fans sometimes wonder if we're talking about real or fictional crimes.

Correct the unclear pronoun reference in the following sentences by replacing each underlined pronoun with a noun.

6. Luis and Rob saw a movie version of Poe's *The Murders in the Rue Morgue*. He thought the ending was disappointing.
7. Poe and his hero C. Auguste Dupin shared a love of mystery. He had a brilliantly logical mind.
8. In the bedroom, the window and door are both closed. Yet it must have been opened by the murderer.
9. The police and family members are baffled by the murders. They arrest a tradesman for the crime.
10. In the end, an orangutan, not the tradesman, turns out to be the killer. He lived in an East Indian forest and was brought to France by a sailor.

10. More Pronoun Problems (links to exercise A, p. 82)

→ **1.** I **2.** me

Write the correct pronoun to complete each sentence.

1. My friends and (I, me) were talking about alien life.
2. We wondered whether life on earth, in all its many forms, had (its, their) origin in space.
3. Miguel and Jake, friends of my brother's, said that (he, they) think alien life is a joke.

4. They laughed at Denise and (I, me) when we disagreed.
5. (She, Her) and I have read about projects that search for alien life in space.
6. Some scientific projects, such as SETI, are clear about (its, their) goal—finding and contacting extraterrestrials.
7. I believe that the SETI program, which uses radio telescopes to detect signals from space, interests (me, I) the most.
8. SETI stands for "Search for Extraterrestrial Intelligence," Denise and (I, me) explained to Jake.
9. Scientists at NASA have (its, their) own organization to explore questions about extraterrestrial life.
10. This group is called the Astrobiology Institute, the librarian told Denise and (I, me).

4 Verbs

1. What Is a Verb? (links to exercise A, p. 94)

➜ **1.** may be **3.** sail

Write the verb in each of the following sentences.

1. *Antz* is an example of feature-length animation.
2. The filmmakers created the graphics on computers.
3. The ants in the movie behave a lot like people.
4. Real ants, of course, are nothing like the ones in this film.
5. In the movie, a worker ant falls in love with a princess ant.
6. The worker and the princess escape to the outside world.
7. However, their home colony faces a serious threat.
8. The whole ant population appears in danger of destruction.
9. The worker and the princess return to the colony just in time!
10. The humble worker becomes a hero to the other ants.

2. Action Verbs and Objects (links to exercise A, p. 97)

➜ **1.** *people,* direct object
2. *members,* indirect object; *assignments,* direct object

Write the 15 complements in these sentences, identifying each as a direct object or an indirect object.

1. Steven Spielberg has given us many hit movies, including *Jaws, Raiders of the Lost Ark*, and *E.T. the Extra-Terrestrial.*
2. Spielberg made his first film at the age of 12.
3. He staged the wreck of two toy trains.
4. That experience gave him a taste for spectacular stunts.

5. He used everyone around him in his movies.
6. He gave his mother starring roles in many home movies.
7. When he was 13, Spielberg joined a Boy Scout photography program.
8. He made the scout troop a three-minute movie about a stagecoach robbery.
9. The movie won Spielberg his first filmmaking award—a merit badge.
10. At the age of 16, Spielberg made *Firelight*, his first science fiction movie.

3. Linking Verbs and Predicate Words (links to exercise on p. 99)

➜ **1.** *are,* linking verb; *scary,* predicate adjective
3. *was,* linking verb; *hit,* predicate noun

Identify each linking verb, predicate noun, and predicate adjective in the sentences below.

1. The job title "continuity clerk" may seem unimpressive.
2. But a continuity clerk is an important person on a movie set.
3. The order in which scenes are shot is not the order in which they will appear in the film.
4. Footage from different days can be part of the same scene.
5. Such footage must appear continuous.
6. The continuity clerk's tasks are very tedious.
7. Most people would grow bored by all the details.
8. Good continuity clerks, however, are perfectionists.
9. They remain attentive to the tasks.
10. Some continuity clerks even become directors.

4. Principal Parts of Verbs (links to exercise on p. 101)

➜ **1.** present **2.** past participle

Identify each underlined principal part as the present, the present participle, the past, or the past participle.

1. Photography has <u>existed</u> for only about 150 years.
2. Eadweard Muybridge <u>created</u> some of the first stop-action photographs.
3. In 1877 he <u>arranged</u> 12 cameras in a row.
4. Then he <u>snapped</u> photos, in sequence, of a galloping horse.
5. Some people had <u>claimed</u> that a running horse always has two feet on the ground.
6. Muybridge's photos <u>proved</u> that all four feet are off the ground at some points.

7. A real horse never assumes a rocking-horse position, with two legs stretched forward and two back.
8. By 1900 Muybridge had mastered the art of stop-action photography.
9. He had produced many series of photos of people running and jumping.
10. Readers are still enjoying these photos in books and magazines today.

5. Irregular Verbs (links to exercise on p. 104)

➜ **1.** seen **4.** made

In the sentences below, choose the correct forms of the verbs in parentheses.

1. The popular musical *Annie Get Your Gun* was (wrote, written) about a real person, Annie Oakley.
2. Annie Oakley had (grown, growed) up on a farm in Ohio.
3. She (beginned, began) teaching herself to hunt at an early age.
4. She (brought, bringed) home game to feed her family.
5. At the age of 15, she (winned, won) a shooting contest against Frank E. Butler, a well-known target shooter.
6. Before long, she had (given, gave) Butler her hand in marriage.
7. The two (shot, shooted) targets together in circuses and shows.
8. Oakley was so accurate with a rifle that she (hit, hitted) dimes thrown into the air.
9. If someone tossed a playing card into the air, she could riddle it with holes before it (fell, fallen) to the ground.
10. When Oakley performed with Buffalo Bill's Wild West Show, audiences (knew, knowed) her as Little Sure Shot.

6. Simple Tenses (links to exercise A, p. 107)

➜ **1.** future **3.** present

Identify each underlined verb form as present, past, future, present progressive, past progressive, or future progressive.

1. Gwilym Hughes watched his first movie at the age of seven.
2. After that, he was viewing movies on a regular basis.
3. In the next 46 years he watched more than 24,000 feature films.
4. That is a record.
5. It represents more than one-tenth of all the feature films ever made.
6. Hughes lives in a remote corner of Wales.

7. The nearest theater <u>is</u> 20 miles away.
8. Yet Hughes <u>sees</u> nearly 20 movies every week.
9. He says he <u>will keep</u> up that pace.
10. He <u>will hold</u> the record for many years.

7. Perfect Tenses (links to exercise A, p. 110)

➜ **1.** *had looked,* past perfect
2. *have found,* present perfect

Identify the verb in each sentence, and indicate whether its tense is present perfect, past perfect, or future perfect.

1. Audiences have watched motion pictures for more than a century.
2. Before 1900, movies had lasted as little as a minute or two.
3. These brief films had showed simple scenes, such as ocean waves.
4. Since the 1903 film *The Great Train Robbery,* movies have featured complete stories.
5. Westerns and thrillers have attracted audiences ever since that time.
6. Even a century from now, thrillers will surely have lost none of their appeal.
7. Before the maturation of the film industry, most producers had filmed movies in New York and New Jersey.
8. Because of its year-round good weather, southern California has become the biggest movie-making center in the United States.
9. By the year 2050, however, several other parts of the country will probably have developed into important centers of film production.
10. The movie business has come a long way since *The Great Train Robbery.*

8. Using Verb Tenses (links to exercise A, p. 114)

➜ **1.** were using **2.** lacked

In each sentence, choose the correct verb form in parentheses.

1. Television (had been, has been) around for less than 70 years.
2. Experiments with television broadcasting (begin, began) in the early 1930s.

3. Before TV sets became available commercially, scientists (will have demonstrated, had demonstrated) television at the 1939 New York world's fair.
4. Color television (made, will make) its first appearance in 1954.
5. Now virtually all television programs (air, aired) in color.
6. Early home TV sets (have, had) large cabinets but very small screens, never larger than 12 inches.
7. Some of today's televisions (feature, will feature) screens more than 60 inches in width.
8. In the near future, thin, flat TVs (will become, became) common.
9. Since the 1960s communications satellites (will enable, have enabled) television broadcasts from anywhere in the world.
10. In 1969 viewers (see, saw) one of the greatest thrills of the television era: astronauts on the moon.

9. Troublesome Verb Pairs (links to exercise A, p. 117)

➜ **1.** can **5.** sat

Choose the correct word or words in parentheses in each of the following sentences.

1. Do the most talented artists (raise, rise) to the top?
2. In Hollywood, they (may not, cannot).
3. Most studio heads don't want to (sit, set) down with anyone who hasn't made a successful commercial movie.
4. But film festivals give young filmmakers a chance to (lie, lay) their reputations on the line.
5. They (raise, rise) the hopes of artists who might otherwise not have a chance.
6. They (sit, set) their sights on quality instead of money.
7. Winning at a festival can help a filmmaker (raise, rise) money for distributing his or her film.
8. Success (lies, lays) ahead for some of these artists.
9. They (sit, set) a festival's tone with movies about important themes.
10. Festival participation might not help, but it (may not, cannot) hurt.

5 Adjectives and Adverbs

1. What Is an Adjective? (links to exercise on p. 128)

→ **1.** some, inventors; successful, inventors; mature, scientists
3. cold, ears; red, ears; harsh, winters; Northeastern, winters

Write each adjective and the noun it modifies. Do not include articles.

1. Alison DeSmyter is an inventive teenager from Texas.
2. Alison has a muscular disability and uses a wheelchair.
3. She invented a portable ramp that helps disabled people move over curbs.
4. She had only a few weeks to create an original design for a local contest.
5. She first considered and rejected an awkward ramp made of rubber.
6. Then she imagined an inflatable ramp, but who would blow it up?
7. Finally Alison created a lightweight metallic ramp and named it the Rampanion (ramp companion).
8. Alison made the exact measurements herself, and her father helped her build the ramp of aluminum.
9. The Rampanion weighs four pounds and comes in a handy bag.
10. Her invention won the grand prize for the fifth grade in a statewide contest.

2. Predicate Adjectives (links to exercise A, p. 130)

→ **1.** common, wipers **2.** dangerous, trolleys

Write each predicate adjective and the noun or pronoun it modifies.

1. Many inventions have been useful to the food industry.
2. In a refrigerator, an apple remains tasty for a long time.
3. Thanks to canning, foods do not become spoiled.
4. But if they smell moldy, they should not be canned!
5. Dried foods stay edible for a long time.
6. Dried fruits are tasty even after long storage.
7. Dried eggs become usable when water is added.
8. Freeze-dried meals are expensive in comparison with other forms of dried food.
9. But they also taste better.
10. Of course, fresh food always seems best of all.

3. Other Words Used as Adjectives (links to exercise A, p. 132)

➜ **1.** Most; human **3.** Our

Write each noun or pronoun that is used as an adjective.

1. What if you did not have clothing fasteners or book-bag snaps?
2. All zippers, buttons, clasps, and laces on your belongings are important.
3. But a more recent invention is replacing these fasteners.
4. Velcro was invented in 1955, long before its widespread use.
5. One of George de Mestral's nature walks led to a startling idea.
6. He found many burs with their tiny hooks clinging to his pants.
7. Burs carry seeds from their parent plants.
8. De Mestral spent some years creating Velcro, which makes our lives more comfortable.
9. A Velcro fastener consists of a hook strip and a loop strip.
10. Perhaps someday most fasteners will be made of Velcro.

4. What Is an Adverb? (links to exercise A, p. 136)

➜ **1.** experimentally, were flying (verb)
2. yet, had flown (verb); successfully, had flown (verb)

Write each adverb and the word it modifies. Then label each modified word as a verb, an adjective, or an adverb. There may be more than one adverb in a sentence.

1. If you have ever failed at inventing something, join the club.
2. The history of invention is full of extremely embarrassing events.
3. Robert Goddard eventually invented the liquid-fueled rocket.
4. But Goddard's first rocket rose rapidly upward and then crashed into his aunt's garden!
5. John Baird made highly important contributions to the invention of television.
6. He also tried to make self-warming socks, a device that failed quite miserably.
7. In 1882 Henry Seeley invented a very early version of the electric iron.
8. But hardly any homes had electricity, so Seeley sold few irons!
9. Hubert Booth cleverly invented an early vacuum cleaner.
10. Because it was too large to move by hand, horses pulled it from house to house!

5. Making Comparisons (links to exercise A, p. 139)

➜ **2.** more important **4.** newest

Choose the correct comparative or superlative form to complete each sentence.

1. The traffic signal is one of the (more important, most important) of all safety inventions.
2. The three-way traffic signal was not the (earlier, earliest) form of traffic control.
3. However, it was (more practical, most practical) than the previous model.
4. Garrett Morgan, who was granted a patent for the traffic signal in 1923, was one of the (more inventive, most inventive) minds of this century.
5. Because Morgan was black, however, his inventions were received (less enthusiastically, least enthusiastically) than those of white inventors.
6. For example, Morgan invented a gas mask that allowed rescue workers to enter gas-filled tunnels (more safely, most safely) than before.
7. In 1916 Morgan and some volunteers who were (braver, bravest) than average wore his masks to rescue 32 men after an underground explosion.
8. Two men with Morgan gas masks were (more effective, most effective) in the first 15 minutes of fighting a fire than a whole company without the masks.
9. Yet when Morgan brought his (later, latest) gas mask to the South, a white companion had to demonstrate it.
10. In World War I, soldiers used Morgan's gas masks to protect themselves from the (deadlier, deadliest) battlefield poison—chlorine gas.

6. Adjective or Adverb? (links to exercise on p. 141)

➜ **1.** really (adverb)

For each sentence, choose the correct modifier from those given in parentheses. Identify each word you choose as an adjective or an adverb.

1. What makes an invention (good, well)?
2. Is a new device (real, really) good if people use it (bad, badly)?
3. The writer Jared Diamond describes the history of some (really, real) helpful inventions that were not used (good, well) at first.

4. For example, the wheel was not a (real, really) advantage for the people of ancient Mexico.
5. Without animals to pull vehicles, they (real, really) couldn't use wheels.
6. An inventor may create something unique without knowing what it is (good, well) for.
7. This happened to Thomas Edison, who did very (good, well) as an inventor.
8. But his plans for the phonograph give us a (good, well) laugh today.
9. Some (bad, badly) ones included using it to teach speech or to record the words of dying people.
10. When businesspeople began playing music on the phonograph, Edison thought this was a (real, really) mistake!

7. Avoiding Double Negatives (links to exercise A, p. 143)

➜ **1.** can **3.** are

Write the word in parentheses that correctly completes each sentence.

1. No one (can, can't) expect all new inventions to be successful.
2. Consider the poor inventor of the "parachute hat," who (had, hadn't) no luck.
3. The invention didn't (ever, never) work, and the inventor broke his neck trying it out!
4. In 1912 Mr. S. I. Russell (couldn't, could) give no reason why his electric heating pad burned.
5. The reason was that the wiring in the device (wasn't, was) no good.
6. Thomas Adams (had, hadn't) no luck in turning chicle into a substitute for rubber.
7. He tried to use chicle for toys and boots, but he (could, couldn't) hardly succeed.
8. Chewing chicle one day, Adams regretted that it barely (had, hadn't) any flavor.
9. He added flavor and invented chewing gum, but doctors warned that it wouldn't be (no, any) good for people.
10. Today chewing gum is very popular, but you (should, shouldn't) never chew too much.

6 Prepositions, Conjunctions, Interjections

1. What Is a Preposition? (links to exercise on p. 154)

➜ **1.** to, fires **2.** from, miles

Write the preposition in each sentence, along with its object.

1. Many people are afraid of bugs.
2. They run from anything "creepy."
3. True, some types of insects are deadly.
4. But very few insects are actually harmful to people.
5. Ant tunnels let air into the soil.
6. Without insect predators, pests would devour farm crops.
7. Bees and butterflies carry pollen between plants.
8. Plants cannot produce fruits or vegetables without pollination.
9. Spiders destroy thousands of flies and other insects.
10. Bugs are a vital link in our ecosystem.

2. Using Prepositional Phrases (links to exercise A, p. 157)

➜ **1.** of spiders, kinds (adj. phrase)
2. to people, dangerous (adv. phrase)

Write the prepositional phrase in each sentence, along with the word it modifies. Then indicate whether the phrase is an adjective phrase or an adverb phrase.

1. Most people are afraid of tarantulas.
2. They are actually less harmful to people than wasps or bees.
3. They would probably run from you and not attack.
4. Many people keep them as pets.
5. The goliath tarantula is the largest spider in the world.
6. It can grow to be a foot in length.
7. However, this spider tips the scales at only about two ounces.
8. If you meet a goliath tarantula, beware the sharp barbs on its abdomen.
9. It can flick the barbs at attackers, causing an itchy rash.
10. Luckily for us, South America is the goliath tarantula's home.

3. Conjunctions (links to exercise A, p. 160)

➜ **1.** and (lenses, light waves)
2. but (Light waves show the details of ordinary objects, the waves are too long to reveal the smallest structures)

Write the conjunction in each sentence, along with the words or groups of words that it joins.

1. The firefly and the lightning bug are the same insect.
2. Females lay eggs in soil, and four weeks later the eggs hatch into larvae.
3. These larvae, or glowworms, are carnivorous.
4. Despite their small size, they can eat slugs and snails.
5. Not only adults but also some larvae glow.
6. The larvae spend the winter in small tunnels and come out again in spring.
7. Adult fireflies feed on pollen and nectar.
8. Both male and female fireflies light up.
9. On summer days fireflies rest on plants or in trees.
10. Fireflies produce light, yet they don't produce heat.

7 Verbals and Verbal Phrases

1. Gerunds (links to exercise on p. 171)

➜ **1.** riding **4.** Waiting

Write the gerunds in these sentences.

1. Helping people in wheelchairs is one job of service dogs.
2. People who are dedicated and good with animals are needed for educating the dogs.
3. Loving the animals is the first requirement for trainers.
4. Training a dog in obedience takes two to three months.
5. The next few months are devoted to teaching special skills.
6. The dog focuses on learning exactly the tasks it will need to perform for its new owner.
7. Retrievers are especially good at fetching things for disabled people.
8. Their favorite activity is helping people.
9. Matching each dog with a particular person is important.
10. New owners learn about feeding and exercising their dogs.

2. Participles (links to exercise on p. 173)

➜ **1.** *acting,* participle
3. *Training,* gerund

Write the participles in these sentences, identifying each as a present participle or a past participle. Also write the noun or pronoun that each participle modifies.

1. Indian Red was a horse living in Ontario.
2. Walking along a road one night, he stopped suddenly.
3. Chilled and fatigued, he should have been seeking shelter.
4. Instead he neighed and whinnied, trying to get cars to stop.
5. Only a few speeding drivers were out on that cold night.
6. Those who came by ignored the horse, driving right past him.
7. Finally, one driver, his curiosity aroused, stopped to see what was wrong.
8. Searching a snow-covered ditch near the horse, the man discovered an old woman.
9. The woman, now numbed by the cold, had fallen into the ditch.
10. Not even knowing her, Indian Red wanted to get help for her.

3. Infinitives (links to exercise A, p. 175)

→ **2.** To play **4.** to let

Write the infinitives in these sentences. Identify whether each is used as a noun, an adjective, or an adverb.

1. Jackie Geyer liked to feed raccoons in her yard.
2. One day a badly injured raccoon came to eat.
3. The raccoon needed to limp to the feeding station because its right hind leg was injured.
4. "Chloe" seemed a good name to give the raccoon.
5. One day Chloe was missing, and Jackie began to worry.
6. Finally Chloe appeared, using only her front legs to walk to the food bowl.
7. Jackie was surprised to see that Chloe's other hind leg was now injured.
8. Luckily, to walk on her "hands" was not very hard for a talented raccoon like Chloe.
9. Chloe had decided that Jackie's was the only place in town to eat.
10. Chloe's injured legs were quick to heal, and she has now been dining at Jackie's place for eight years.

4. Verbal Phrases (links to exercise A, p. 177)

→ **1.** *Strolling around the neighborhood,* gerund phrase
2. *slightly spoiled,* participial phrase

Write the verbal phrases in these sentences, identifying each as a gerund phrase, a participial phrase, or an infinitive phrase.

1. Many animals, including chimpanzees and elephants, have learned to draw or paint.

2. A chimp named Alpha preferred drawing pictures to eating meals.
3. She would beg visitors, fascinated by her behavior, to give her paper and a pencil.
4. Researchers asked a chimp named Moja to draw various things, including a basketball.
5. Seeing vertical zigzags on the paper, they thought that she had just scribbled.
6. Then they realized that the zigzags might represent the ball's up-and-down bouncing.
7. An elephant named Ruby loves to paint abstract pictures.
8. Choosing colors is a creative act for her.
9. A visitor who enjoyed watching Ruby paint fell ill, and paramedics in blue uniforms came to help him.
10. After they left, Ruby expressed herself by painting a blue blob surrounded by a swirl of red.

8 Sentence Structure

1. What Is a Clause? (links to exercise A, p. 187)

→ **1.** dependent clause **5.** independent clause

Identify each underlined group of words as an independent clause or a dependent clause.

1. <u>Dalié Jiménez was concerned</u> that disadvantaged children were not getting books read to them often enough.
2. She had learned in her psychology class <u>that reading to young children was very important</u>.
3. Children need this experience <u>so that their brains can develop properly.</u>
4. <u>When she was 14 years old</u>, Dalié began volunteering at a Head Start program in her hometown of Miami, Florida.
5. She liked this work <u>because she was interested in children</u>.
6. When she told her friends about her work, <u>they wanted to volunteer too</u>.
7. Dalié and about 30 of her friends started a children's library <u>that consisted of donated books</u>.
8. They used puppets to act out stories <u>while they read</u>.
9. When Dalié heard that Head Start's funding was going to be cut by one-third, <u>she lobbied lawmakers</u>.
10. <u>Because they worked so hard</u>, she and her friends were able to help save the Head Start program.

2. Simple and Compound Sentences (links to exercise A, p. 190)

→ **1.** simple **2.** compound

Identify each sentence as simple or compound.

1. Justin Lebo of Saddle Brook, New Jersey, loved bikes.
2. He and his dad shared an interest in bicycle racing.
3. They had their garage set up like a bike shop; they worked there on their bikes all the time.
4. Justin bought a couple of rundown bikes, and he fixed them up.
5. The bikes looked as good as new, but Justin didn't need any more bikes himself.
6. He decided to donate them to the Kilbarchan Home for Boys.
7. Justin liked the idea of people fixing up bikes for those less fortunate, so he continued to do so in his spare time.
8. Many people offered him their old bikes for free.
9. The donations were helpful for a time, but soon Justin ran out of space in his small garage.
10. Justin fixed 250 bikes, and he gave them all away.

3. Complex Sentences (links to exercise A, p. 193)

→ **1.** Independent clause: *many people do not know about it;* dependent clause: *Although the Foster Grandparent Program is more than 30 years old*
2. Independent clause: *This program was established;* dependent clause: *so that hospitalized and institutionalized children could get special attention*

Write these sentences on a sheet of paper. Underline each independent clause once and each dependent clause twice.

1. National Youth Service Day is not well-known, although it has been celebrated for more than ten years.
2. This national event was founded so that young people's volunteer work would be recognized.
3. National Youth Service Day is a two-day event that brings together student volunteers working on community projects.
4. After they work on a project, the volunteers have a deep sense of satisfaction.
5. In Washington, D.C., an old building was turned into a community center so that children would have a safe place to go.
6. Because they wanted to help beautify their city, some volunteers in Atlanta, Georgia, painted a playground.
7. Although adult volunteers helped, most of the work was done by elementary-school and middle-school students.

8. Since they were interested in identifying major problems in their neighborhood, about 90 high school students in San Francisco conducted a community survey.
9. Because they wanted to improve the environment, volunteers in Troutdale, Oregon, planted new vegetation at a state park.
10. Nearly 3 million volunteers worked on one recent National Youth Service Day, so that many communities benefited.

4. Kinds of Dependent Clauses (links to exercise A, p. 197)

➜ **1.** *who are visually challenged,* adjective clause
2. *because they help the people get around in daily life,* adverb clause

Write these sentences on a sheet of paper. Underline each dependent clause, identifying it as an adjective clause, an adverb clause, or a noun clause.

1. Christian Miller, who is a young animal lover, cared for sea turtles on a beach near his home in Palm Beach, Florida.
2. You may know that sea turtles are endangered.
3. Until he received training from the Florida Department of Natural Resources, Christian could not work with the turtles.
4. During the turtles' nesting season, which lasts from May to October, Christian help the turtles for two to three hours a day.
5. After the turtles hatch in the sand, they head for the ocean.
6. Baby turtles that have a hard time digging themselves out of the sand may need extra help.
7. Those that were in need of help were lucky to have Christian to assist them.
8. Christian knows where most of the 400 to 600 nests on his beach are.
9. He keeps careful records of his beach patrols so that he can send his findings to the U.S. Department of Natural Resources.
10. Although the job of monitoring sea turtles is hard, Christian finds it very rewarding.

5. Compound-Complex Sentences (links to exercise A, p. 199)

➜ **1.** complex **2.** compound

Identify each sentence as compound, complex, or compound-complex.

1. When she was four, Mandy Van Benthuysen learned that she had muscular dystrophy.
2. Later she volunteered for the Muscular Dystrophy Association, which works to find treatments for neuromuscular diseases.

3. Neuromuscular diseases are diseases that affect both the nerves and the muscles.
4. Mandy, who was a college student, traveled around the country, and she urged other young people to volunteer.
5. She said that volunteering helps those in need; it also "makes you a better person all around."
6. For more than 30 years, the comedian Jerry Lewis has hosted a telethon that raises money for the Muscular Dystrophy Association.
7. Celebrities who want to help volunteer to be on the show.
8. Among the stars who have volunteered are Mariah Carey, Jason Alexander, Judge Judy, and Cher.
9. Television viewers call in with pledges while they watch the show.
10. Millions of dollars have been raised, and this money has helped many Americans with neuromuscular diseases.

9 Subject-Verb Agreement

1. Agreement in Number (links to exercise A, p. 210)

➜ **1.** have **2.** create

Rewrite these sentences so that verbs agree in number with their subjects. If a sentence contains no error, write *Correct.*

1. According to legend, the model for *kente* cloth were a spider's web.
2. The word *kente* come from *kenten,* which means "basket."
3. *Kente* cloth resembles the woven pattern of a basket.
4. This finely woven cloth are made on homemade looms.
5. Weavers moves the looms with strings tied to their big toes.
6. Traditionally, *kente* cloth is made from silk.
7. These days the cloth don't always contain silk.
8. Rayon threads serves as an inexpensive substitute.
9. Weavers creates four-inch strips of cloth and then weaves the strips together to make larger garments.
10. Every design has a name, such as "crocodile tears."

2. Compound Subjects (links to exercise A, p. 212)

➜ **1.** Correct **2.** A basket or pot serves a practical function, such as food storage.

Write the verb form that agrees with the subject of each sentence.

1. Written reports and speeches (has, have) their limitations.
2. Many politicians and business executives (prefers, prefer) using multimedia presentations.
3. CDs and other technology (provides, provide) new ways of reaching audiences.
4. Text, images, and sound (combines, combine) to convey messages effectively.
5. A photograph, art reproduction, or video clip (grabs, grab) the audience's attention.
6. Recorded speech or music (enlivens, enliven) a presentation.
7. Charts and graphs (allows, allow) people to absorb information quickly.
8. Skill and imagination (contributes, contribute) to a presentation's success.
9. Either fuzzy images or poor sound quality (makes, make) a presentation less effective.
10. Poor organization and dull ideas also (displeases, displease) audiences.

3. Agreement Problems in Sentences (links to exercise A, p. 215)

➜ **1.** Do your classmates collect posters?
2. Correct

Rewrite these sentences so that verbs agree with their subjects. If a sentence contains no error, write *Correct*.

1. Posters is an effective way to sell goods and services.
2. Has you ever seen a poster that sells war?
3. Propaganda posters during wartime has performed this function.
4. Such posters are sometimes an important part of a war effort.
5. There is many examples from the two world wars.
6. The slogan on one of the World War I posters are "Food *is* ammunition—Don't waste it."
7. There is wartime posters designed to promote patriotism.
8. Hatred and fear are other emotions that can be stirred up by propaganda posters.
9. Through posters is recruited many volunteers for the military.
10. Advertising specialists and artists hired by the government are the creative force behind wartime posters.

4. Indefinite Pronouns as Subjects (links to exercise A, p. 218)

➜ **1.** Many know the saying "A picture's worth a thousand words." **2.** Correct

Rewrite these sentences so that verbs agree with their subjects. If a sentence contains no error, write *Correct*.

1. One glimpses 19th-century slum life in Jacob Riis's *How the Other Half Lives*.
2. Another of his influential books are *Children of the Poor*.
3. Each of these books contain photographs that convey the problems of immigrants.
4. Many of the photographs document conditions in New York City tenements.
5. All of Riis's photographs exposes the horrors of overcrowding and malnutrition.
6. Both of these problems was common in 19th-century cities.
7. Few has captured urban poverty as vividly as Riis did.
8. None of the written accounts so dramatically demonstrate the plight of the urban poor.
9. Most of Riis's photographs illustrates problems caused by rapid growth.
10. Nearly everyone credit Riis with helping to improve conditions.

5. Problem Subjects (links to exercise A, p. 221)

➜ **1.** describes **2.** travels

Write the form of the verb that agrees with the subject of each sentence.

1. Three and a half years (seems, seem) a short amount of time for planning and finishing the Vietnam Veterans Memorial.
2. Economics (is, are) always a concern in designing a large project.
3. About eight months (is, are) how long it actually took to construct the memorial.
4. The public (lines, line) up to view the wall and nearby statues at this popular site.
5. "Heroes in Black Stone" (is, are) a song about Vietnam veterans and the people who visit the memorial.
6. Politics (is, are) not the point of the wall.
7. A committee of distinguished sculptors and architects (is, are) to be congratulated for choosing such an effective tribute.
8. Only 600 feet (separates, separate) the wall from the Lincoln Memorial.

9. *Offerings at the Wall,* a book by Thomas Allen, (contains, contain) pictures of items left at the wall by visitors.
10. The National Park Service staff (collects, collect) personal items left at the wall.

10 Capitalization

1. People and Cultures (links to exercise on p. 232)

➜ **2.** Mr. Jones, Knight, Glubok, Tamarin

Write the words and abbreviations that should be capitalized but are not in these sentences. Capitalize each correctly.

1. Last week coach jackett told us a story about one of the most interesting tennis matches of the 20th century.
2. It all started with a man by the name of robert larimore riggs.
3. bobby riggs, as he was known in the tennis world, won the Wimbledon title in 1939.
4. Our coach said that mr. riggs won three U.S. Open championships but became famous for his weird tennis matches.
5. My friend roberta said that her aunt a.j. once played a match against riggs while he sat on a chair.
6. The one event that i found most interesting occurred when riggs challenged the australian margaret court to a tennis match.
7. Most people—including my aunt, who was a tennis fan—expected court to beat riggs because she was 25 years younger than he.
8. Riggs won that tennis match but later met another female challenger, billie jean king, who defeated him easily.
9. The match became one of the most publicized events in american sports, attracting 50 million viewers.
10. Years later, in another gender battle, riggs and vitas gerulaitis lost a doubles match to martina navratilova and pam shriver.

2. First Words and Titles (links to exercise A, p. 235)

➜ **1.** How, Equipment, Baseball, Bat **2.** Whoever

Write the words that should be capitalized but are not in these sentences, capitalizing them correctly. If there are no errors in a sentence, write *Correct*.

1. on July 20, 1998, the Special Olympics celebrated its 30th anniversary.

2. *the today show* and *parade magazine* have featured inspiring stories about the courage of athletes in the Special Olympics.
3. The Special Olympics oath is "let me win. but if I cannot win, let me be brave in the attempt."
4. In 1997 a Christmas album benefiting the Special Olympics was produced, with songs like "blue christmas" and "the christmas song."
5. The Special Olympics has its own magazine, entitled *spirit*.
6. On February 11, 1990, the television drama *life goes on* devoted an hour-long episode to the Special Olympics.
7. In 1987 more than 4,700 athletes participated in the Special Olympics, the year's largest amateur sports event.
8. The event was covered in *sports illustrated* and *time*.
9. For information on how to get involved, write a letter to Special Olympics headquarters, beginning "dear Sir or Madam."
10. If you would like to research the Special Olympics, you may want to make an outline that begins like this:
    I. general information
        a. athletes
        b. families
        c. volunteers
        d. national and worldwide chapters

3. Places and Transportation (links to exercise A, p. 239)

➜ **1.** North America **3.** Appalachian Mountains

Write the words that should be capitalized but are not in these sentences, capitalizing them correctly. If there are no errors in a sentence, write *Correct*.

1. Have you ever wondered where the word *marathon* originated?
2. The first marathon was held during the first modern Olympics in athens, greece, in 1896.
3. The race was named for an ancient battle near the Greek town of marathon.
4. According to legend, the soldier Pheidippides raced from marathon to athens (about 25 miles) with news of the Greeks' victory over the Persians and then immediately died.
5. Today, marathons are held all over the world, in places like london, england; sydney, australia; and dublin, ireland.
6. Whether in the northern or the southern part of the country, on the east coast or the west coast, you'll find marathons.
7. For example, the one in new york city begins on staten island, at the verrazano-narrows bridge, and ends in central park.

8. There's even a marathon called Grandma's Marathon in duluth, minnesota, with a scenic course along lake superior.
9. Perhaps you'd be more interested in the Rock 'n' Roll Marathon, with a course that travels through the san diego zoo and along highway 163.
10. Known for its difficult course, the Boston Marathon begins in hopkinton and ends in copley square.

4. Organizations and Other Subjects (links to exercise on p. 241)

→ **1.** North Side Junior High

Write the words that should be capitalized but are not in these sentences, capitalizing them correctly. If there are no errors write *Correct.*

1. Records show that as early as 400 b.c. the Chinese were playing a game similar to soccer.
2. Some early footballs were stuffed with hair or rags.
3. The term *soccer* was first used at oxford university.
4. James Richardson Spensley, founder of the genoa cricket and football club, introduced the game of soccer to Italy in 1893.
5. On may 21, 1904, an international soccer federation was formed in paris, France.
6. The first world cup finals were held in Uruguay, but the teams could not agree on the size of the ball; therefore, different-sized balls were used in the two halves.
7. During world war II (1939–1945), the world cup was canceled.
8. The oneidas of boston, the first organized soccer club in America, were undefeated from 1862 to 1865.
9. The first series of games known as the women's world cup was played in China in 1991.
10. On saturday, july 10, 1999, the U.S. women's team won its second world cup title in Pasadena's rose bowl stadium.

11 Punctuation

1. Periods and Other End Marks (links to exercise A, p. 252)

→ **1.** ? **2.** !

Write the punctuation end mark that should replace each numbered blank.

You don't have to use a code to keep a message secret__1__ You can use invisible ink. What substance should you use__2__ Well, lemon juice works well__3__ No kidding__4__ Dip a toothpick or brush into the juice and use it to write your message. Let the juice dry__5__ Your message will be invisible. Now, hold the paper so that it touches a hot light bulb. Be careful__6__ Don't burn yourself. The words of your message will appear. Amazing__7__ Do you want to try a different kind of ink__8__ Write your message in milk and let it dry. Now, empty pencil-sharpener shavings over the flat paper__9__ The shavings will stick to the invisible words and make the message appear__10__

2. Commas in Sentences (links to exercise on p. 255)

➜ Think of this, readers,

Rewrite this paragraph, adding commas where they are needed.

Some cultures lived in America for many centuries but then they disappeared. They left tools pottery and other artifacts behind. They also left carvings and paintings on rocks called rock art. Petroglyphs (rock carvings) show human figures animals and some designs that are not easily explained. Artists made petroglyphs with small pointed rocks or flat stones. They used these as knives picks and chisels to carve shapes on large stones. Pictographs (rock paintings) on the other hand were made with paint from berries or vegetables. Native American artists may have painted for pleasure or they may have painted to communicate with one another. In any case the pictures are like a form of code to us.

3. Commas: Dates, Addresses, and Letters (links to exercise A, p. 257)

➜ New York, NY February 20, 2000

Rewrite the following letter, adding missing commas.

April 27 2000

Manuel Rojas
123 Maple Ave.
Los Angeles California

Dear Manny

Today I learned another interesting fact about secret codes. I found out how spies sent secret messages through the mail during World War II. It worked like this. A spy in London England might write a normal letter that contained no secret information. The spy would then address the envelope to his or her superior in Paris France. In the upper right-hand corner of the envelope, the spy would write a tiny message in code. When the spy placed a stamp over the message, no one could detect the message. When the letter arrived, the recipient would steam off the stamp and decode the message. Even if enemy agents opened the letter, it would not arouse suspicion.

By the way, I read in the newspaper that a speaker will give a presentation at our local library about how information is coded in computers. The presentation is on May 18 2000. Would you like to go with me when you visit?

Your friend who loves codes

Jack

4. Quotation Marks (links to exercise A, p. 261)

➜ "Are you nuts?"   “I do,” said Jay,” and

Rewrite the following passage, correcting errors in the use of quotation marks.

“Some codes are spoken rather than written, Julia said. A whole town once used a secret language called Boontling.”

“Why was it called that? asked Paul.

“The town was Boonville, California,” Julia explained, “and the word *Boontling* stood for *Boonville lingo*”.

Paul asked, “Is lingo the same as slang?”

“That’s right! Julia exclaimed. “From the 1880s to the 1930s, nearly everyone who lived in Boonville could speak the lingo.” She went on to say that “a few people still know it today.”

“Give me some examples,” Paul said, of Boontling words.”

“Some combine parts of English words,” said Julia. “For example, a schoolteacher is a schoolch.” A rail fence is a relf.”

Paul pointed out that “those words weren’t too hard to decipher.”

“No,” said Julia, but other words are less obvious. A storyteller is called a bearman because the best storyteller in town hunted bears.”

5. Semicolons and Colons (links to exercise A, p. 263)

➜ messages: a folk song;

Rewrite this paragraph, correcting errors in the use of semicolons and colons.

The ancient Celts used: a form of written communication called the ogham alphabet. This alphabet can still be seen in inscriptions on stones in fact, more than 350 such stones have survived. They are found in: Ireland, Wales, Scotland, southern England, and the Isle of Man. During the time of ogham's use (about 600 B.C. to 700 A.D.), few people could read and write. To write a message in ogham, a person would draw or chisel a long, straight line. Each letter would be represented by one to five short lines, which might extend to the left of, to the right of, or completely through the long line. A message could also be written on a stick, the letters were cut into its edge. The ogham alphabet had 20 letters, each named for a tree; a shrub or other plant, or a natural element, like lightning or the sea. Among the trees represented were the following, the birch, the oak, and the hawthorn. Nose ogham and shin ogham were variations in which people used their fingers to form the cross-strokes of the letters against the straight line of their nose or shinbone.

6. Hyphens, Dashes, and Parentheses (links to exercise on p. 265)

➜ **1.** — **2.** -

Indicate what punctuation mark—hyphen, dash, or parenthesis—should replace each numbered blank in this paragraph. If no mark is needed, write *None*.

Imagine living in the Victorian era __1__ a time when messages had to be carried hundreds of miles on horseback or sent on ships that traveled across the ocean __2__. It may have taken days, weeks, or even months for a message to reach its destination. This was how people communicated over long distances in the 1800s. What a tremendous improvement __3__ a leap in technology __4__ the invention of the telegraph was to the people of the Victorian era. Samuel Morse was one of the inventors of the telegraph. In 1844, at the age of fifty __5__ three, Morse demonstrated that messages could be sent quickly from Washington, D.C., to Baltimore, Maryland, __6__ by using his electric telegraph. Morse also invented his own code __7__ the Morse code __8__, which is a system of long and short clicks used to transmit messages by means of the telegraph. When Morse code is written out, the letters of the alphabet appear as groups of dots and dashes. The most famous message in Morse code is (· · · – – – – – · · ·), or SOS, the widely recognized distress call.

7. Apostrophes (links to exercise A, p. 267)

➜ another's, Cryptoanalysts

Rewrite this paragraph, correcting errors in the use of apostrophes and possessive pronouns.

Its easy to make a simple cipher called a scytale, which was invented by the Spartan's in ancient Greece. To make you're own scytale, youll need a long strip of plain paper and a cylinder, such as a pencil or the cardboard tube from a paper-towel roll. Wrap the strip of paper in a spiral around the cylinder. Then begin writing your message along the length of the cylinder. Write each letter on a different part of the paper spiral. Dont use punctuation. When you reach the end of a line, continue writing on the next line until your message is complete. Now unroll the paper from the cylinder. It'll look like a long strip of letters in a single column. To read your message, the recipient must wrap the strip of paper around a cylinder of the same size that you used in writing the message. Whose going to read your message? Lysander, an ancient Greek military leader, once received a scytale and used the information in it to win an important battle for the Greek's.

8. Punctuating Titles (links to exercise A, p. 269)

➜ <u>Polygraphia</u> <u>The Journal of Cryptology</u>

Read this paragraph and rewrite the titles in it, using either quotation marks or underlining as appropriate.

Countries have spied on each other for centuries. In China 2,500 years ago, Sun Zi described how to organize military intelligence in his book The Art of War. In his epic poem the Iliad, Homer discussed spying during the Trojan War. Spying helped the Allies win World War II, as William Stevenson explains in his book A Man Called Intrepid. Codebreaking helped the Allies sink the German battleship *Bismarck*. Broadcast over the BBC, the first lines of Paul Verlaine's poem Chanson d'Automne warned the French Resistance that the Normandy invasion was imminent. Shortly after the war, an American engineer developed information theory in an article called A Mathematical Theory of Communication. Even works of entertainment, like the 1960s TV show Secret Agent, have depicted the pressures of being a spy who can trust no one. Johnny Rivers sang about this dangerous life in the show's theme song, Secret Agent Man. Contemporary movies, such as Mission Impossible and Tomorrow Never Dies, still thrill audiences with their tales of espionage.

Quick-Fix Spelling Machine

QUICK–FIX SPELLING MACHINE: PLURALS OF NOUNS

SINGULAR	RULE	PLURAL
skateboard painting ticket	Add *-s* to most nouns.	skateboards paintings tickets
WATCH OUT	The exceptions to this rule are nouns whose plurals are formed in special ways such as *man (men), woman (women)* and *child (children).*	
hiss dish ditch box buzz	Add *-es* to nouns that end in *s, sh, ch, x,* or *z.*	hisses dishes ditches boxes buzzes
auto igloo radio	Add *-s* to most nouns that end in *o.*	autos igloos radios
potato tomato mosquito	Add *-es* to a few nouns that end in *o.*	potatoes tomatoes mosquitoes
flurry deputy battery dairy	For most nouns ending in *y,* change the *y* to *i* and add *-es.*	flurries deputies batteries dairies
alley play turkey	Just add *-s* when a vowel comes before the *y.*	alleys plays turkeys
calf thief wife leaf knife	For most nouns ending in *f* or *fe,* change the *f* to a *v* and add *-es* or *-s.*	calves thieves wives leaves knives
belief muff safe	Just add *-s* to a few nouns that end in *f* or *fe.*	beliefs muffs safes
series sheep species aircraft	Keep the same spelling for some nouns.	series sheep species aircraft

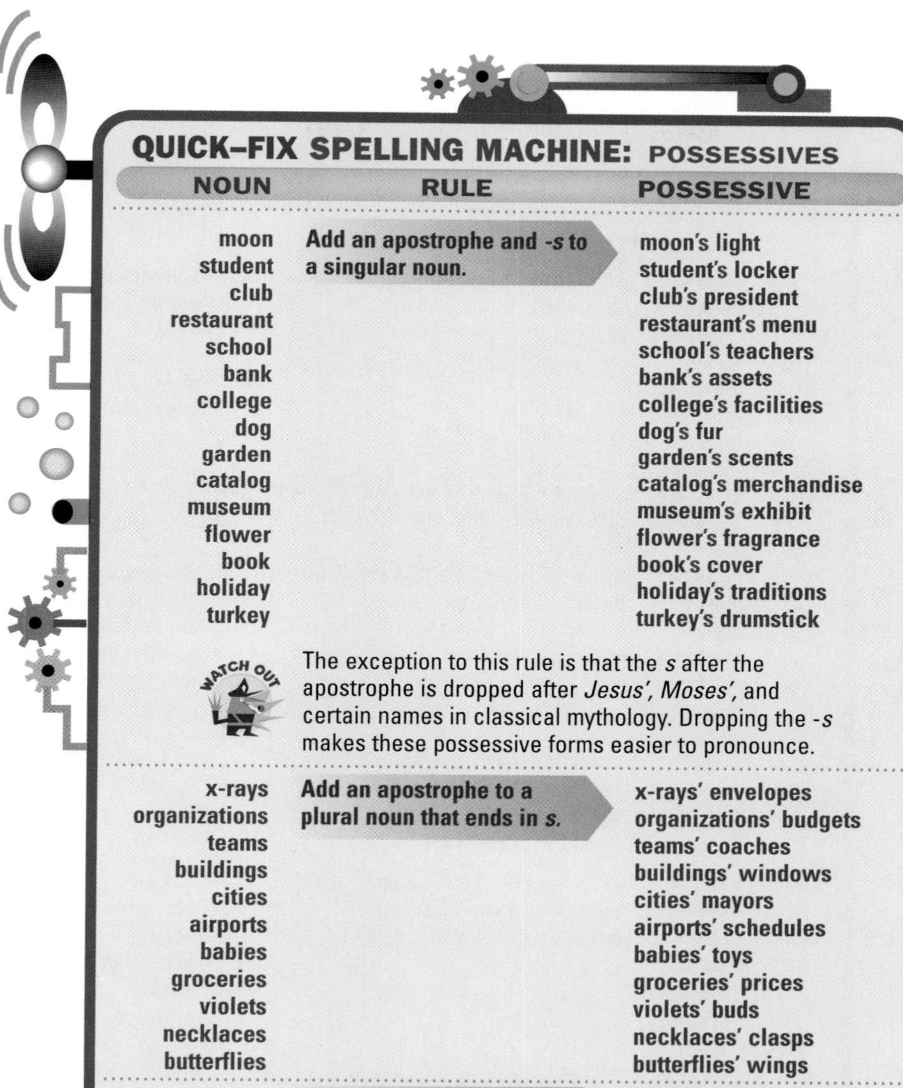

QUICK–FIX SPELLING MACHINE: POSSESSIVES

NOUN	RULE	POSSESSIVE
moon	Add an apostrophe and *-s* to a singular noun.	moon's light
student		student's locker
club		club's president
restaurant		restaurant's menu
school		school's teachers
bank		bank's assets
college		college's facilities
dog		dog's fur
garden		garden's scents
catalog		catalog's merchandise
museum		museum's exhibit
flower		flower's fragrance
book		book's cover
holiday		holiday's traditions
turkey		turkey's drumstick

The exception to this rule is that the *s* after the apostrophe is dropped after *Jesus', Moses',* and certain names in classical mythology. Dropping the *-s* makes these possessive forms easier to pronounce.

NOUN	RULE	POSSESSIVE
x-rays	Add an apostrophe to a plural noun that ends in *s.*	x-rays' envelopes
organizations		organizations' budgets
teams		teams' coaches
buildings		buildings' windows
cities		cities' mayors
airports		airports' schedules
babies		babies' toys
groceries		groceries' prices
violets		violets' buds
necklaces		necklaces' clasps
butterflies		butterflies' wings
deer	Add an apostrophe and *-s* to a plural noun not ending in *s.*	deer's hoofs
oxen		oxen's load
salmon		salmon's gills
stepchildren		stepchildren's names
sheep		sheep's wool
mice		mice's nests
people		people's languages

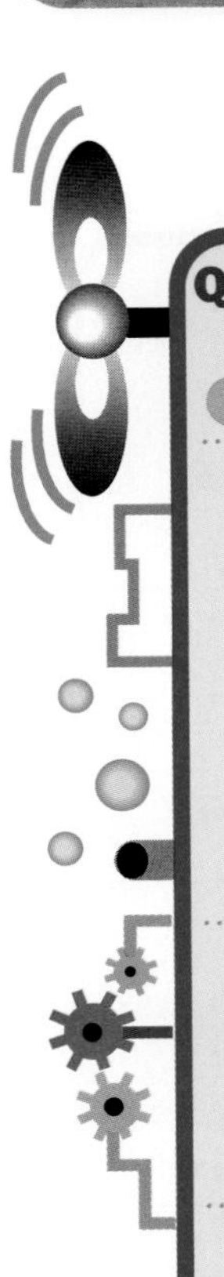

QUICK–FIX SPELLING MACHINE: WORDS ENDING IN SILENT *e*

WORD	RULE	CHANGE
home engage hope tune shame state	Keep the silent *e* when a suffix beginning with a consonant is added to a word that ends in a silent *e*.	homeless engagement hopeful tuneless shameful statement

WATCH OUT Some words that are exceptions include *truly, awful, argument, ninth,* and *wholly.*

WORD	RULE	CHANGE
peace courage manage salvage outrage charge	Keep the silent *e* when a suffix beginning with an *a* or an *o* is added to a silent *e* word if the *e* follows a soft *c* or *g*.	peaceable courageous manageably salvageable outrageous chargeable
agree woe	Keep the silent *e* when a suffix beginning with a vowel is added to a word ending in *ee* or *oe*.	agreeable woeful
flake elevate haze institute shake create	Drop the silent *e* from the base word when you add a suffix beginning with *y* or a vowel.	flaky elevation hazy institution shaky creative

WATCH OUT Exceptions to this rule are such words as *changeable* and *courageous.*

QUICK–FIX SPELLING MACHINE: WORDS ENDING IN *y*

WORD	RULE	CHANGE
happy thirty merry greedy sneaky deputy	Change the *y* to *i* to add a suffix to a word ending in *y* if the *y* follows a consonant.	happiness thirtieth merriest greedily sneakier deputies
rally marry tally fry	Keep the *y* when adding *-ing* to a word ending in *y* if the *y* follows a consonant.	rallying marrying tallying frying
joy pay boy	Keep the *y* when adding a suffix to a word ending in a vowel and *y*.	joyous payable boyish

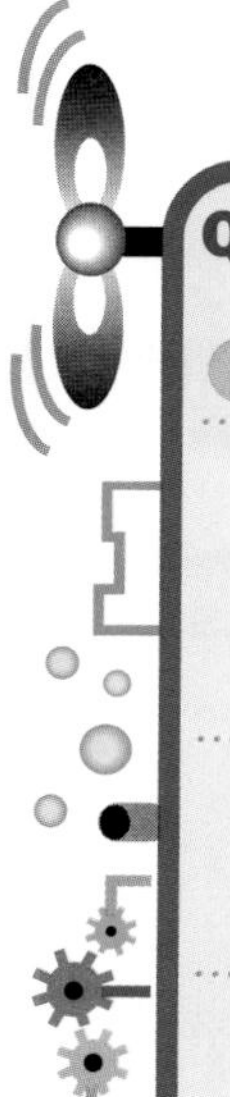

QUICK–FIX SPELLING MACHINE: WORDS ENDING IN A CONSONANT

WORD	RULE	CHANGE
mat slip hit dim	If a one-syllable word ends in a consonant preceded by a vowel, double the final consonant before adding a suffix beginning with a vowel.	matting slipped hitter dimmest
heap steal scoot meat	If a one-syllable word ends in a consonant preceded by two vowels, do not double the final consonant.	heaped stealing scooted meaty
transfer admit allot permit	Double the final consonant in a word of more than one syllable only if the word is accented on the last syllable.	transferring admitted allotting permitting

QUICK-FIX SPELLING MACHINE: ADVERBS

ADJECTIVE	RULE	ADVERB
sudden bad rapid	Add *-ly.*	suddenly badly rapidly
true	Drop *e,* add *-ly.*	truly
angry heavy steady	Change *y* to *i,* add *-ly.*	angrily heavily steadily

QUICK–FIX SPELLING MACHINE: COMPOUNDS

	SINGULAR	RULE	PLURAL
One word	dishcloth supermarket airport	Add *-s* to most words.	dishcloths supermarkets airports
Two or more words	feather bed atomic bomb attorney general	Make the main noun plural. The main noun is the noun that is modified.	feather beds atomic bombs attorneys general
Hyphenated words	son-in-law half-dollar vice-president	Make the main noun plural.	sons-in-law half-dollars vice-presidents

QUICK-FIX SPELLING MACHINE: OPEN AND CLOSED SYLLABLES

An *open syllable* ends in one vowel and has a long vowel sound.	baby labor fable cedar	ba by la bor fa ble ce dar
A *closed syllable* ends in a consonant and has a short vowel sound.	ladder mischief problem plunder	lad der mis chief prob lem plun der

QUICK-FIX SPELLING MACHINE: CONTRACTIONS

WORDS	RULE	CONTRACTION
I am	Combine a personal pronoun with a verb by adding an apostrophe in place of the missing letters.	I'm
you are		you're
he is		he's
she is		she's
it is		it's
we are		we're
they are		they're
I would		I'd
you would		you'd
he would		he'd
she would		she'd
we would		we'd
they would		they'd
I will		I'll
you will		you'll
he will		he'll
she will		she'll
it will		it'll
we will		we'll
they will		they'll
I have		I've
you have		you've
we have		we've
they have		they've
I had		I'd
you had		you'd
he had		he'd
she had		she'd
we had		we'd
they had		they'd
do not	Otherwise, combine two words into one by adding an apostrophe in place of the missing letters.	don't
where is		where's
there is		there's
could not		couldn't
would not		wouldn't
should not		shouldn't
is not		isn't
was not		wasn't
who is		who's

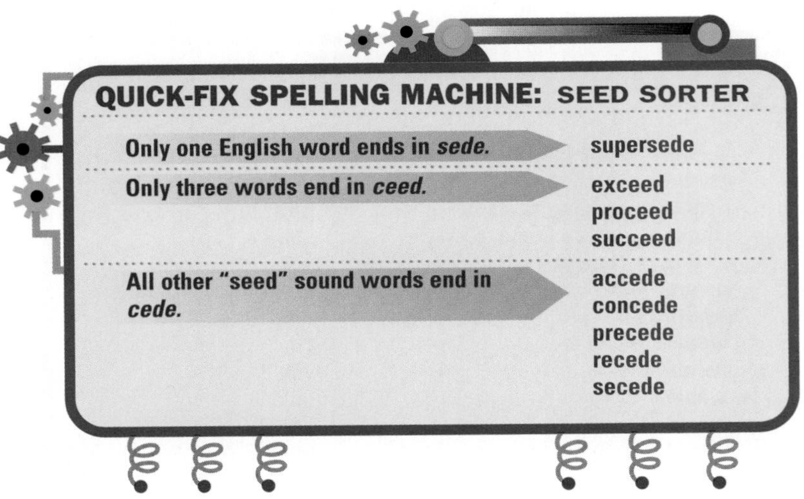

QUICK-FIX SPELLING MACHINE: SEED SORTER

Only one English word ends in *sede.*	supersede
Only three words end in *ceed.*	exceed proceed succeed
All other "seed" sound words end in *cede.*	accede concede precede recede secede

QUICK–FIX SPELLING MACHINE: *ie* AND *ei* ENGINES

If you are unsure whether to use *ie* or *ei,* the better choice is usually *ie,* unless the letters follow *c,* or sound like *a.*

i BEFORE *e*	EXCEPT AFTER *c*	SOUNDS LIKE *a*	EXCEPTIONS
field	receipt	eight	their
chief	deceive	weight	height
piece	deceit	sleigh	counterfeit
grief	conceit	neigh	heir
belief	receive	feign	sheik
niece	perceive	vein	neither
priest	ceiling	skein	leisure
thief		rein	seize
relief		reign	either
brief		neighbor	weird
achieve			species
shield			financier
shriek			
believe			

QUICK-FIX SPELLING MACHINE: BORROWED WORDS

Over the centuries, as English speakers increased their contact with people from other lands, English speakers "borrowed" words from other languages. The English language began to grow in new directions, and became the colorful tapestry we know today.

Spelling follows certain patterns in every language. For example, some letter patterns in French, Spanish, and Italian appear in words commonly used in English.

PATTERN	WORD
Some borrowed words keep their original spellings and pronunciations.	
In many words taken from French, a final *t* is silent.	ballet beret buffet
In both English and French, a soft *g* is usually followed by *e, i,* or *y.*	mirage region energy
A hard *g* is followed by *a, o,* or *u.*	vague
Many words taken from the Dutch language have *oo* in their spellings.	cookie snoop hook caboose
Many words borrowed from Spanish end in *o.*	taco tornado rodeo bronco
Many words that were plural in Italian end in *i.*	spaghetti macaroni ravioli
Some words from other languages were changed to fit English rules of pronunciation and spelling.	
Many words in Native American languages contain sound combinations unlike those in English words. English speakers found these words to be useful but difficult to pronounce, so they used more familiar sounds and letter combinations.	topaghan = toboggan tamahaac = tomahawk pakani = pecan squa = squaw wampumpeag = wampum qajaq = kayak

Commonly Misspelled Words

A
abbreviate
accidentally
achievement
analyze
anonymous
answer
apologize
appearance
appreciate
appropriate
argument
awkward

B
beautiful
because
beginning
believe
bicycle
brief
bulletin
business

C
calendar
campaign
candidate
caught
certain
changeable
characteristic
clothes
column
committee
courageous
courteous
criticize
curiosity

D
decision
definitely
dependent
description
desirable
despair
desperate
development
dictionary
different
disappear
disappoint
discipline
dissatisfied

E
eighth
eligible
eliminate
embarrass
enthusiastic
especially
essay
exaggerate
exceed
existence
experience

F
familiar
fascinating
favorite
February
foreign
fourth
fragile

G
generally
government
grammar
guarantee
guard

H
height
humorous

I
immediately
independent
irritable

J, K, L
judgment
knowledge
laboratory
library
license
lightning
literature
loneliness

M
mathematics
minimum
mischievous

N
necessary
nickel
ninety
noticeable
nuclear
nuisance

O
obstacle
occasionally
once
opinion
opportunity
outrageous

P
parallel
particularly
people
permanent
persuade
pleasant
pneumonia

possess
possibility
prejudice
principal
privilege
probably
psychology
pursue

R
realize
receipt
receive
recognize
recommend
reference
rehearse
repetition
restaurant
rhythm
ridiculous

S
sandwich
schedule
scissors
separate
sergeant
similar
sincerely
souvenir
specifically
strategy
success
surprise
syllable
sympathy
symptom

T
temperature
thorough
throughout
tomorrow
traffic
tragedy
transferred
truly
Tuesday
twelfth

U
unnecessary
usable

V
vacuum
vicinity
village

W
weird

Commonly Confused Words

Good writers master words that are easy to misuse and misspell. Study the following words, noting how their meanings differ.

accept, except *Accept* means "to agree to something" or "to receive something willingly." *Except* usually means "not including."
Did the teacher *accept* your report?
Everyone smiled for the photographer *except* Jody.

advice, advise *Advice* is a noun that means "counsel given to someone." *Advise* is a verb that means "to give counsel."
Jim should take some of his own *advice.*
The mechanic *advised* me to get new brakes for my car.

affect, effect *Affect* means "to move or influence" or "to wear or to pretend to have." *Effect* as a verb means "to bring about." As a noun, *effect* means "the result of an action."
The news from South Africa *affected* him deeply.
The band's singer *affects* a British accent.
The students tried to *effect* a change in school policy.
What *effect* did the acidic soil produce in the plants?

all ready, already *All ready* means "all are ready" or "completely prepared." *Already* means "previously."
The students were *all ready* for the field trip.
We had *already* pitched our tent before it started raining.

all right *All right* is the correct spelling. *Alright* is nonstandard and should not be used.

a lot *A lot* may be used in informal writing. *Alot* is incorrect.

borrow, lend *Borrow* means "to receive something on loan." *Lend* means "to give out temporarily."
Please *lend* me your book.
He *borrowed* five dollars from his sister.

bring, take *Bring* refers to movement toward or with. *Take* refers to movement away from.
I'll *bring* you a glass of water.
Would you please *take* these apples to Pam and John?

can, may *Can* means "to be able," or "to have the power to." *May* means "to have permission to." *May* can also mean "possibly will."

We *may* not use pesticides on our community garden.
Pesticides *may* not be necessary, anyway.
Vegetables *can* grow nicely without pesticides.

capital, capitol, the Capitol *Capital* means "excellent," "most serious," or "most important." It also means "seat of government." A *capitol* is a building in which a state legislature meets. *The Capitol* is the building in Washington, D.C., in which the U.S. Congress meets.

Going to the beach is a *capital* idea.
Is Madison the *capital* of Wisconsin?
Protesters rallied at the state *capitol.*
A subway connects the Senate and the House in *the Capitol.*

desert, dessert *Desert* (des´ ert) means "a dry, sandy, barren region." *Desert* (de sert´) means "to abandon." *Dessert* (des sert´) is a sweet, such as cake.

The Sahara in North Africa is the world's largest *desert.*
The night guard did not *desert* his post.
Alison's favorite *dessert* is chocolate cake.

fewer, less *Fewer* refers to numbers of things that can be counted. *Less* refers to amount, degree, or value.

***Fewer* than ten students camped out.**
We made *less* money this year on the walkathon than last year.

good, well *Good* is always an adjective. *Well* is usually an adverb that modifies an action verb. *Well* can also be an adjective meaning "in good health."

Dana felt *good* when she finished painting her room.
Angela ran *well* in yesterday's race.
I felt *well* when I left my house.

its, it's *Its* is a possessive pronoun. *It's* is a contraction for *it is* or *it has.*

Sanibel Island is known for *its* beautiful beaches.
***It's* great weather for a picnic.**

lay, lie *Lay* is a verb that means "to place." It takes a direct object. *Lie* is a verb that means "to be in a certain place." *Lie,* or its past form *lay,* never takes a direct object.

The carpenter will *lay* the planks on the bench.
My cat likes to *lie* under the bed.

lead, led *Lead* can be a noun that means "a heavy metal" or a verb that means "to show the way." *Led* is the past tense form of the verb.

***Lead* is used in nuclear reactors.**
Raul always *leads* his team onto the field.
She *led* the class as president of the student council.

learn, teach *Learn* means "to gain knowledge." *Teach* means "to instruct."

Enrique is *learning* about black holes in space.
Marva *teaches* astronomy at a college in the city.

leave, let *Leave* means "to go away from" or "to allow to remain." *Leave* can be transitive or intransitive. *Let* is usually used with another verb. It means "to allow to."

Don't *leave* the refrigerator open.
She *leaves* for Scotland tomorrow.
Cyclops wouldn't *let* Odysseus' men *leave* the cave.

like *Like* used as a conjunction before a clause is incorrect. Use *as* or *as if.*

Ramon talked *as if* he had a cold.

lose, loose *Lose* means "to mislay or suffer the loss of something." *Loose* means "free" or "not fastened."

That tire will *lose* air unless you patch it.
My little brother has three *loose* teeth.

passed, past *Passed* is the past tense of *pass* and means "went by." *Past* is an adjective that means "of a former time." *Past* is also a noun that means "time gone by."

We *passed* through the Florida Keys during our vacation.
My *past* experiences have taught me to set my alarm.
Ebenezer Scrooge is a character who relives his *past.*

peace, piece *Peace* means "a state of calm or quiet." *Piece* means "a section or part of something."

Sitting still can bring a sense of *peace.*
Here's another *piece* of the puzzle.

principal, principle *Principal* means "of chief or central importance" or refers to the head of a school. *Principle* means "a basic truth, standard, or rule of behavior."

Lack of customers is the *principal* reason for closing the store.
The *principal* of our school awarded the trophy.
One of my *principles* is to be honest with others.

raise, rise *Raise* means "to lift" or "to make something go up." It takes a direct object. *Rise* means "to go upward." It does not take a direct object.

The maintenance workers *raise* the flag each morning.
The city's population is expected to *rise* steadily.

set, sit *Set* means "to place" and takes a direct object. *Sit* means "to occupy a seat or a place" and does not take a direct object.

He *set* the box down outside the shed.
We *sit* in the last row of the upper balcony.

stationary, stationery *Stationary* means "fixed or unmoving." *Stationery* means "fine paper for writing letters."

The wheel pivots, but the seat is *stationary.*
Rex wrote on special *stationery* imprinted with his name.

than, then *Than* is used to introduce the second part of a comparison. *Then* means "next in order."

Ramon is stronger *than* Mark.
Cut the grass and *then* trim the hedges.

their, there, they're *Their* means "belonging to them." *There* means "in that place." *They're* is the contraction for *they are.*

All the campers returned to *their* cabins.
I keep my card collection *there* in those folders.
Lisa and Beth run daily; *they're* on the track team.

to, too, two *To* means "toward" or "in the direction of." *Too* means "also" or "very." *Two* is the number 2.

We went *to* the mall.
It's *too* risky riding without a helmet.
***Two* amusement parks are offering reduced rates for admission.**

whose, who's *Whose* is the possessive form of *who. Who's* is a contraction of *who is* or *who has.*

***Whose* parents will drive us to the movies?**
***Who's* going to the recycling center?**

your, you're *Your* is the possessive form of *you. You're* is a contraction of *you are.*

What was *your* record in the fifty-yard dash?
***You're* one of the winners of the essay contest.**

Index

A

RESOURCES

INDEX

D

INDEX

I, J, K

L

INDEX

M

N

O

P

INDEX

Q

R

INDEX

S

T

U, V

W, X, Y, Z

Acknowledgments

For Literature and Text

Atheneum Books for Young Readers: Excerpts from "Eleanor Roosevelt," from *Great Lives: Human Rights* by William Jay Jacobs. Copyright © 1990 by William Jay Jacobs. Reprinted with the permission of Atheneum Books for Young Readers, an imprint of Simon & Schuster Children's Publishing Division.

Brandt & Hochman Literary Agents: Excerpts from "The Serial Garden," from *Armitage, Armitage, Fly Away Home* by Joan Aiken. Copyright © 1966 by Macmillan & Co., Ltd. Copyright renewed © 1994 by Joan Aiken. Reprinted by permission of Brandt & Hochman Literary Agents, Inc.

Hill and Wang: Excerpt from "Thank You, M'am," from *Short Stories* by Langston Hughes. Copyright © 1996 by Ramona Bass and Arnold Rampersad. Reprinted by permission of Hill and Wang, a division of Farrar, Straus & Giroux, LLC.

Gish Jen: Excerpt from "The White Umbrella" by Gish Jen, first published in *The Yale Review.* Copyright © 1984 by Gish Jen. Reprinted by permission of the author

Random House: Excerpt from "Homeless," from *Living Out Loud* by Anna Quindlen. Copyright © 1987 by Anna Quindlen. Used by permission of Random House, Inc.

Scholastic: Excerpt from "A Crush," from *A Couple of Kooks and Other Stories About Love* by Cynthia Rylant. Copyright © 1990 by Cynthia Rylant. Reprinted by permission of Scholastic, Inc.

Viking Penguin: "Mooses," from *Under the North Star* by Ted Hughes. Copyright © 1981 by Ted Hughes. Used by permission of Viking Penguin, a division of Penguin Putnam, Inc.

Table of Contents

v Illustration by Todd Graveline; **vi** © Reporters/Verpoorten/Leo de Wys, Inc.; **vii** Illustration by Todd Graveline; **viii** © Dick Young/Unicorn Stock Photos; **ix top** © 1999 Harry Walker/AlaskaStock.com; **bottom** Illustration by Todd Graveline; **x** The Purcell Team/Corbis; **xi** © Getty Images; **xvi background** © Andrea Pistolesi/Getty Images; **xiii** Illustration by Todd Graveline; **1** Illustration by Todd Graveline.

Illustrations by Todd Graveline

6, 8, 16, 17 top right, **27, 32, 33** top, center, **38** center left, **39, 43, 44, 52, 55, 71, 76–77, 88, 89, 105, 113, 116, 123, 130, 143, 148, 152, 156** top, **167, 177, 182, 183, 189, 204, 205, 227, 235, 236, 246, 247, 257, 272** bottom right, **274, 276, 284, 286.**

Art Credits

COVER © Ryan Aldrich/McDougal Littell

CHAPTER 1 **2–3** © William Swartz/Index Stock Imagery/PNI; **4** © Reporters/Verpoorten/Leo de Wys, Inc.; **7** Richard A. Cooke/Corbis; **8** © 1999 Harry Walker/AlaskaStock.com; **15** © Corbis; **17 bottom** FoxTrot copyright © 1988 Bill Amend. Reprinted with permission of Universal Press Syndicate. All rights reserved; **25** © Pacific Pictures/John Penisten/Liaison Agency; **29** © SuperStock.

CHAPTER 2 **34** Illustration by John Roman; **36** © FogStock LLC/Index Stock Imagery; **38 bottom right** Farcus® is reprinted with permission from LaughingStock Licensing Inc., Ottawa, Canada. All rights reserved; **40** American Jewish Joint Distribution Committee Photo Archives; **41** The Purcell Team/Corbis; **48** © David Burnett/Contact/Camp; **49** Illustration by John Condon; **50 top** © Rob Boudreau/Getty Images; **50–51** Illustration by John Roman; **51 bottom right** © Donovan Reese/Getty Images.

CHAPTER 3 **56** © Photofest; **59** © Paul Chesley/National Geographic Image Collection; **60** © Michael Melford/Getty Images; **61** © Victor R. Boswell, Jr./National Geographic Image Collection; **63** © Owen Franken/Stock Boston/PNI; **66** © Victor H. Mair; **69** Corbis; **72** Roman Soumar/Corbis; **74** Corbis-Bettmann; **78** AP/Wide World Photos; **79, 80** © Getty Images; **83 top** © Corbis.

CHAPTER 4 **90, 93, 99** © Photofest; **101** AP/Wide World Photos; **108** © Photofest; **111, 112** © Photofest; **118** Photos by Sharon Hoogstraten; **120** © Time-Life Films/The Museum of Modern Art/Film Stills Archive.

CHAPTER 5 **124 left, center** Corbis-Bettmann; **top right** © George Hall/Check Six/PNI; **126, 131** © Getty Images; **139 left** David G. Houser/Corbis; **center** Galen Rowell/Corbis; **right** Lowell Georgia/Corbis.

CHAPTER 6 **150** © Dr. Morley Read/Science Photo Library/Photo Researchers, Inc.; **153** Corbis; **154** The Granger Collection, New York; **156 bottom** © 1994 Kim Taylor/PNI; **157** © Getty Images; **158 left** © K. G. Vock/OKAPIA 1989/Photo Researchers, Inc.; **right** © Andrew Syred/Science Photo Library/Photo Researchers, Inc.; **161** IN THE BLEACHERS © 1996 Steve Moore. Reprinted with permission of UNIVERSAL PRESS SYNDICATE. All rights reserved; **162 background** Photo by Sharon Hoogstraten; **163** © Des & Jen Bartlett/National Geographic Image Collection; **164** © Mervyn Rees/Getty Images.

CHAPTER 7 **168** © 1996 Robert Allison/Contact Press Images; **170** W. Perry Conway/Corbis; **171, 178, 179 background** Photo by Sharon Hoogstraten; **179 foreground montage** Paolo Koch/Photo Researchers, Inc.; © Marilyn Silverstone/Magnum Photos, Inc.; Jim Merli/Visuals Unlimited; **180** IN THE BLEACHERS © 1999 Steve Moore. Reprinted with permission of UNIVERSAL PRESS SYNDICATE. All rights reserved.

CHAPTER 8 **184 background** © D. Young-Wolff/PhotoEdit; **186** © Myrleen Ferguson/PhotoEdit; **188** © Martin H. Simon/Corbis; **194** © Mary Kate Denny/PhotoEdit/PNI; **195** © PhotoDisc, Inc.; **197** © Charles Gupton/Stock Boston/PNI; **200** UPI/Bettmann.

CHAPTER 9 206 Courtesy of Boston Youth Fund; **210** Photo by Sharon Hoogstraten; **216** Model for East Building Mobile (1972), Alexander Calder. Painted aluminum and steel wire, .289 x .692 (11 3/8 x 27 1/4). National Gallery of Art, Washington, D.C. Gift of the Collectors Committee; **218** Photo by Dorothea Lange. Courtesy of the Library of Congress; **222** Courtesy of The Historical Scenic Collection, School of Theatre and Dance, Northern Illinois University, DeKalb, Illinois, Alexander Adducci, curator; **224** © Getty Images.

CHAPTER 10 228 background David Lees/Corbis; **foreground** © Getty Images; **231** The Granger Collection, New York; **233** Detail of Baseball Scene of Batter, Catcher, and Umpire (1915), Joseph Christian Leyendecker. Photo courtesy of the Archives of the American Illustrators Gallery, New York. © 1995 ARTShows and Products of Holderness 03245; **237** © Getty Images; **239** Illustration by David Fuller, DLF Group; **242–243 background** © Sovfoto/Eastfoto/PNI; **242 foreground, 244 background, foreground** © Getty Images.

CHAPTER 11 248 foreground Photo by Sharon Hoogstraten; **265** Mark Gibson/ Corbis; **269** Barnes Foundation, Merion, Pennsylvania/SuperStock; **271** © Getty Images; **272 top** © Corbis.

The editors have made every effort to trace the ownership of all copyrighted material found in this book and to make full acknowledgment for its use. Omissions brought to our attention will be corrected in a subsequent edition.